D1068279

EXPLORATIONS

IN

INTERPERSONAL COMMUNICATION

SAGE ANNUAL REVIEWS OF COMMUNICATION RESEARCH

Other Books in this Series:

Volume I – *Current Perspectives in Mass Communication Research*
F. Gerald Kline and Phillip J. Tichenor, Editors

Volume II – *New Models for Communication Research*
Peter Clarke, Editor

Volume III – *The Uses of Mass Communications: Current Perspectives on Gratifications Research*
Jay G. Blumler and Elihu Katz, Editors

Volume IV – *Political Communication: Issues and Strategies for Research*
Steven H. Chaffee, Editor

Volume V

SAGE ANNUAL REVIEWS OF COMMUNICATION RESEARCH

Explorations in Interpersonal Communication

GERALD R. MILLER
Editor

SAGE PUBLICATIONS / Beverly Hills / London

For information address:

SAGE PUBLICATIONS, INC.
275 South Beverly Drive
Beverly Hills, California 90212

SAGE PUBLICATIONS LTD
St George's House / 44 Hatton Garden
London EC1N 8ER

Printed in the United States of America
ISBN No. 0-8039-0665-X (cloth)
ISBN No. 0-8039-0666-8 (paper)
Library of Congress Catalog Card No. 76-6315

FIRST PRINTING

CONTENTS

EXPLORATIONS

IN

INTERPERSONAL COMMUNICATION

FOREWORD

Gerald R. Miller

INEVITABLY, I SUSPECT, editors of collected papers commence their tasks with optimistic–perhaps even grandiose–expectations of achieving a synthetic *coup.* Visions stubbornly persist of some abstract conceptual scheme that will magically impose order on the assorted scholarly creations of the contributors. In the end, however, the editor is rudely jolted back to reality, realizing that his efforts to impose unity and focus have yielded only modest returns.

This volume has proved no exception. Its title is appropriate, for the papers which follow constitute diverse "explorations" in interpersonal communication. Such diversity is not only predictable but *desirable,* since, unlike some of the other volumes in this series, the book's content boundaries, denoted by the label "interpersonal communication," are broad and varied. In a sense, the contributors have provided the reader with an intellectual smorgasbord.

But to say that the reader is to be served a smorgasbord need not deny the possibility of imposing at least some planning on the meal. Thus, while the papers in this volume are not rigidly organized according to an overall master plan, they do reflect several current issues of deep concern to students of interpersonal communication. My major aim in this Foreword is to identify these issues and to indicate specific papers that bear upon them. Since we have lingered long enough at cocktails, pick up some silverware and a napkin and follow me to the smorgasbord table.

ISSUE 1: HOW IS THE INTERPERSONAL COMMUNICATION PROCESS TO BE CONCEPTUALIZED?

As I have noted elsewhere (Miller, 1976), the relatively recent interest of communication researchers in the problem area of interpersonal communication can be traced to several origins. Among individuals in speech communication, the realization that much everyday discourse occurs in small, face-to-face settings and consists of brief, punctuated exchanges between the communicators suddenly assumed added import. Moreover, the "times" reinforced the shift in emphasis from public platform to private dialogue: encounter groups and sensitivity sessions stressed communicative purposes other than persuading and informing large, heterogeneous audiences, and students themselves began to demand answers about how to relate communicatively with their acquaintances, close friends, and romantic partners. Suddenly, the phrase "interpersonal communication" became a hot pedagogical, consultative, and research item.

Along with this development, researchers in social psychology and sociology were continuing to expand the empirical frontiers of such investigative areas as person perception, interpersonal attraction, and nonverbal communication. Findings relating to these topics, as well as others, had something to say to students of interpersonal communication; and, as a consequence, early courses and texts relied heavily on these findings for their content.

Although not totally related to the research mission, these historical happenings largely explain initially dominant conceptualizations of the interpersonal communication process. In a few instances, the phrase "the initial *lack* of conceptualizations of the interpersonal communication process" would be more accurate, since some writers and researchers refused to tackle thoughtfully the issue of conceptual definition. For instance, one text defined "interpersonal communication" as "communication between persons"—a definition that captures the etymology of the terms "inter" and "personal" but does nothing to distinguish interpersonal communication from all other human communicative transactions. Indeed, if one accepts this definition, it implies that this volume is the fifth *Sage Annual Reviews of Communication Research* dealing with interpersonal communication, rather than the first one.

When conceptualizations were attempted, they usually centered on *situational* criteria: face-to-face message exchanges, a relatively small number of communicators, maximum number of sensory channels activated, immediate feedback, etc. Although this approach goes beyond the *nonconceptualization* tactic mentioned above (at least, it eliminates the difficulty involved in classifying other volumes of this series as works about interpersonal communication), it still produces some counterintuitive outcomes. For example, it mandates that a one-sentence greeting exchange between total strangers should be counted as an instance of interpersonal communication, but a 15-minute telephone conversation between a wife and her husband should not. And from a research perspective, it provides minimal guidance, save for suggesting that researchers manipulate this or that situational variable to determine its impact on the communication process.

Recent theoretical and empirical ventures have sought to provide richer, potentially more heuristic conceptualizations of the interpersonal communication process. The contributors to this volume manifest the quest for conceptual advancement. Donald P. Cushman and Robert T. Craig adopt a *systems* perspective, treating interpersonal communications systems *functionally* and arguing that the function of such systems is development of self-conception. Using mathematical modeling as a foundation, Joseph N. Cappella conceives of certain interpersonal communication systems as pairs of machines coupled through feedback—an approach based on cybernetic systems theory. Moreover, a number of other papers occasionally make use of systems theory concepts, a tendency that reflects the movement away from the traditional covering law-model view of theory construction to a greater reliance on systems theory explanations.

In a similar vein, W. Barnett Pearce's paper details a theoretical conception of interpersonal communication grounded in *rules,* rather than *laws.* His rules-centered approach stresses the communicator as an active agent who makes choices about the way to communicate in various episodic encounters. Such a position represents a radical break with prevailing mechanistic views of human behavior, which often picture communicators as relatively passive, helpless automatons at the mercy of antecedent genetic and environmental forces impinging upon them. Stated differently, people are not always at the mercy of immutable, deterministic laws that despotically dictate their communicative transactions; instead, they themselves play a role in creating the rules that govern their various message exchanges. Moreover, the greater their individual contributions in creating the relational rules—i.e., the more idiosyncratic the rules guiding particular relationships—the more interpersonal the relationship and the communication accompanying it. Forging these rule systems is itself a complex process. Randall P. Harrison points out how the rich variety of cues associated with the face may signal successful or unsuccessful negotiation, while Teru L. Morton, James F. Alexander, and Irwin Altman underscore the problems involved in negotiating relative spheres of influence, or spans of control, in ongoing relationships.

In my view, however, the term that best captures the prevailing conceptual shift in the study of interpersonal communication is the term *developmental.* Most of the contributors agree that initial encounters do not involve interpersonal communication. Instead, relationships begin noninterpersonally (or impersonally, or nonintimately, or whatever term one may prefer). Given preliminary contacts, one of three outcomes may occur: one or more of the parties may decide that the relationship has little to offer and act immediately to terminate it (as when further contact is avoided after one or two short, casual chats); the relationship may persist over time at a friendly yet impersonal level (as when two commuters visit on the train each morning about the news, weather, and baseball scores); or, *if certain conditions exist,* the relationship may move from impersonal acquaintanceship to intense intimacy (as when an initial encounter eventually develops into a close friendship or a romantic bonding). This *qualitative shift* in the relationship is marked by a *qualitative change* in the communication transactions which occur—a change from relatively noninterpersonal to relatively interpersonal communication.

What qualitative changes take place as a relationship moves along the continuum from noninterpersonal to interpersonal? A number of the papers deal with this question. Two factors emerge consistently: First, as a relationship develops and becomes more interpersonal, greater differentiation occurs–i.e., the participants begin to perceive each other as *individuals,* rather than undifferentiated occupants of *social roles.* For example, the papers by Charles R. Berger, Royce R. Gardner, Malcolm R. Parks, Linda Schulman, and Gerald R. Miller and by Michael E. Roloff argue that participants base an increasing number of predictions about message outcomes on psychological level data–i.e., data that differentiate the person from other members of his or her social groups–with a corresponding decrease in the number of predictions based on cultural and sociological level data–i.e., data that rely on grouping the person with other members of particular social groups. Accompanying this transition is a process of *uncertainty reduction;* initial interactions produce information which causes the participants to perceive that they are getting to "know" each other better. While using a somewhat different vocabulary, Steve Duck makes a similar argument, contending that individuals communicate information about their personality structure and content in subtly different ways at various stages of a relationship and that this shared information permits increasingly accurate judgments about personality similarity and the relative attractiveness of the relationship itself.

The second factor marking the transition from noninterpersonal to interpersonal relationships is a change in message content. As Shirley J. Gilbert notes, genuine self-disclosure is seldom observed at the beginning stages of a relationship; rather, messages *sometimes* become more intimate as the relationship progresses. Moreover, Michael E. Roloff points out the content of control strategies and communicative modes of reducing conflict changes from noninterpersonal to interpersonal relationships. These content changes correspond with the shift from generalization to differentiation mentioned earlier: initial message exchanges are largely governed by cultural and social norms; given the right circumstances for relational development, later message content evolves from shared idiosyncratic rules or predictions based on individual differentiation.

Doubtless a great deal more could be said about the issue of conceptualizing the interpersonal communication process; in fact, as I have implied, the various papers go far beyond my brief remarks. Despite the many remaining explicational problems, this section can close on a note of optimism: the degree of concern for conceptual matters found in these papers considerably outdistances most earlier work. Hopefully, the result is a richer, more heuristic conceptualization (or more properly, conceptualizations) of the interpersonal communication process.

ISSUE 2: HOW IS THE INTERPERSONAL COMMUNICATION PROCESS TO BE RESEARCHED?

Obviously, the issues raised in this Foreword are not mutually exclusive; consequently, my previous comments on conceptualization offer some clues concerning potentially fruitful research postures. In this section, however, I want to mention several research trends represented by the present papers.

A number of the papers, at varying degrees of explicitness, reflect a change in emphasis from the *individual,* as the primary unit of analysis, to the *relationship.* Stated differently, communication researchers are becoming increasingly aware of the potential theoretical and empirical advantages of dealing with relational level variables. Frank E. Millar and L. Edna Rogers sketch the rationale for such an analytic shift, as well as presenting a system for coding message exchanges relationally. Morton, Alexander, and Altman stress the potential importance of a construct labeled *mutuality of relationship definition* and describe a conceptual scheme for analyzing and researching interpersonal communication from a relational perspective. The research of Cappella and of Leonard C. Hawes and Joseph M. Foley has a strong relational flavor, since both their papers present data pertaining to the sequencing of series of messages. Even Harrison's discussion of facial communication and Gilbert's analysis of self-disclosure point out the advantages of investigating these constructs within a relational context.

This development is long overdue, for students of interpersonal communication have typically pursued their theorizing and their researching at different levels of abstraction. Theoretical concern has usually centered on the *interpersonal relationship,* a level of abstraction that subsumes the individuals involved in the transaction. By contrast, most research undertakings have relied on data concerning *individual communicators,* thereby producing empirical findings that are at least one level of abstraction below the original theoretical starting point. To the extent that such theoretical-operational schizophrenia can be reduced by greater attention to, and reliance upon, relational measures, more powerful and useful tests of theoretical propositions are assured.

Closely linked to this development is a second trend reflected in several of the papers: the use of more complex and powerful mathematical models and techniques in the conduct of research. Cappella presents mathematical models of several two-person interpersonal systems and summarizes the results of several studies designed to test the empirical fit of each of the models. Hawes and Foley apply stochastic modeling to the process of group decision making. Although their work at this stage consists largely of preliminary testing, stochastic processes have the potential for identifying the major phases of the group decisioning process and for providing insights into the rules governing group decision making.

The potential advantages of these mathematical approaches are at least twofold. At the theoretical level, the casting of interpersonal communication systems into mathematical models permits derivation of a number of implications and hypotheses not easily discernible in verbally stated theories. In other words, mathematical specification of relationships produces a precision and parsimony not found in verbal constructions. At the research level, more powerful mathematical techniques allow the researcher to milk maximum information from the data and permit closer approximation of the processual complexities of interpersonal communication. As with the shift from individual to relational levels of analysis, these possibilities bode well for fitting data closely to theoretical interests.

A major outstanding question, of course, concerns the extent to which certain assumptions of these models can be met in the domain of "real world" data. Both Cappella and Hawes and Foley address this question extensively, and their current results, while but a beginning, are encouraging. Unquestionably, they will be joined by an expanding group of like-minded explorers as their research continues.

Thus far, the research trends mentioned represent instances of "making new friends"; I want to end this section by noting one line of investigation that involves "keeping the old." As the papers by Hawes and Foley and by Douglas R. Vaughn and Michael Burgoon reveal, interest persists in the ways that interpersonal communication functions within particular situational contexts. Certainly, this is as it should be, since situations such as the therapist-client relationship and the decision-making small group represent pervasive social phenomena. In particular, it is important to discover whether certain features of such settings prescribe specific conceptual models of the interpersonal communication process if task goals are to be accomplished. In this respect, it is interesting to note that Vaughn and Burgoon advocate an approach to interpersonal communication in the therapeutic setting that departs markedly from prevailing viewpoints.

The reader will probably spot other theoretical and methodological trends in the various papers. Taken as a whole, the vantage points of the contributors offer a reasonable sample of current thinking regarding potentially useful research strategies for studying the interpersonal communication process.

ISSUE 3: WHAT ASPECTS OF THE INTERPERSONAL COMMUNICATION PROCESS MERIT RESEARCH SCRUTINY?

Once again, this section is bound to overlap with the previous two, since conceptual postures and research preferences mirror assumptions about the investigational priorities that should be assigned to the interpersonal communication process. Nevertheless, I will conclude by underscoring several of the key problem areas explored in these papers.

Both the verbal and nonverbal code systems used to communicate interpersonally receive attention. Harrison's paper provides a useful overview of theoretical and empirical work on facial communication, and concludes by relating this area of nonverbal communication to the evolution of interpersonal relationships. Roloff details the content of various compliance-gaining strategies and modes of conflict resolution and, as mentioned earlier, contrasts the kinds of modes and strategies likely to be used in noninterpersonal and interpersonal relationships. Gilbert discusses the possible effects of self-disclosing messages on relational development and also considers how positive and negative self-disclosure may differ in their impact on other communicators. Cappella presents a model which focuses on interactional style as an important regulator of interpersonal systems, while Berger and his associates examine the content of various knowledge-gathering strategies used to elicit information at early stages of a relationship. Pearce introduces the construct of *coordinated management of meaning* as a central dimension of his rules-centered approach to interpersonal communication. Even the relational coding scheme of Millar and Rogers hinges on drawing inferences about the structure of the relationship from the content of message exchanges.

This interest in symbolic transactions, verbal and nonverbal, is entirely in keeping with a scholarly emphasis on interpersonal *communication.* Too often, researchers have been satisfied to hold communication constant while varying other antecedent variables (personality traits, situational constraints, etc.) to determine their influence on relational outcomes. Although such studies sometimes provide valuable information about certain social processes, they tell us little or nothing about the role of communication in shaping these processes. And since communication is the chief tool for establishing and developing human relationships, it is essential to understand how variations in its structure and content affect the genesis and evolution of such relationships.

The preceding observation leads to a final point, one that actually echoes a refrain from the beginning section of this Foreword. *Understanding the interpersonal communication process demands an understanding of the symbiotic relationship between communication and relational development: communication influences relational development, and in turn (or simultaneously), relational development influences the nature of the communication between parties to the relationship.* Hence, interpersonal communication can be studied most fruitfully as a developmental process; cross-sectional, ahistorical "laws" can provide, at best, only limited insights. To recite again the papers that manifest a concern for relational development would constitute little more than an exercise in redundancy; suffice it to say that the reader will encounter this developmental flavor throughout the volume.

Hopefully, our brief excursion to the smorgasbord table has been but an appetizer that has whetted the reader's appetite for the main courses which follow. These papers are indeed "explorations"; the contributors have sought to identify and to examine some relatively new areas in the study of interpersonal communication. Consequently, the volume is not only a review; it is also an invitation for other interested explorers of interpersonal communication to join in forthcoming expeditions.

REFERENCE

MILLER, G.R. (1976). "Foreword." In K.L. Villard and L.J. Whipple, Beginnings in Relational Communication. New York: John Wiley.

Chapter 1

THE COORDINATED MANAGEMENT OF MEANING: A RULES-BASED THEORY OF INTERPERSONAL COMMUNICATION

W. Barnett Pearce

THIS PAPER DESCRIBES continuing development of a theory of interpersonal communication. The focus of the theory is on the ability of two persons to engage in conversation.[1]

An analysis of conversations provides a convenient entry point into the study of human experience generally. The social sciences have traditionally been concerned more with the bizarre than with the normal, more with the improbable than with the commonplace. Of course, events three standard deviations from the mean are inherently interesting–a journalist sees news value in "man bites dog" but not in "dog bites man"–but the glamour of studies of genius or depravity may mask the importance of accounting for what usually happens. Recalling the old adage about the fish being the last to discover the existence of water, the social sciences have only recently developed an explicit interest in the development and function of social routines, talk, and the formation of interpersonal relationships (Douglas, 1970). The study of everyday life quickly focuses on interpersonal communication–the sequencing of messages in conversations and the sequencing of conversations into relationships–as the primary activity in human sociation and has demonstrated that apparently simple acts of conversation are in fact incredibly complex feats which even social scientists can perform better than they can explain.

For quite different reasons, persons in a number of disciplines have felt it in their interest to develop an understanding of some phase of interpersonal communication. A patient detective could find fingerprints enough to indict half of academe for improper fondling (see Budd and Ruben, 1972), but explanations of human ability to participate in conversations are unsatisfactory.

Theoretic offerings are based on different orienting assumptions, vary in scope, and possess quite different amounts and types of explanatory power.

This theory is identified by the phrase "the coordinated management of meaning," which is offered both as an ancestral term under which the fuller explication of the theory may be subsumed and as a useful descriptor of what persons do when they communicate. The coordinated management of meaning differs from other treatments of interpersonal communication largely because it is avowedly general, unabashedly theoretical, deliberately based on a set of assumptions differing from recent orthodoxy, and self-consciously two levels of abstraction away from observable exchanges of messages. The theory was briefly described in Pearce (1976) for an undergraduate audience. In this paper, the assumptions behind the theory are articulated, some conceptual problems are solved, and the methodological implications of the theory are described. If the coordinated management of meaning meets the usual criteria for a theory, I will make this rather extravagant claim [2] : it provides an integrating perspective which forces the inclusion of concerns traditionally associated with anthropology, sociology, and psychology, as well as communication studies, and structures an explanatory framework which indicates how the different contributions of each of these disciplines function in an adequate explanation of human sociation.

ASSUMPTIONS

The term "preparadigmatic" well describes the current condition of the social sciences (Kuhn, 1970). Normal science occurs when there is relatively full communication among scientists and they render relatively unanimous professional judgments. This happy state is attained when scientists share a common socialization and adhere to a common disciplinary matrix involving "symbolic generalizations," beliefs in particular models, common values, and acceptance of particular exemplars of how to do research (Kuhn, 1970:177-187). This is far from the state of the social sciences today. [3]

According to Harré and Secord (1973:27-28), the recent orthodoxy is based on (1) a mechanistic model of man, (2) a Humean conception of cause, and (3) a logical positivist methodology. Although the radical behaviorism which consistently follows from these premises has been successively revised (Koch, 1964), only recently have coherent packages of alternative assumptions been offered, and none has been widely accepted as a new paradigm. [4] As a result, current research on human sociation lurches about, unguided by theory and frequently based on unstated and untenable premises (Harré and Secord, 1973:27-83).

The assumptions of the coordinated management of meaning may be summarized as stipulating (1) a diverse set of models for man, (2) a set of alternative modes of explanation for human action, and (3) a social science characterized as pluralistic and naturalistic.

The theory stipulates that human action is diverse, being both proactive and reactive, caused and purposive, and that each form of action requires a different explanatory model. A useful typology differentiates between *controlled, influenced,* and *creative* action in such a way that the appropriate explanatory mode for each can be determined (Harris, 1975). Controlled behavior is reactive or "caused" (in a Humean sense) and is appropriately explained by identifying antecedents and subsuming the particular instance under a nomothetic law (Hempel, 1966). A person's meanings or volition have no effect on controlled behavior: if a person steps from a curb and is hit by a speeding Mack truck, none of these will change the distance, direction, and trajectory of his body. Influenced behavior is structured by socialization and is appropriately explained by describing the rules which persons follow as they conduct purposive action. This explanation follows the form of a somewhat modified practical syllogism (Von Wright, 1971). Influenced behavior varies as a function of the actor's meanings and volition. For example, a person probably would not step from a curb to pick up a dime from the street (or would reinterpret this act of basic greed) if he self-consciously weighed the gain of the dime against the danger of being hit by a truck or if he followed a rule which specified a scramble in the gutter for a dime as indecorous. Examples of influenced behavior include kneeling in the presence of royalty, using a "demand ticket" to get into a conversation (Nofsinger, 1975), or employing turn-taking cues to manage interaction while conversing (S. Duncan, 1972). Finally, creative behavior is a product of individual choice which is not the normal, expected meaning or movement. Creativity may involve following rules in a novel way or acting independently of the rules. It is not clear what explanatory mode is appropriate for creative behavior. Perhaps no more can be done than an explicative history.

Interpersonal communication probably includes elements of all three types of action, but for the most part it consists of influenced behavior in which individuals allow their actions to be governed and guided by rules (Cushman and Whiting, 1972; Pearce, 1973). But the transactive nature of human communication (Rossiter and Pearce, 1975) requires an explanatory procedure which goes beyond a listing of the rules or a description of how individuals follow rules. Since the outcome is the result of a frequently nonsummative input of both persons, the conversation which actually occurs may not resemble the rule-governed behaviors of either person independently. As a result, an explanation must be able to account for the effect of each person on the other as well as each person's rule-governed behavior.

The assumptions that human action is diverse and that each type of behavior necessitates a different form of explanation have significant implications for the nature of social science. Specifically, a science which is appropriate for studying interpersonal communication must be pluralistic and naturalistic. It must be pluralistic in that it grants legitimacy to a variety of forms of research and theoretic formulations and—most importantly—in that the decisions about how to do research and how to frame explanations are determined by the characteristics of the phenomena being studied. For example, it must admit teleological as well as causal explanatory frameworks and must contain criteria by which to determine when each is appropriate. It must be naturalistic[5] in that it is at least sometimes based on actor-defined variables rather than exclusively on observer definition. Meanings as well as movements must be understood to account for actions, and in influenced behavior an observer must elicit the actor's meanings rather than superimpose his own.

These assumptions are to an extent the direct denial of yesterday's orthodoxy and are consistent with what I view as an emerging consensus on an "anthropomorphic" concept of man (Harré and Secord, 1973). However, there is little agreement about the shape of a coherent theory and a viable methodology built on these assumptions. The following sections present a new attempt to work out the implications of these assumptions.

THE COORDINATED MANAGEMENT OF MEANING

These paragraphs present a perspective from which to think about interpersonal communication. The picture is of persons who have learned a set of rules which describe how they and others should behave in conversation and who make strategic choices about which rules to follow and which persons to converse with in order to achieve a satisfactory mode of sociation. The joke is that the rules frequently contradict each other and fail to cover some situations and that everybody learns a different set of rules. Keeping score in the resulting confusion is difficult for both communicators and social scientists. The coordination problems in the management of meaning are like those of five musicians suddenly thrust before an audience, who must simultaneously perform and collectively decide what numbers to play, how fast to play them, and who should play what parts. The element of surprise in the joke is that people so frequently produce such good music.

Meaning

Since communication must be understood as action (interpreted movement) rather than simply as movements, an explanation of communication must account for the communicators' meanings as well as the messages they exchange. Without attempting to construct a comprehensive theory of meaning, this theory specifies meaning in interpersonal communication as *episodic.*

Communicators do not perceive their conversations as an undifferentiated stream of experience. Rather, they punctuate them into units, each of which situates particular interpretations of messages *synchronically,* by locating them within a context of related meanings (e.g., "this comment was made during a brainstorming session"), and *diachronically,* by providing an interpretation of past messages and a prediction of future ones (e.g., "we are trying to generate as many ideas as possible regardless of merit; we'll evaluate them later"). These units of meaning have been variously described, but the concept of episode is perhaps the most useful.

The definition of episode—"any part of human life, involving one or more people, in which some internal structure can be determined" (Harré and Secord, 1973:153)—is useful because it is purposefully imprecise, being determined by the actors rather than an observer; because it indicates that episodes may vary widely in scope (from "having coffee with" to "having an affair with"); and because it defines episodes interpersonally.

A description of an episode answers the question, "What does he think he is doing?" Whether or not a particular lexicon has an appropriate word for it, the enactment of an episode constitutes a sequence of actions which are perceived as entities and thus are "noun-able." Particular conversations may be described as "having a fight," "making up," "culturally appropriate greeting rituals," "bull sessions," etc. But notice that the rules in each of these differ: behaviors which are expected and legitimate in making up do not exist in greeting ritual, and those appropriate in bull session do not exist in church.

A cluster of rules which specify legitimate and expected behaviors and meanings may be considered an operational definition of an episode, with the implicit instruction: "to enact episode X, do this. . . ." Actually, the task confronting communicators is usually the other way around: they are presented with behavior and must reason "if he is doing this, he must be enacting episode X, and given episode X, I should do this. . . ." This mental process is comparable to abstraction and generalization in concept-formation (Bruner et al., 1956) and explains the process behind H.D. Duncan's (1968:32) insistence on the interrelation between form (*how* we communicate) and content (*what* we communicate).

Specifying meaning as episodic orients analysis to integrated patterns of meaning with behavioral implications, but there is still considerable equivocation in the use of the term. To avoid paralyzing confusion in the explanation of communication, it is necessary to differentiate three referents for episode, designated by subscripts

Episodes$_1$ consist of patterns of meanings and behaviors which are culturally sanctioned and which exist independently of any particular individual or dyad. These are the public symbols necessary for meaning to be shared and seem identical with the concept of "significant symbols" described by Mead (1934) and H.D. Duncan (1968). Traditionally studied by anthropologists and sociologists, Episodes$_1$ include social institutions and related rituals such as marriage and rites of passage, and ritualized ways of dealing with particular situations such as greeting rituals, patterns of social deference, and treatments of humor or sarcasm.

Episodes$_2$ consist of patterns of meanings and behaviors in the minds of individuals and are similar to discussions of images (Boulding, 1956), plans (Miller et al., 1960), acts (Morris, 1946), or definitions of situations (McHugh, 1968). These are private symbols which express individuals' understanding of the forms of social interaction in which they are participating, or in which they want to participate. To the extent that a person's Episodes$_2$ resemble society's Episodes$_1$, the person will be able to converse easily, understanding and being understood. To the extent that the Episodes$_2$ are idiosyncratic, the person will have greater coordination problems.

Episodes$_3$ consist of the communicators' interpretation of the actual sequence of messages which they jointly produced. Episodes-as-coenacted have been studied by Cicoural (1974) and Garfinkel (1967) among others, but explanations of conversations are barren unless they are integrated with analysis of Episodes$_1$ and Episodes$_2$.

When two people communicate, the Episodes$_1$ which they have learned from their cultures provide them with a repertoire of patterns of actions which they may assume are common to both (the "assumption of reciprocal perspectives," Cicourel, 1974, or "background expectancies," Garfinkel, 1967). From this repertoire, both persons select and/or construct the Episode$_2$ which reflects their particular interpretation of what they want to enact or what they feel is appropriate. As each person begins to enact his Episode$_2$, the combination of both their actions structure Episode$_3$. A coordinated management of meaning can easily be achieved when both persons share an Episode$_1$, when both want to enact the same Episode$_2$, and when the structure of the Episode$_1$ equals Episode$_2$. In this instance, both know the rules for enacting the Episode$_3$; they understand what to expect and what is expected of them. When heads of state meet for a summit conference, it is mutually desirable that at least their public conversations proceed smoothly. The function of protocol officers is to identify an Episode$_1$ common to both and to get their principals to internalize it as their Episodes$_2$ so that the Episode$_3$ will proceed smoothly. In these contexts, statesmen sacrifice spontaneity and individuality for a performance which looks good for the cameras.

Most people must muddle through life deprived of the services of protocol officers, however, and their conversations may be expected to flow smoothly if they and their conversational partners are willing to take complementary roles and if they share definitions of Episodes$_1$. This is why communication within tribal society is easy: everyone knows his roles, and there is a ritualized pattern for handling all of the usual interactions (Albert, 1972). Modern Western society is not like that: it is characterized by an acceptance of change, recognized interdependency, and a celebration of heterogeneity. This frequently leads to communication between persons who do not have a common repertoire of Episodes$_1$ or who have conflicting Episodes$_2$, and coordination problems in their management of meanings is the result.

Management

Kelly (1955) forcefully argued that persons are the prisoners of neither their history nor their heredity. They can manage their meanings even though they cannot change their environment or themselves. People are "always free to reconstrue what they cannot deny." This ability accounts for the fact that people can transcend their cultures (their $\text{Episodes}_2 \neq$ their Episodes_1) and that people can produce and understand an Episode_3 which may differ from either communicator's Episodes_1 or Episodes_2.

Management of meaning may take several forms, an observation which itself bodes ill for methodology. In the simplest case, a person might shift from one episode to another as that which best identifies a particular sequence of behaviors. Alternatively, a person might redefine the structure of an episode by changing the cluster of rules comprising it or by changing the perception of its boundaries or internal structure. The most complex form of management of meaning involves shifting the level of abstraction. As Russell demonstrated with the theory of types, it is impossible to perceive the world without paradox unless levels of abstraction are granted such that one statement will be seen as describing a class of others without itself being a part of that class. In much the same way, persons manage their meanings by changing level of reflexive self-awareness. [6]

An adequate explanation of interpersonal communication must account for the fact that people not only can but regularly do manage their meanings. Discussion of meaning management is facilitated by two analytic devices: an adaptation [7] of the process model of coorientation (Pearce and Stamm, 1973) and the concept of enigmatic episodes (Harré and Secord, 1973).

The process model of coorientation assumes that persons interact with others on the basis of perceived agreement or disagreement about what episode is being enacted and that these expectations are subject to confirmation or disconfirmation by the other person's subsequent acts. The model identifies four coorientational states: predicted agreement confirmed (PAC), predicted agreement disconfirmed (PAD), predicted disagreement confirmed (PDC), and predicted disagreement disconfirmed (PDD). The hypothesis on which the model is built states that persons communicate differently depending on what their expectation is and whether it is confirmed or disconfirmed. The management of meaning is of particular importance in the two states in which the expectation is disconfirmed. In each instance, persons must reevaluate the meanings of previous messages and change their expectations for the meanings and behaviors which will occur subsequently.

The explanatory power of this concept of the management of meaning may be demonstrated by contrasting Rogerian client-centered therapy with gestalt counseling. Rogers employs "unconditional positive regard" and reflective statements which in effect support the client's definition of his Episode_2 (by inducing the agreement states of PAC or PDD) and encourage him to explore it. Gestalt therapists deliberately refuse to enact the $Episode_3$ (inducing the disagreement states of PAD or PDC) requested by the patient, forcing the patient to reconstrue his $Episodes_2$. These distinctions clearly demonstrate the different strategies and objectives (exploration versus reconstruction of $Episodes_2$) of the two approaches. (Based on the model, one would expect a difference between Rogerian clients in PAC and those in PDD and between Gestalt clients in PAD and those in PDC.)

The enactment of enigmatic episodes also necessitates the management of meaning. An episode is enigmatic if its expression in the form of rules is inadequate as a guide for action. There are two forms of enigmatic episodes. *Equivocal* episodes are those in which a particular pattern of behaviors is interpretable in two or more contradictory ways or in which a particular interpretation fits two or more patterns of behavior. Episodes in which the rules do not describe appropriate behaviors specifically or completely enough to guide actions or interpretations are designated as *ambiguous.*

For most people, communicating with the terminally ill is an enigmatic (ambiguous) episode. Partly because we institutionalize seriously ill patients, most people have not learned an $Episode_1$ which could guide them. Thrown into relying on their own ingenuity, these conversations are more troublesome and require more management of meanings than the enactment of a nonenigmatic episode.

Coordination

The study of communication properly centers on the coordination procedures by which individuals intermesh their own actions with those of someone else to produce $Episodes_3$. Just as five virtuoso musicians cannot play together unless they achieve some system of tacit agreements which enables them to coordinate their performance, so the success of a conversation depends on the coordination achieved by both persons, as well as their individual merits.

Coordination is achieved when the communicators "contract" (Carson, 1969) with each other to enact a particular episode. The early phases of conversations frequently are best understood as negotiations in which each requests the other to enact his preferred $Episode_2$, and these requests are either accepted or rejected, usually with a counterrequest. Once a request is accepted, each knows what to expect and what is expected–*if* their understandings of the rules of the episode are similar.[8]

Coordinating the management of meaning becomes quite a problem when the communicators have different $Episodes_2$ which they need/want to enact or when their definition of an $Episode_2$ is similar enough that they think that they share rules which in fact differ. (This is, of course, the origin of the plot line of many TV situation comedies.)

The essential condition of coordination is consensual rules. Given a set of rules common to both communicators, each can accurately predict what the reaction to his behaviors will be and can reliably interpret the significance of what the other does. Without consensual rules, conversational chaos and frustration result. One important topic for communication theory is the manner in which consensual rules are developed in particular conversations. A tentative taxonomy identifies three coordination strategies: *casting, mirroring,* and *negotiation.*

Coordinating conversations by casting occurs when a person has a preferred $Episode_2$ (or repertoire of $Episodes_2$) and he develops or terminates interpersonal relationships depending on the other person's ability to participate in the $Episode_3$ that he wants to enact. A useful analogy is that of an actor who has found a script with a part in it which he wants to play but who must find a stage upon which to perform and a group of people to fill the other roles. When coordinating by casting, a person communicates by recruiting others to enact particular roles and training them for the part. Casting has an imperative tone: others are offered an opportunity to interact with the caster only if they are willing to play the game, but there may be a wide range of stylistic variations. Sophisticated casting may be subtle, humorous, or deliberately blatant.

Coordinating conversations by mirroring is just the opposite of casting. Desiring above all else participation in an interaction with other people or with a particular other, a mirrorer is willing to take any role in any $Episode_3$ proposed by the other person. When coordinating by mirroring, persons communicate by seeking to discover what the other person wants them to do and eliciting feedback to see if they are doing well. Mirroring has a dependent, acquiescent tone and may perhaps best be detected by observing chameleonlike changes as the person moves between various relationships and situations.

Coordinating conversations by negotiation is more complicated than doing so by either mirroring or casting. In negotiation, a person is willing to compromise between his $Episode_2$ and that of the other person. Successful negotiations frequently result in an $Episode_3$ unlike either of the $Episodes_2$. Four negotiation strategies have been described at some length (Pearce, 1976). *Invocation* occurs when a person begins to enact an $Episode_3$, inviting the other to take the complementary role. *Ingratiation* (better described as bargaining) occurs when a person enacts an episode which the other person finds desirable with the assumption that the other will then reciprocate. Negotiation by *creating shared experiences* is a way of structuring a common background which provides a pattern for future interactions. *Metacommunicating* consists of talking explicitly about the episodes which are or might be enacted.

All these coordination strategies comprise a repertoire of techniques by which people can manage each other and their own meanings. Sometimes it works well and usually well enough for people to get by, but these successes do not disguise the fact that good communication is a highly sophisticated form of action requiring considerable competency to perform or to study.

METHODOLOGICAL ISSUES

The assumptions on which this theory is based necessitate a pluralistic and naturalistic methodology, but the precise shape of a research program which would be appropriate for this theory is far from clear. In fact, one of the highest prices paid for abandoning the positivist paradigm is that one must renounce a comfortably elaborated methodology for which laudable virtues—objectivity, replicability, etc.—are claimed.

There have been many calls for a nonpositivist research program in the last 15 years, and social scientists are rightly impatient with self-selected sirens whose songs do not describe how to get to work. Before this theory or any other can claim to be a viable alternative way of studying communication scientifically, it must at least show that it is possible to do legitimate research consistent with its premises.

Type of Behavior

Since the methodology required by this theory is pluralistic, researchers must choose between various models for the appropriate description of the phenomena they want to study. This choice may be expressed as a hypothesis that the phenomena possess the criterial attributes of controlled, influenced, or creative behavior. For several reasons (space, author's interests, applicability to conversations), this discussion will deal only with influenced behavior.

The hypothesis that a particular aspect of conversation consists of influenced behavior implies that the behavior is rule-governed. The hypothesis may be tested by answering five questions based on the characteristics of rules.

(1) Is there a logically or empirically necessary relationship between antecedents and consequents? This question must be answered "no" by demonstrating the possibility of alternative sequences. An affirmative answer would suggest that the behavior be conceptualized as controlled and would be explained very differently.

(2) Is the observed pattern a recurring one? This question must be answered "yes" by demonstrating a statistical regularity. In the absence of any necessary relationship, this regularity attests to the presence and function of rules which account for structure, differentiating it from creative behavior.

(3) Can the communicators generate these sequences? This question must be answered "yes" by demonstrating that informants can interpolate and extrapolate to complete fragments of the pattern. For example, if presented a transcript in which some messages have been deleted, the informants could supply the missing messages or variants of them which they and others will perceive as functionally synonymous. This ability demonstrates that the actors perceive the internal structure of the episode.

(4) Can the communicators perceive alternative sequences of messages which are inappropriate? This question is another attempt to tap into the internal structure of the episode, this time by negation, and must be answered "yes."

(5) Are sanctions (positive or negative) applied to deviations from the pattern? Although the existence of observable sanctions is not a necessary condition,[9] the presence of negative sanctions is one indication that a rule has been violated (see Garfinkel, 1967).

If each of these questions is answered in the indicated way, the researcher can conclude that the conversation in question is rule-governed, and this decision determines the rest of his procedure.

Description

A naturalistic methodology stresses the importance of describing the phenomena. The ultimate descriptive phrase for influenced behavior in conversations is to say that "they enacted an Episode_3 of ritualized insults" where the episode named can be described in at least two ways. The first description is external to the episode and may follow an organizing scheme similar to Burke's dramatistic pentad. The five terms in the pentad can be adapted to social action by specifying the *scene* as the socially defined interpersonal context, the *act* as the effect of what is done in the social institutions, the *agency* as the medium in which communication takes place, and the *purpose* as the struggle to achieve the consensus necessary to integrate social action (this is slightly revised from H.D. Duncan, 1968:19). Duncan correctly identified the pentad as a way of accounting for the structure of social action but not its function. For that, episodes must also be defined by describing the cluster of rules which translate between the symbolic meaning and the patterns of inferences and behaviors which constitute the episode.

Rules may be stated in a number of ways, but should be reducible to a form such as "If we are enacting Episode_3 A, and he does Act B, then I am expected to or legitimately may do Act C" (this is an adaptation of Gottlieb, 1968). The first phrase establishes a boundary condition; the second ties into the particular structure of the Episode_3 as it is being enacted; and the third expresses the role of rules in establishing acts/meanings which are required for the episode to be enacted (*constitutive* rules) and the array of allowable acts from which the person may choose (*regulative* rules). Both descriptions may be validated by comparing them with the actors' perceptions and behavior (although the actors should not be expected to be fully aware of or able to articulate either rules or symbolic meanings).

If the communicators are following the same rules, their coordination problems are easy and an observer can readily describe their conversation by identifying the rules. Both coordinating the management of meaning and describing the ensuing conversation are more difficult when the communicators follow different rules (e.g., their $Episodes_2$ are different) or when $Episode_3$ is enigmatic (e.g., the rules do not adequately specify meanings and behaviors). In these instances, a researcher must identify those sequences of messages which are based on a consensually shared rule and those which are not. The latter may be described in terms of each communicator's $Episode_2$ and his use of coordination strategies. For example, this conversational excerpt shows a quickly corrected coordination problem:

TOM: Hey, did you hear what happened downtown today?

DICK: Tell me.

TOM: No, I was asking you.

DICK: Oh, well, there was a demonstration at the post office. . . .

To describe this sequence of messages, it is necessary to contrast Tom's and Dick's $Episodes_2$. Tom wanted to enact a *question-answer* sequence based on an $Episode_1$ which legitimates this pattern (Schlegloff, 1968). Dick interpreted what Tom and he were doing as a three-message sequence which functions to give Tom an extended speaking turn during which he can play newscaster. This interpretation is also based on a common $Episode_1$ (Sacks, 1967, 1972). Tom's second message acknowledged the coordination problem and used the negotiation strategy of metacommunication (Pearce, 1976). Dick's second statement is an appropriate response to Tom's first remark, indicating his awareness of and willingness to follow the rules of a question-answer episode.

For some purposes, additional descriptors can be used. For example, the $Episodes_1$ may be identified as enigmatic because the opening for each is the same. The question "Did you hear . . . ?" does not differentiate between "question-answer" and "three utterance turn-request." Further, Dick's first response put Tom in a coorientational state of predicted agreement disconfirmed, and Tom's second message put Dick in the same state, while Dick's second response put Tom in a state of predicted agreement confirmed, which shows that his coordination strategy was successful. Of course, a description may be more or less detailed depending on the researcher's purpose, but the apparatus necessary for a highly detailed description should be included in a theory which is based on the assumptions articulated above and which will be tested by naturalistic research.

Explanation

A two-step explanation is necessary for conversations. First, each person's behavior must be explained in answer to the question, "Why did he do that?" But conversations are transactive and cannot be explained adequately even by a full explication of each person's actions individually. The second step in explanation is to account for the $Episode_3$.

The practical syllogism (Von Wright, 1971) is a viable explanatory model for each person's rule-governed actions. Two characteristics of the model make it particularly appropriate: it explains actions teleologically, in terms of reasons or goals to be achieved rather than in terms of antecedent causes, and it explains an action by showing that it is a reasonable choice without assuming that it was logically or empirically necessary.

The practical syllogism takes this form:

> A wishes B to occur;
>
> A knows/believes that he must do X if B is to occur;
>
> Therefore, A does X.
>
> where: A is a person,
>
> B is an episode, and
>
> X is a particular behavior given meaning by its location in the episode.

The first premise poses a statement of purpose ("He wanted to do B") as a "final" explanatory principle for the observed behavior.[10] As any five-year old child can demonstrate, a series of "why" questions may be extended beyond anyone's ability to answer. Certainly it can be asked, "Why does he want B to occur?" Although this is an interesting question, it is external to the theory of the coordinated management of meaning; rather, it is more suitable to the mythology of motivation, reinforcement schedules, needs, etc. The more appropriate question is, "How do you know that A wishes B to occur?" which is answered with reference to interview and observational techniques.

The second premise links the occurrence of the desired episode to the production of the observed behavior. As stated in the syllogism, however, the connection between B and X is simply assumed. The warrant which justifies the second premise is a statement of the rules which comprise the episode. These rules are generated by the descriptive procedures discussed in the previous section.

Given the ability to specify the statements which function as the first and second premises of the practical syllogism and to state the rules which are the warrant for the second premise, the observed behavior can be explained by demonstrating that it logically follows. An explanation of a well-coordinated conversation—such as the enactment of a "Hi, how are you?" greeting ritual—is straightforward. A poorly coordinated conversation, however, is more difficult, in part because the same syllogism cannot be used for both communicators. The coordination problem may be traced to a difference in one or both of the premises, and the communication problem may be explained by contrasting the syllogisms which explain the behavior of each individual.

Note the difference between explaining an instance of an actor's behavior, which requires a single syllogistic form, and explaining a conversation. Unless the communicators have achieved a high degree of coordination, explaining a conversation requires constructing a practical syllogism for each person and comparing them. The appropriate explanatory terms for uncoordinated conversations are those which describe the fit between the syllogisms, such as "One person was enacting $Episode_2$ B and the other $Episode_2$ C" or "Their understanding of the rules for $Episode_1$ D differed." Ultimately, it will be desirable to develop a set of terms describing different kinds of coordination problems and to determine which coordination strategies are most frequent and most effective in each.

Prediction and Control

In addition to description and explanation, potential for prediction and control are frequently cited as criteria for scientific theory. In fact, those in the positivist tradition sometimes argue that prediction and control are essential for a theory to be considered scientific (Kaplan, 1964; Rudner, 1966), and several audiences have criticized preliminary statements of this theory because of its supposed inability to predict or control. These criticisms may be responded to in two ways. The weaker reply—albeit a valid one—is that prediction and control are neither necessary nor sufficient conditions of a scientific theory (as Toulmin, 1961, has lucidly demonstrated). The stronger reply is that this theory does have the capacity to predict and confers at least some ability to control, but in a special way, consistent with its own assumptions.

A theory of rules-based social action is necessarily two steps removed from behavior. This type of theory will not predict behavior with any consistency because the actors' interpretive activities and choices intervene between the observer's theoretical postulates and the observable behaviors. However, the theory may well predict the way actors engage in interpretive activities and make choices.

The concept of a theory two steps removed from the actual exchanges of messages can be clarified by contrasting it with a one-level theory (see Bergmann, 1954). In the dream world of a naive positivist, there is no "slippage" between the world of things and the symbolic system which represents them. A necessary, consistent, one-to-one relationship between concepts and variables is structured by the alchemy of operational definitions and other magic potions. Prediction and control are possible, in part, because symbolic manipulations of concepts are considered isomorphic with operational manipulations of things.

The assumptions of isomorphism between observed and theoretic terms cannot be sustained when dealing with rule-governed human action. A given behavior may mean many things depending on how the actor construes its signification and significance (Morris, 1964), and quite different behaviors may be interpreted by the actor as functionally synonymous. But slippage occurs even in these actor-defined relations between events and their interpretation as the actors "manage" their meanings.

However, a theory of social action can develop predictive utility about the way persons construe their experience. Specifically, the theory of the coordinated management of meaning may develop propositions about communication situations in which coordination problems are likely, about persons who will be more or less able to coordinate their management of meanings with specific others, and about the effect of using particular coordination strategies.

Consistent with the principle of methodological pluralism, some of these propositions may invoke a causal explanatory model and some a rules-based model. For example, it may be argued that ongoing patterns of interpersonal relationships and communication are systemic in nature (Watzlawick et al., 1967). If so, the network of interrelationships necessitates that a given system-state precludes some alternatives and that a given input will have certain kinds of effects. This proposition (based on Pearce, 1976) is based on a systemic view of communication: the use of metacommunication as a negotiation strategy in the coordinated management of meaning inevitably leads to an alteration in the relationship between the communicators by introducing an irreversible increase in the level of their self-awareness. The explication of such propositions depends on an assumption of causality (or necessary interdependency) among the components of the communication system.

Other propositions assume a structure of meta-rules which describe rule-utilizing action. Consider the problem of sequencing a set of episodes during the course of an evening or a lifetime. One negotiation strategy is bargaining (called "ingratiation" in Pearce, 1976) according to a meta-rule of equity. The problem is solved by enacting a sequence of episodes such that every second one is preferred by each person. The selection of episodes is explained by stipulating that the persons wanted a continuing relationship; they each believed that they had to enact some episodes which "favored" the other person if the relationship was to succeed (because of the meta-rule of equity); therefore they acted as they did.

Propositions based on assumptions of necessary relations among components of a system confer ability to predict and control based on an understanding of the structure of the phenomena. Propositions based on an explication of meta-rules allow an observer to develop better than chance expectancies about what will happen by reconstructing at least part of the person's decision making procedure, but they do not permit confident predictions or the ability to control.

The difference between the two is best illustrated by the observer's response if the unexpected occurs. If a prediction based on causal or structural assumptions is wrong, this constitutes an anomaly and the observer must rethink the theory. If an expectation based on meta-rules is wrong, this may require a reworking of the theory or may indicate that the person is engaging in creative action—which cannot be predicted but might be understood.

The value of predictive and controlling ability is obvious, but there is also value in propositions based on meta-rules. For one, an analysis of meta-rules permits the theory to be extended to a level permitting symbolic manipulation and hypothesis development. Consider the hypothesis that interpersonal relationships in Western society are governed by two meta-rules, one which specifies an equitable distribution of values (Brittan, 1973) and the other which legitimates a hierarchical order (H.D. Duncan, 1968). Assuming that these are rules which warrant inferences about particular behaviors in specific situations, various patterns of expected behavior can be hypothesized. Further, these hypotheses may be contrasted with those drawn from intellectually constructed societies based on other rules such as inequity (unabashed exploitation) and egalitarianism. This symbolic manipulation permits nonempirical construction of alternative societies and empirical tests of the goodness-of-fit between various constructions and the actual structure of interpersonal relationships.

CONCLUSION

The theory described in this report differs significantly from conventional orthodoxy because it is explicitly based on a set of assumptions unlike those of the still-dominant paradigm. One claim for the value of the theory rests on the judgment that its assumptions are better: they admit the diversity of human actions; they stress the importance of actors' meanings; and they structure teleological as well as causal explanatory models. A second claim for the value of the theory rests on its ability to integrate into one coherent framework many strands of social science without imposing a doctrine of conceptual or methodological monism. Rather than amalgamating the social sciences, it demonstrates the relations between them. Specifically, the methodology of studying rule-governed action requires an understanding of culturally sanctioned $Episodes_1$ and individual choice of $Episodes_2$ as well as the coordination strategies used in a particular conversation. A third claim for the value of the theory is that it is heuristic. The theory sensitizes an observer to aspects of communication which were not previously identified and poses questions not previously asked. The question remains, however, whether this perspective is more useful than others. Ultimately, this will be answered with data rather than by argument. Research presently being conducted is designed to test some of the implications of the theory.[11]

NOTES

1. Although interpersonal communication is not limited to dyads, my discussion will be, primarily for syntactical reasons.

2. . . . he said, somewhat nervously. (See Rossiter and Pearce, 1975:60.)

3. Full communication among scientists is certainly not the norm, as evidenced by the

frustrating public exchange between Westley (1973) and Darnell (1971, 1973), neither of whom could understand or would grant even provisional legitimacy to the perspective of the other. And professional judgments are hardly uniform, as evidenced by the pointed exchange between critics and authors of the "Top Three" competitively selected papers in the Interpersonal and Small Group Division of SCA at its 1975 convention. At issue were disagreements about whether data are inevitably theory-laden, the function of concepts in research, and the most productive forms of research.

4. Harré and Secord (1973) are no exception. In my judgment, their attack on the old paradigm is brilliant and their discussion of ethogeny as a research program is provocative, but their work does not achieve the status of a viable alternative. This is due to at least three factors. First, the admitted (p. 9) overemphasis on self-directed behavior and the decision to use this as a prototype limits their ability to account for a variety of behavior and in particular masks the role of self-awareness in rule-following. Second, the discussion of episode is equivocal (Harré, 1974, and Toulmin, 1974, do better, but choose the wrong bases to make distinctions). Third, the discussion of methodology is admittedly incomplete (pp. 295-296) and unsatisfying. More disturbing, in a small lecture-discussion in November 1975, Secord was unwilling or unable to go beyond the suggestions in the book.

5. I hesitate to use the term "naturalistic" because of its vagueness. I do *not* mean field studies as opposed to lab studies, because location is not the criterion; nor do I mean atheoretic exploration, because there is no such thing as non-theory-laden observation. The proper reference for naturalistic inquiry is that which studies entities and variables defined by the actors in an attempt to account for their experience. Thus defined, naturalistic inquiry gains the advantage of forcing observers to respect the experience of the actors and draws on their tacit knowledge as a source of information.

6. Because of its reflexive nature, self-awareness is a difficult concept. Consider this schema:

meta meta awareness:	He was aware of being aware of being aware of hitting the ball.
meta awareness:	He was aware of being aware of hitting the ball.
awareness:	He was aware of hitting the ball.
direct action:	He hit the ball.

These propositions follow: (1) There is a possibility of an infinite regress (at least far enough to disrupt the ability to act). (2) A person can volitionally move to the next higher level of awareness, but cannot move to the next lower. The problem is like that of deciding to forget the number 9; one must remember what it is that he is trying to forget. (3) A person cannot choose to act at a particular level. That choice itself is at the next higher level. (4) All levels of awareness are potentially available to a person, but most behavior is somnambulant, in which higher levels are disattended to. The procedure by which this is accomplished is an important area of study. (5) The level of awareness at which a person acts makes an important difference in the meaning of the action. For example, a person may be proud to have hit the ball (direct action), ashamed of himself for being proud (awareness), proud of himself for feeling ashamed to be proud (meta awareness), and ashamed for feeling proud for feeling ashamed for feeling proud (meta meta awareness). Now ask him, "How do you feel about hitting the ball?"

7. The adaptation consists of substituting episodes for attitudes or beliefs as the object toward which the persons are simultaneously oriented while retaining the basic structure of the model. Although this introduces some difficult methodological problems, it brings the coorientation paradigm into line with the assumptions of the theory of the coordinated management of meaning.

8. . . . and if both are willing to abide by the contract. I have not included in this report a discussion of "fraudulent contracts" in which a person proposes a coenactment of a

particular episode just so that he can "set up" and exploit the other (see Carson, 1969). This topic presents no insurmountable problems, but does create complications with levels of self-awareness.

9. Among other reasons, sanctions are not necessary conditions of episode enactment because (1) sanctions vary as a function of the importance/significance of the episode and (2) sanctions are applied when a negatively evaluated episode is enacted as well as when a person fails to enact a positively evaluated episode.

10. The fact that the person participates in the episode is sufficient to say that he "wishes" it to occur since he could refuse the enactment if he chose. To say that he did not really "want" to enact the episode or that it was the only alternative available to him is irrelevant for explanatory purposes since "wishes" carries the meaning of *purposeful intent* rather than *evaluation.*

11. I refuse to end this paper by saying that more research needs to be done, but it does, and I hope that others will find this theoretic framework useful for their own work.

REFERENCES

ALBERT, E.M. (1972). "Culture patterning of speech behavior in Burundi." Pp. 72-105 in J. Gumperz and D. Hymes (eds.), Directions in sociolinguistics. New York: Holt, Rinehart and Winston.

BERGMANN, G. (1954). The metaphysics of logical positivism. New York: Longmans, Green.

BOULDING, K. (1956). The image. Ann Arbor: University of Michigan Press.

BRITTAN, A. (1973). Meanings and situations. Boston: Routledge and Kegan Paul.

BRUNER, J., GOODNOW, J., and AUSTIN, G. (1956). A study of thinking. New York: John Wiley.

BUDD, R., and RUBEN, B. (1972). Approaches to human communication. New York: Spartan.

CARSON, R. (1969). Interaction concepts of personality. Chicago: Aldine.

CICOUREL, A. (1974). Cognitive sociology. New York: Free Press.

CUSHMAN, D., and WHITING, G. (1972). "An approach to communication theory: Toward consensus on rules." Journal of Communication, 22:217-238.

DARNELL, D. (1971). "Toward a reconceptualization of communication." Journal of Communication, 21:5-16.

--- (1973). "To Bruce Westley, with love." Journal of Communication, 23:476-478.

DOUGLAS, J. (1970). Understanding everyday life. Chicago: Aldine.

DUNCAN, H.D. (1968). Symbols and society. New York: Oxford University Press.

DUNCAN, S., Jr. (1972). "Some signals and rules for taking speaking turns in conversations." Journal of Personality and Social Psychology, 23:283-292.

GARFINKEL, H. (1967). Studies in ethnomethodology. Englewood Cliffs, N.J.: Prentice-Hall.

GOTTLIEB, G. (1968). The logic of choice. New York: Macmillan.

HARRE, R. (1974). "Some remarks on 'rule' as a scientific concept." In T. Mischel (ed.), Understanding other people. Oxford: Basil Blackwell.

HARRE, R., and SECORD, P. (1973). The explanation of social behavior. Totowa, N.J.: Littlefield, Adams.

HARRIS, L. (1975). "Construction and preliminary testing of a behavior continuum." Unpublished paper.

HEMPEL, C. (1966). Philosophy of natural science. Englewood Cliffs, N.J.: Prentice-Hall.

KAPLAN, A. (1964). The conduct of inquiry. San Francisco: Chandler.

KELLY, G. (1955). The psychology of personal constructs. New York: Norton.

KOCH, S. (1964). "Psychology and emerging conceptions of knowledge as unitary." Pp. 1-41 in T.W. Wann (ed.), Behaviorism and phenomenology. Chicago: University of Chicago Press.

KUHN, T. (1970). The structure of scientific revolutions (2nd ed.). Chicago: University of Chicago Press.

McHUGH, P. (1968). Defining the situation. Indianapolis: Bobbs-Merrill.

MEAD, G.H. (1934). Mind, self and society. Chicago: University of Chicago Press.

MILLER, G., GALANTER, E., and PRIBRAM, K. (1960). Plans and the structure of behavior. New York: Holt, Rinehart and Winston.

MORRIS, C. (1946). Signs, language and behavior. New York: George Braziller.

--- (1964). Signification and significance. Cambridge, Mass.: Massachusetts Institute of Technology Press.

NOFSINGER, R., Jr. (1975). "The demand ticket: A conversational device for getting the floor." Speech Monographs, 42:1-9.

PEARCE, W.B. (1973). "Consensual rules in interpersonal communications: A reply to Cushman and Whiting." Journal of Communication, 23:160-168.

--- (1976). An overview of communication and interpersonal relationships. Palo Alto, Calif.: Science Research Associates.

PEARCE, W.B., and STAMM, K. (1973). "Coorientational states and interpersonal communication." Pp. 177-204 in P. Clarke (ed.), New models for communication research. Beverly Hills, Calif.: Sage.

ROSSITER, C., and PEARCE, W.B. (1975). Communicating personally. Indianapolis: Bobbs-Merrill.

RUDNER, R. (1966). Philosophy of social science. Englewood Cliffs, N.J.: Prentice-Hall.

SACKS, H. (1967, 1972). "Mimeographed lecture notes." University of California, Berkeley.

SCHEGLOFF, E. (1968). "Sequencing in conversational openings." American Anthropologist, 70:1075-1095.

TOULMIN, S. (1961). Foresight and understanding. Bloomington: Indiana University Press.

--- (1974). "Rules and their relevance for understanding human behavior." Pp. 185-215 in T. Mischel (ed.), Understanding other people. Oxford: Basil Blackwell.

VON WRIGHT, G.H. (1971). Explanation and understanding. Ithaca, N.Y.: Cornell University Press.

WATZLAWICK, P., BEAVIN, J., and JACKSON, D. (1967). Pragmatics of human communication. New York: Norton.

WESTLEY, B. (1973). "Darnell reconceptualized." Journal of Communication, 23:187-194.

Chapter 2

COMMUNICATION SYSTEMS: INTERPERSONAL IMPLICATIONS

Donald P. Cushman and Robert T. Craig

> Future historians who record what is being said and done today will find it difficult to avoid giving a prominent place to our preoccupation with communication. Communication does not signify a problem newly discovered in our time, but a fashion of think and a method of analyzing which we apply in the statement of all fundamental problems.
>
> Richard McKeon (1957:89)

COMMUNICATION: A MAJOR THEME OF OUR AGE

ALMOST AS INTERESTING AS COMMUNICATION itself is the fact that people today are so interested in communication. The "problem of communication" is a major theme of our age. It fills our bookshelves and the advice columns of our newspapers. It spawns endless methods, therapies, and courses in the name of self-improvement, interpersonal adjustment, salesmanship, or whatever. It explains–and, we hope, solves–all other problems. If you want to find a mate . . . save a marriage . . . get a job . . . sell a used car . . . educate the public . . . prevent a war . . . then communicate!

Why have people recently become so interested in problems of communication? According to the distinguished philosopher Richard McKeon (1957) our preoccupation with communication today is no accident, but rather a response to the convergence of three trends in contemporary society.

The first is a trend toward an increase in tolerance for cultural, group, and individual diversity. The United States fought World War I and World War II to make the world safe for democracy. We did not consult the world's cultures to ask if they wanted to be free; instead we assumed an eminence for our way of life and sought to extend it to others. Within the United States, political, social, and religious groups proceeded in a similar manner. If you were a Democrat, a liberal, and a Catholic you sought to convert others to your political, social, and religious beliefs. Republicans, conservatives, and Protestants were in error in their point of view and thus required conversion. Interpersonal relationships with families, friends, and acquaintances were primarily based on commonalities of attitudes, values, and beliefs.

The latter half of the 20th century has witnessed an increase in our tolerance for cultural, group, and individual diversity. The United States as a nation has begun to recognize the legitimacy of alternative political, social, and economic institutions. Detente with China and Russia and our new nonalignment policies in Southeast Asia and the Middle East are evidence of our recognition of the legitimacy of diverse cultural systems. Within the United States, the rise of ticket splitting in politics, women's liberation and the recognition of minorities in the social areas, and ecumenism in religion are all signs of our increased tolerance for group diversity. This same tolerance is manifest in family, friendship, and acquaintance patterns. People often choose interpersonal associations with others who are quite different from themselves. A recent field study of interpersonal attraction (Curry and Kenny, 1974) indicates that similarity of values is a poorer predictor of interpersonal attraction in natural settings than laboratory studies have led us to believe (Byrne, 1971; Huston, 1974). The increased tolerance for diversity is clearly evident in the reduced "social distance" between Americans and various racial and national groups over a 40-year period as reported by Bogardus (1967).

A second trend recognizable in today's world is an increase in interdependence both between and within cultures. The 20th century has witnessed a rapid growth in population throughout the world which has placed a serious strain upon the world's resources. The unequal distribution of these resources has forced an interdependence between cultures. We are in need of European manufactured goods, Arab oil, and rare minerals found in Africa, Asia, and Latin America; and the countries overseas, in turn, are in need of our food, arms, and technology. America's national interests and goals can be achieved only with the cooperation of other nations. Each culture is capable, if it withdraws its resources, of inflicting serious harm upon other cultures.

Similarly we have witnessed a growth in interdependence between people within the same culture. Industrialization, urbanization, and their companions, high specialization of function and strict division of labor, have made people within the same culture interdependent in regard to goods and services. We live in nations, cities, and families in which, respectively, a strike by airline employees, a boycott by doctors, or the illness of a family member can seriously impair our capacity to pursue our individual interests and goals. Our interdependence and our diversity require that we take account of others who frequently view the world in a somewhat different way than we do. Our failure to take into account other people who may differ with us in point of view will lead to the withdrawal of their cooperation and resources and the disruption of our capacity to achieve individual or group goals.

A third trend discernible in contemporary society is an increase in the availability of communication. Increased access to the means of communication has made each of us aware of our diversity and our interdependence. Television has made most Americans as familiar with some of the attitudes, values, and beliefs of Southeast Asians, Arabs, and Irish as they are with the opinions of their friends and co-workers. The mass media have familiarized us with the plight of blacks, Chicanos, and the poor. The telephone allows members of the same family to be scattered throughout the country and yet be able to maintain regular and close interpersonal contact. Because of this rapid expansion in the available means of communication, we have been thrust into a "global village" where we are confronted with people who follow different religions, pursue different interests, and have different political philosophies, but with whom we must cooperate if we are to achieve our national, group, and individual goals.

The preoccupation of people today with the problem of communication is no accident, but rather a response to the situations which confront us. When the problems we face are broad and complex, when the people capable of solving those problems have divergent and sometimes competing frames of reference, and when people require the cooperation of others for a satisfactory solution to their problems, then the initial distinctions necessary for examining problems as well as the means for achieving cooperation in the solution of problems must be found in communication (McKeon, 1957).

However, growth in our tolerance for diversity and in our interdependence has placed stress upon the primary function of communication—namely, the motivation and coordination of collective action necessary for the solution of the common problems which confront interdependent groups. Communication aimed at motivating collective action in regard to our common problems depends on our establishing agreements regarding meanings, purposes, and values. Tolerance for diversity poses a substantial barrier to achieving the precise understandings and agreements on purposes and values necessary to direct and motivate collective action in regard to serious and complex problems. Such barriers may lead to confusion, misunderstanding, and insufficient commitment to motivate collective action. Yet the awareness of our interdependence suggests that the common problems which confront us and which require the cooperation of diverse others for their resolution will, if we fail to act, continue to grow in intensity.

Communication: The Need For a Paradigm Shift

The convergence of these three trends suggests a shift in our assumptions about the basic mechanisms which give efficiency to communication processes. Several implications can be drawn from our previous analysis for the construction of a new perspective on the communication process.

First, the primary impulse for communication has shifted from persuasion and conversion to understanding and negotiation. Whereas previously the impulse to communicate arose within systems seeking means to achieve agreed-upon ends consistent with common values, such conditions no longer should be assumed to obtain. In their place, the conditions of diversity and interdependence now give rise to the impulse to communicate. Previously, communication sprang from a desire to persuade or convert people to a common set of values as a prerequisite for the solution of problems which optimizes those values. Solutions thus located were optimal from the viewpoint of both the interdependent system and the individuals who constituted it, because all participants shared a common set of values. But when our values and interests are no longer shared—as they are not under conditions of diversity and interdependence—the impulse to communicate accompanies a recognition that differing parties possess differing conceptions of their mutual problems. In such circumstances it is necessary to understand and recognize the legitimacy of alternative conceptions of a problem. Our understanding of the diverse points of view toward a problem allows for the negotiation of a solution which is optimal for the system of interdependence, but which almost always is suboptimal from each individual's perspective. The realization by diverse individuals that they are interdependent provides the pressure for the negotiation and acceptance of courses of action which are suboptimal from each individual's perspective.

Second, the efficacious use of communication has shifted from a reliance upon symbols which are value-laden to a reliance upon symbols which are neutral in regard to diverse and sometimes competing value systems. Previously, the efficacious use of communication was achieved by the use of symbols which were endowed with consensual meaning and motivational force because they were grounded in a common value system. Diversity and interdependence preclude such an approach. Value-laden symbols would introduce a whole array of prejudices in favor of one value system and give rise to a heightened awareness of diversity, thus generating disagreements and conflicts. Instead a symbol system is required which is neutral in regard to diverse value systems, but which is endowed with consensual meanings and motivational force because participants engaged in a common task have found it productive for coordinating their activities.

Third, the conditions for the evolution and disintegration of communication relations have shifted from a focus on an awareness of our common values to an awareness of our interdependence. Whereas previously the growth of communication relations began with an awareness of our common values and expanded in accordance with our awareness of the problems confronting those values, diversity and interdependence now preclude such a focus. In its place, the recognition of diversity and a heightened awareness of our interdependence now provide the basis for the growth of communication relations. The disintegration of communication relations results from a failure to recognize diversity and to see interdependence where it exists.

Understanding Human Communication as a System

The purpose of our previous analysis has been to indicate why communication in general and interpersonal communication in particular can best be understood by understanding the systems in which communication takes place. The concept *system* refers to a set of components which influence each other and which constitute a whole or unity for the purpose of analysis. To call a set of components a system implies that the components are *organized* in some way and that we are interested in the principles of organization or interdependence that make the whole work, rather than in the parts in their own right. It happens, however, that there are several points of view that one can take in describing the organization of a system. The three most important of these are function, structure, and process.

Simply defined, a *function* is something that a system does. More exactly, it is something that the system *must* do, in the sense that if the function were not performed the system would break down. Thus, respiration is a function of the human body; maintaining internal order is a function of a political system; and regulating the level of expressed affection is a function of an interpersonal relationship.

The *structure* of a system is the set of connections or relationships among its components. If a functional analysis answers the question, "What does the system do?" a structural analysis answers the question, "How is the system put together?" These two questions are obviously closely related, in that what a thing does depends very much on how it is put together, and how we put a thing together depends on what we want it to do. Structure and function are just two ways of describing a single fact, a system's principle of organization. The structure of an engine is a set of components and mechanical linkages; the structure of a human relationship is a set of rules governing behavior.

The *processes* of a system are the changes which the system undergoes over time. This is a third way of describing the organization of a system. Here we describe the system as a temporal continuum or a sequence of events and become interested in how the system functions and evolves–how it responds by rule to situations which it assimilates to its structure, and how it accommodates or fails to accommodate to novel developments, thus growing or decaying.

At the most basic level, what are the functions, structures, and processes of *communication* systems? We have argued that the contemporary problem of communication is how to ensure cooperation among people who are diverse in perspectives and interdependent in regard to the resolution of mutual problems. Following Cushman and Whiting (1972:219) we suggest that three propositions undergird that analysis: (1) that cooperative action is required to resolve common problems, (2) that communication facilitates cooperative action, and (3) that communication requires consensus upon communication rules. The basic *function* of human communication in such a system is to regulate consensus–to adjust consensus to the need for coordination. The *structure* of a communication system is the set of rules which constitutes the consensus of the system at a given moment. These rules are of two general types: *code* rules, which regulate the usage of symbols, thus structuring the content of communication, and *network* rules, which regulate the channels, circumstances, and manner of communication, thus structuring communication relations. To describe the structure of a communication system is to describe the set of rules which ensures coordinated collective responses in defined situations (if there is consensus on the rules). It is, in other terms, to describe a repertory of "episodes" (Harré and Secord, 1973; Pearce, Chapter 1 in this volume). The *process* of human communication is the functioning and evolution of a system-in-context: the assimilation of concrete situations as they are codified and transmitted within the system, and the simultaneous accommodation of the system to the more recalcitrant aspects of those same situations.

The three perspectives correct one another. Process corrects the more static implications of structure. Structure reminds us that process does not preclude relative invariances, patterns persisting across situations. Function, finally, implies that those patterns are not arbitrary, but rather are explicable in terms of the design or evolution of the class of systems which they describe. A complete description of a communication system requires all three points of view.

The General Levels of Communication Systems

We find it both aesthetically pleasing and intellectually fruitful to think of human civilization as one great communication system. As we argued above, the people of the world have become interdependent; so the regulation of consensus on a worldwide scale has become a need—and, to some degree, an accomplished fact. If you accept the basic idea of a world system, then it is only a small step to think of that system as organized in hierarchical levels, as systems generally are. Within the great network there are clusters, and clusters within clusters, and so on. The structure of the world network is very complex, with clusters overlapping each other at many levels. For the sake of grasping the world intellectually, however, it helps to tidy things up by imposing some clearly defined categories. It is in that spirit that we ask you to consider a scheme called the general levels of communication systems. Table 1 presents the three general levels, and indicates how we distinguish between them from the standpoints of function, structure, and process.

Cultural communication systems are, generally speaking, the largest and longest-lived clusters in the world network. The basic function of such systems is *to regulate consensus with respect to institutions*—established values, beliefs, assumptions, expectations, and patterns of behavior. Institutions underlie the sense of unity that we feel with the other members of such networks as nations, regions, and social classes. People can identify with each other to the extent that they speak the same language, wear the same styles of dress, and support the

TABLE 1
THE GENERAL LEVELS OF COMMUNICATION SYSTEMS

		Typical Structures		
System Level	*Basic Function*	*Networks*	*Codes*	*Typical Processes*
Cultural	consensus about institutions	nation, culture, class, subculture, region, community, family	language, dialect, accent	diffusion, especially via mass media; customs and rituals
Social Organization	consensus about production	organization, group, role	jargon, technical terminology	leadership, control, information exchange, bargaining, negotiation, discussion
Interpersonal	consensus about self-concepts	dyadic relationships within friendship, family networks	personal style, personal reference	development, presentation and validation of self-concepts

same forms of government. The structure—code and network rules—of a cultural system is standardized throughout a nation, culture, subculture, social class, region, or community. The communication processes that most typically occur in cultural systems are (1) the customs and rituals that are the concrete expression of institutions and (2) processes of diffusion or the spread of ideas that change institutions or create new ones.

We add one final comment about the cultural level. In view of the above, we might reformulate the modern problem of communication as a problem of regulating consensus in a world where traditional institutions have broken down. Our identification within cultural systems has been weakened. There is less diversity among cultures as a world culture emerges, but more diversity within cultures as diffusion processes accelerate. As part of the same process, social organizational and interpersonal communication have increased in importance as bases for human cooperation. These shifts have made communication problematic.

Social organizational communication systems, from a functional standpoint, are systems which *regulate consensus with respect to production.* People can cooperate in performing a task to the extent that each performs work that complements the work of the others. Thus, the focus of social organizations is upon the division of labor, the definition and performance of differentiated and integrated rules in the collective performance of some task. Structurally, such systems range from great, complex organizations like national governments and General Motors, to small informal groups working together to solve a homework problem or paint a house. The network rules of social organizational communication systems tend to be more formal (explicit) than those of a culture. Authority relations are especially important. With respect to code rules, a social organization tends to evolve a jargon or technical terminology having to do with objects important to the organization's task. The communication processes that most typically occur in social organizations include (1) processes of leadership and control, such as orders, directives, and reports to superiors, (2) exchanges of information, and (3) formal and informal bargaining, negotiation, and discussion.

Finally, *interpersonal communication systems,* functionally speaking, are systems which *regulate consensus with respect to individual self-conceptions.* A person's self-conception is the person's set of ideas about the kind of person that he or she is.[1] Clyde considers himself an American, a bank teller, handsome, intelligent, a bad driver, quick-tempered, attractive to women, a joker, and afraid of snakes—these are all elements of Clyde's self-conception. The key points about self-conceptions are two. First, unlike institutions and organizational roles, self-conceptions are *unique* to individuals. Second, there is a mutual causal relationship between a person's self-conception and what *others* think of the person; a person's presentation of self to others, in other words, affects the impressions that others have of the person, and the reactions of others to the person in turn affect the person's conception of self. One's sense of self—both one's general sense of being a unique person and the more specific elements of self-conception—depends absolutely upon participation in a certain kind of close, personal relationship with others. We call these interpersonal relationships.

The *structures* of an interpersonal system are not imposed from without, but emerge from the interaction of the people. The typical network form of an interpersonal system is the *dyad* (two people) within a friendship or family network. An interpersonal system tends to evolve a private code based on the personal styles and experiences of the individuals. The typical *processes* of interpersonal communication systems are those involving the development, presentation, and validation of self-conceptions. The individual in interaction proposes identities for self and other. The proposed conceptions are accepted or rejected by the other in a kind of tacit negotiation. By such processes individuals develop, present, and validate self-conceptions, creating thereby a relationship responsive to their needs—and needs responsive to their relationship.

The last point to be made about the general levels of communication systems is perhaps the most important, because it explains why we should be concerned with cultural and social organizational communication in what will be a theory of interpersonal communication. The point is that the general levels are both mutually exclusive and interdependent. On the one hand, defining the three levels helps us to understand what *is* interpersonal communication by contrasting it with what is *not* interpersonal communication. Given the definitions of the three levels, it ought, in principle, to be possible to divide the content of any set of messages or the rules of any network into three piles: cultural, social organizational, and interpersonal. In that sense the levels are mutually exclusive. On the other hand, understanding the general levels helps us to understand interpersonal communication because the three levels are *interdependent*—they affect one another. Cultural and social organizational systems constrain and influence interpersonal systems and vice versa. For example, the smooth working of a social organization depends upon what is called the interpersonal climate—the quality of the personal relations between organizational members. Or again, marriage is a cultural institution, but marriage is also the formal framework for the most intimate of interpersonal relationships. In short, we cannot understand an interpersonal communication system without understanding its social organizational and cultural environment. In the final analysis, the world network is all of a piece.

In conclusion we indicate three significant implications of our analysis for the development of interpersonal communication theory and practice:

(1) We characterized the modern problem of communication as one of discovering and building upon consensus, which in the flux of the modern world cannot be assumed. The thrust of this argument is that as the unique self becomes more and more free to vary, more and more dominant in the behavior of individuals, then more and more of the communication between individuals must become interpersonal, as opposed to cultural or social organizational. The problem of communication is in essence a problem of *negotiating* communication systems to relate people who are not sufficiently related by preexisting social organizational or cultural systems. Understanding the unique function, structures, and processes of interpersonal communication systems is thus responsive to its very core to the contemporary problem of communication.

(2) We have defined a system as a set of components that are interdependent and constitute a whole or unity for purposes of analysis. The system perspective on interpersonal communication should be seen in contrast to the major alternative, an atomistic perspective that views interpersonal communication strictly from an individual standpoint. This issue arose earlier in the context of characterizing our contemporary communication environment as made up primarily of diverse individuals who are interdependent with others for the solution of their mutual problems. We argued that the basic function of communication systems in such a context is the regulation of consensus. There we suggested that the consensus approach was useful because what was an optimal solution to a problem from the invididual's point of view may not be optimal from the point of view of the system. Interpersonal communication involves more than just individuals; it involves individuals *in a relationship;* and, furthermore, the relationship itself is always embedded in systems at the social organizational and cultural levels. Tensions among the needs of systems at different levels sometimes create interesting problems. A woman may come to feel the need for a kind of independence that her relationship with a particular man does not allow. A pair of co-workers might want to develop an intimate relationship, but the conditions of their employment do not permit it. Thus, important problems of communication often arise because individuals, interpersonal systems, and higher-level systems do not have the same needs. That this

sort of analysis is possible would alone warrant a systems approach to interpersonal communication.

(3) Interpersonal communication is that communication which occurs in interpersonal communication systems. Interpersonal communication systems are distinguished from other general levels in terms of function, structure, and process, but primarily in terms of function. Function is the leading aspect because communication systems, like naturally occurring, living systems generally, are *assumed* to "work" in some way—the explanation of this is left to a theory of evolution. The basic function of such a system thus becomes a starting point, itself requiring no explanation, which can be called upon to explain other features of the system. In that sense function explains structure and process. So interpersonal communication is first of all defined by its unique function, which is to regulate consensus regarding individual self-conceptions.

The peculiar function of interpersonal systems implies peculiar structures and processes. An interpersonal system is marked by the evolution of a private code, especially having to do with persons and personal experiences. A well-defined interpersonal system is necessarily a *small* system—paradigmatically a dyad—for only a small number of people can simultaneously orient toward each others' unique selves. Relationship issues like affection and openness, and processes of development, presentation, and validation of self-conceptions seem necessary in view of the basic function of interpersonal systems.

Thus, interpersonal communication is defined and warranted as a distinct field of study and practice by the unique function, structures, and processes of interpersonal communication systems. We feel that this way of drawing the distinction raises a set of issues rich in implications for theory and practice. In the next section we develop a more specific paradigm for inquiry in line with our general orientation.

> From the symbolic interactionist posture arose the idea that people develop and support their self-conceptions through interaction with others. In a segmentalized world, one in which diverse values and attitudes can co-exist, the particular shape of any individual's self-conception depends upon the particular individuals from whom he develops them. These particular persons are, following Sullivan, *significant others.* The term significant other seems to designate those persons who are particularly influential in the formation, support or modification of the self-conception of an individual.
>
> A.O. Haller (1970:15)

INTERPERSONAL COMMUNICATION: A PARADIGM FOR INQUIRY

Human communication can be characterized from many vantage points. In a world marked by increased tolerance for cultural, group, and individual diversity and increased interdependence both within and between cultures in regard to the solution of common problems, a particularly fruitful perspective for the development of communication theory is that of symbolic interactionism. The symbolic interactionist perspective focuses on the processes involved in fitting together the lines of behavior of separate individuals into joint action through the transfer of symbolic information (Blumer, 1966:540). If interpersonal communication is to be viewed as the regulation of consensus in regard to the development, presentation, and validation of individual self-conceptions, then it is natural that we draw upon the symbolic interactionist tradition in examining the function and structure of self-conceptions and the interpersonal processes involved in the development, presentation, and validation of self-conceptions.

The Function and Structure of the Self-Conception [2]

Approaching the study of interpersonal communication from a symbolic interactionist perspective, we find a long theoretical heritage which focuses upon the concepts of human action, self-conception, and symbolic interaction. Charles Taylor (1968:33) incisively distinguishes human action from other types of behavior when he notes that to ascribe *action* to a person implies that (1) a certain state of affairs came into existence, (2) the person intended this state of affairs (or something very close to it), and (3) the person's behaviors were, at least in part, instrumental in bringing the state of affairs into existence. Any explanation of human action requires an understanding of the actor's view of his relationship to those objects which he deems relevant to that action. We need a map of the environment as it appears to the actor. This map will not correspond to any "objective" description of the environment since it will exclude much and add more. The map will have to tell us what objects the individual will take into account and how–i.e., what his current conceptions are of his relations to relevant objects. It may be important to determine the degree to which the map is subject to alteration by the individual through a consideration of new objects or new properties of objects. In other words, we need some way of knowing the probable direction and content of changes in the map due to experience and, in particular, due to inputs of appropriately designed information.

Following in the tradition of James, Cooley, and Mead, we shall argue that the self-conception is the generative mechanism of interpersonal choice and that an appropriate analysis of its contents and the processes it involves will provide us such a cognitive map. In the words of Herbert Blumer (1966:535), "The possession of a self provides the human being with a mechanism of self-interaction with which to meet the world–a mechanism that is used in forming and guiding his conduct." For Mead, the self meant that the human being is an object to himself. The individual may then perceive himself as others do, communicate with himself, have a conception of who he is, and act toward himself and others. Blumer (1966:536) says, "With the mechanism of self-interaction the human being ceases to be a responding organism whose behavior is a product of what plays upon him from the outside, the inside, or both. Instead he acts towards his world, interpreting what confronts him and organizing his actions on the basis of the interpretations."

We regard the self-conception as an organized set of rules which defines the relationship of objects to the individual and which is capable of governing and directing human action. The self-conception, as an organized set of rules, provides the rationale for choice in the form of a valenced repertory of alternative plans of action.

The self-conception has traditionally been viewed as the information an individual has regarding the relationship of objects or groups of objects to the individual (Mead, 1934:243). Man, moving in his environment, is confronted by persons, places, things, messages. Man, when confronted by such an object, must, if he is to commit himself to any action, perform two tasks. First, he must determine what the object of his experience *is* by associating it with and differentiating it from other objects of his experience. Second, he must determine the relationship of the object to him in terms of appropriate actions in appropriate circumstances. Man's knowledge of what objects are and of how he should act toward them is a product of information based on past experience. Obviously, the individual has object relationships in his experiential field which do not include the self as one of the objects. It is equally evident that relationships among objects where the self is not one of the objects cannot contain information regarding an imperative course of action for the individual. Such relationships, in short, would not be a part of the self-conception. For example, the statement, "Aristotle is dead," while providing information about Aristotle, tells an individual nothing about himself. Such a statement would be an example of a relationship which is *not* part of the self-conception. The statement, "I am a teacher," does provide an individual with information about himself and, as such, would be part of the self-conception.

It is important to note that some self-object relationships, in addition to providing information about an individual's relationship to an object, prescribe a plan of action for the use of that object in certain situations. For example, the statement, "I am the kind of person who (given certain circumstances) attempts to be logical," would be part of the self-conception and would serve as a *rule* governing an individual's actions in certain circumstances. The rules which govern an individual's relationship to objects and which serve to direct human action can always be stated such that in circumstance X, some act Y is appropriate (Gottlieb, 1968). Self-conception statements, formulated as rules for action, always contain:

(1) A definition of an object in terms of its relationship to the individual; e.g., "I am the kind of person who attempts to be logical."

(2) An indication of the circumstances in which the rule is applicable; e.g., when dealing with others.

The composite of all the rules an individual has regarding the relationship of objects to him is his self-conception. These rules provide organization which serves to guide human action. It is the stability of this set of rules which makes an individual's actions predictable.

The Interpersonal Communication Processes Involved in the Development, Presentation, and Validation of Individual Self-Conceptions

If the basic determinant of differential human behavior is an individual's rules regarding his relationship to objects then it is apparent that all the ways in which an individual can become aware of those relationships are the ways in which the self-conception is formed. George Herbert Mead argued that the process of self-conception development is basically a process of socialization or enculturation. The individual is born into ongoing cultural and social organizational processes which provide the individual with a repertory of potential self-object relations. Through social-learning processes the person is made aware of sets of rules regarding his relations to objects, including other people.

According to Mead (1934:327) *role-taking* is the central mechanism for the development of a self-conception and for understanding the self-conception of others. The term "role" is defined as a socially prescribed way of behaving in particular situations for any person occupying a given cultural or social organizational position. A role represents what a person is supposed to do in a given situation by virtue of the position he holds. Role-taking is the process whereby an individual imaginatively constructs the attitudes and expectations that others have for him when he assumes a given role. This allows him to predict others' behavior toward him when he occupies the role (Mead, 1934:243). Through the role-taking process, which exhibits a developmental history, an individual is made aware of an increasing range of self-object relationships.

Building on the work of Ralph Turner (1956) and Robert Lauer and Linda Boardman (1971), we shall differentiate four levels of role-taking. *Basic role-taking* is the process whereby an individual imaginatively constructs the attitudes and expectations of cultural and social organizational positions and is consequently able to anticipate and respond to the roles of others. *Reflective role-taking* is the evaluation of various role requirements in regard to an individual's likes and dislikes. Two types of information are required for such a comparison: information regarding the cultural and social organizational role acquired through basic role-taking and information about an individual's self-conception, his or her likes and dislikes. *Appropriative role-taking* entails an individual's evaluation of some aspect of a role positively and the reduction of that self-object relationship to a permanent part of his personality or self-conception. It leads to the acquisition of a self-conception rule. For example, a high school student might be a debater and find that he likes one aspect of the role, namely, the aggressive testing of arguments. He may then make that aspect of the role a permanent part of his personality. This means that even when he leaves the role of debater he will take the opportunity to exercise that aspect of his personality whenever possible. Through appropriative role-taking a person develops a set of self-object relations which are person-dependent rather than role-dependent. Those relations are the set of characteristics that an individual manifests across roles, his self-conception. *Synesic role-taking* is the imaginative construction of the other's self-conception such that not only is his behavior anticipated, but an understanding of his feelings, perceptions, and definition of the situation is gained. Synesic role-taking occurs when a person can separate some other individual from his roles and respond to him as a self.

The stratification of role-taking by awareness levels has several important implications. *Basic, reflective, appropriative,* and *synesic* role-taking represent progressively greater orders of communication awareness. Communication awareness enables individuals to comprehend the expectations of others. *Basic* and *reflective* role-taking are processes one employs to learn and evaluate previously established roles and their expectations. These two levels of role-taking presuppose the existence of mechanisms other than the self-conception to generate such roles. Basic and reflective role-taking are thus restricted to the cultural and social organizational levels of communication systems. *Appropriative* role-taking and *synesic* role-taking are processes that one employs to develop, present, and validate individual self-conceptions. These two levels of role-taking presuppose the existence of the self-conception as the mechanism generating behavior. Appropriative role-taking and synesic role-taking are thus restricted to the interpersonal level of communication systems.

It is our belief that the interpersonal levels of role-taking can be validly and reliably measured by the Twenty Statements Test (Kuhn and McPartland, 1954; Spitzer et al., 1969). This test can be made out either by an individual actor or by other people who observe an individual's actions. The Twenty Statements Test asks one to respond to the statement "I am ---" or "X is ---" with 20 descriptive terms. If one were asked to fill out this questionnaire on himself or on another in a variety of specified roles (i.e., father, teacher, friend, etc.), then those descriptive terms which appeared again and again across observers and role positions would define the focal individual's self-conception. Researchers can employ the Twenty Statements Test to locate the set of rules which make up an individual's self-conception and to follow their development in the process of symbolic interaction (Mahoney, 1973).

Once we locate a given individual's set of self-conception rules we can then treat those rules as the generative mechanism for explaining, predicting, and controlling the regulation of consensus in regard to the self-conception. This can be accomplished by developing categories of interpersonal communication behaviors which are tautological with the set of self-conception rules. The categories of behavior will contain the same distinctions as the role-taking levels, but the subject matter will be regularities of communication behaviors. The communication categories will be conceptually parallel to, but operationally distinct from, the role-taking levels. Table 2 shows how the distinctions underlying the role-taking levels can be replicated in terms of message contents, communication styles, and communication relationships. If the self-conception is indeed the generative mechanism for interpersonal communication, then these conceptual correlations ought to be empirically verifiable.

First we extend the role-taking levels into a set of message content categories for analyzing the *development* of individual self-conceptions. Messages generated by an individual at the basic role-taking level will manifest statements which are *role-prescribed.* The statements will be what is prescribed when one role addresses another, as when the wife asks her husband when he would like his dinner. Reflective role-takers will generate messages containing statements which are *role-evaluative.* They will compare a given role or an aspect of a role to what the individual considers his or her likes and dislikes, as when the wife complains that she has to do all the housework. Messages generated by an appropriative role-taker will take the form of *means-ends* statements aimed at the exercise of the respective appropriative characteristic. They will be communication aimed at achieving a given end—the woman demands a change in the division of labor. Synesic role-taking messages will contain content categories that are *other-oriented* and that recognize the uniqueness of another's self-conception. They will acknowledge the rules of others. Our example is now more difficult to characterize without further knowledge of the situation, but we would generally look for some adaptation of the wife's demand to the husband's feelings.

Second, we extend our analysis to a classification scheme of communication styles employed in the *presentation* of self-conceptions. We would operationalize communication style by means of measures of risk and disclosure (Miller et al., 1971). Risk refers to how a communicator limits others' responses to his

TABLE 2
ROLE-TAKING LEVELS AND COMMUNICATION CONTENTS, STYLES, AND RELATIONSHIPS

Role-Taking Levels	*Message Content Categories*	*Communication Styles*	*Risk*	*Dis*	*Communication Relationships*
1. Basic	Role Prescribed	Conventional	L	L	Independent of Self
2. Reflective	Role Evaluative	Intrapersonal	L	H	Counterdependent on Self
3. Appropriative	Means-Ends	Manipulative	H	L	Dependent on Self
4. Synesic	Other Oriented	Open	H	H	Interdependent Selves

messages. A low risk statement is exemplified by "It's a nice day, isn't it?" The communicator minimizes personal risk by selecting impersonal topics and structuring his statements in a manner that elicits responses acceptable to him. A high risk statement is exemplified by "How do you feel about that?" Such a statement fails to prescribe acceptable responses and hence increases the risk from unknown responses. Disclosure is employed in much the traditional sense of the term. Low disclosure is minimal exposure of information concerning the communicator's self-conception. High disclosure occurs when information is presented which reveals the structure of the communicator's self-conception.

Basic role-takers will generate messages which are *conventional* in terms of the interacting roles. They will be low risk and low disclosure in that they are entirely predictable given the roles. Reflective role-takers will generate messages which are *intrapersonal* in terms of selected roles and specific self-conceptions. Intrapersonal messages will be low risk, since they are merely cognitive comparisons, and high disclosure, since they reveal the relationship of the role to the self. Appropriative role-takers will generate messages which are *manipulative* in nature, aimed at achieving a goal. Such messages will be high in risk because the self will confront or attack the other or will goad the other to disclose–information about the other being needed in order to manipulate him–but low in disclosure because they will reveal little of the self beyond what is objectified in the self-presentation. Here the person "plays himself straight" –no deviations from a predetermined identity–in much the same way as the basic role-taker plays a conventional social role straight. Synesic role-takers will generate messages which are *open* in content, both high risk and high disclosure. When one self fully confronts another, high risk and high disclosure, of necessity, occur. To open oneself is to expose one's identity to the possibility of challenge and change.

Third, we extend our role-taking levels into a description of communication relationships which *validate* the self-conception.[3] Basic role-takers will establish relationships which are *independent* of the self-conceptions of the individuals involved, because they are role-specific. The individual changes, chameleonlike, from role to role, as does the sergeant who is one person before a private and an entirely different person before a lieutenant. Reflective role-takers will establish intrapersonal relationships between cultural and social roles and the self, yielding social relationships which are *counterdependent* on the self-conception. The individual, "playing off" his role, is capable of negotiating a unique variant of his role relationship with a particular other by a process somewhat like Mead's "conversation of gestures" (1934:63). The resulting rules, however, are not transferable from role to role. The person *brings* nothing to the relationship beyond the prescribed role. Our sergeant might become a unique sergeant to his private and another unique sergeant to his lieutenant, but the uniqueness in each case might result purely from the sergeant's adaptation of his role, not from a unique self that he brings to his role.

Appropriative role-takers will generate relationships which are *dependent* upon an individual's specific self-object relationship. Stable relationships can only be formed with others who have complementary self-conceptions. The submissive person requires dominant partners; the political liberal requires politically liberal partners. Synesic role-takers will establish relationships which offer recognition to the other's self-conception and interact in terms of the *interdependence* of two self-conceptions. Here the person maintains his or her identity across relationships, but is capable of negotiating variants of that self-conception which "address," or adapt to, the self-conceptions of others. At this level, interpersonal communication comes into its own as the negotiation of identities. The political liberal and the political conservative can evolve a relationship in which, despite their differences, the two can develop, present, and validate their self-conceptions.

Appropriative and synesic role-takers must be, in some respects, substantively different personalities. Role-taking is more than merely a set of cognitive skills, although role-taking undoubtedly requires certain cognitive skills (Flavell et al., 1968). To ascend from the appropriative to the synesic level of role-taking is to appropriate self-conception rules allowing for other-oriented messages, an open style, and interdependent relationships and is to reject self-conception rules restricting one to means-ends messages, a manipulative style, and dependent relationships. To reach the synesic level the "dominant" person must become less inflexibly dominant, and the political liberal must become tolerant of other views. Personality characteristics like tolerance, openness, and thoughtfulness may be taken as evidence of synesic role-taking, since such characteristics reflect the operation of self-conception rules which are associated with the synesic level. Characteristics which reflect synesic role-taking we call synesic characteristics; characteristics which reflect appropriative role-taking we call appropriative characteristics. There are no "basic" or "reflective" characteristics, since at those levels the self-conception is not coherent and thus not strongly operative.

Let us examine an example of a self-conception which generates interpersonal communication behaviors. Let a set of valid and reliable self-conception categories for Don Cushman be:

(1) Don Cushman is aggressive.

(2) Don Cushman is organized.

(3) Don Cushman is arrogant.

(4) Don Cushman is thoughtful.

(5) Don Cushman is helpful.

Let the first three qualities be appropriative and the last two synesic. The self-conception categories are presumably among those that investigation with the Twenty Statements Test would show are manifest by Don Cushman across role relationships. The self-conception categories would then be classified by trained coders as either appropriative or synesic.

Turning to the message levels, we are suggesting that a content analysis of Don Cushman's interpersonal messages will reflect two primary classes of statements: means-ends statements and other-oriented statements. Means-ends statements will take the form of assertions of aggressiveness, organization, and arrogance, thus reflecting Don Cushman's appropriative qualities. Other-oriented statements will take the form of assertions that Don Cushman can see things from the other's point of view and will manifest his synesic qualities of being thoughtful and helpful. A content analysis of Don Cushman's messages across role relationships should reveal this pattern of statements as the principal configuration in his interpersonal communication behavior.

Turning to communication styles, we are suggesting that Don Cushman's presentation of self will manifest these same qualities. A risk and disclosure analysis of Don Cushman's interactions will reflect both the manipulative and open styles. A manipulative communication style is characterized by high-disclosure and low-risk messages and will allow Cushman to manipulate others in such a manner as to manifest his aggressiveness, organization, and arrogance. An open style is characterized by high-risk and high-disclosure messages; it will allow Cushman to be open to others and to manifest his thoughtfulness of and helpfulness to others.

Turning to the validation of self-conception relationships, we are suggesting that an interaction analysis of Don Cushman's communication will reveal that he manifests dependent and interdependent relationships of a particular form. Dependent relationships will be formed with people who will allow Don Cushman to be aggressive, organized, and arrogant. Interdependent relationships will be formed with people who allow Cushman to be thoughtful and helpful. A particular interpersonal communication relationship might reflect either or both sets of qualities.

If our analysis is correct, then the self-conception can be viewed as the generative mechanism which gives regularity to interpersonal communication. That is an empirical hypothesis, one which can be and, we hope, will be tested. We have presented the general logic of a study which would test the hypothesis.

> Symbolic interaction involves interpretation, or ascertaining the meaning of the actions or remarks of other persons, and definition, or conveying indications to another person as to how he is to act. Human association consists of a process of such interpretation and definition. Through this process the participants fit their own acts to the ongoing acts of one another and guide others in doing so.
>
> Herbert Blumer (1966:537)

A CONCEPTION OF INTERPERSONAL COMMUNICATION COMPETENCE

All human conduct and human experience takes place in the context of our association or joint actions with others. Blumer (1966) points out that a joint action cannot be resolved into a common or similar type of behavior on the part of each system participant because various individuals usually possess divergent attitudes, values, and beliefs, even though they may be interdependent in regard to some common task. In such instances, each individual necessarily has a unique self-conception, acts from that self-conception, and thus emits quite different behaviors. Yet, it is the fitting together of diverse acts that constitutes joint action. How do separate acts come to fit together? How can interpersonal interaction take place?

Individuals can fit their behaviors together into joint action only by interpreting and defining each other's behavior through the process of communication. By *listening* to the cues of the other an individual is able to take the role of the other in such a way as to develop expectations for himself. By *cueing* the other as to his own definition of a situation, an individual provides the other with the information necessary to develop expectations toward his actions. When expectations are unclear, are misinterpreted, or prevent coordination, the *negotiation* of meaning is required to achieve joint action. Listening, cueing, and negotiation skills thus become tools for the regulation of consensus and constitute our conceptual definition of interpersonal communication competence.

Listening skills turn on our ability to recognize differing types of statements and the respective self-object relationships which they designate. Cueing skills turn on our ability to translate our own relationships to objects into the vocabularies of diverse others. Negotiation skills turn on our ability to recognize the positions of others, to cue others as to our position, and to develop the appropriate strategies for reconciling differences in our expectations toward situations. Several effective programs for developing such skills have been designed by researchers (Swensen, 1973). One such program, the Minnesota Couples Training Program (Miller et al., 1971) is particularly suited to the development of listening, cueing, and negotiating skills involved in role-taking.

Data gathered on interpersonal interaction through role, content, interaction, and style analysis will provide communication researchers with diagnostic tools for analyzing, evaluating, and correcting individual and system patterns in listening, cueing, and negotiation skills. Such a set of diagnostic tools will be helpful in revealing the points of stress and the optimal coordination patterns for various systems of interdependence. This data should facilitate the development of a theory of interpersonal negotiation based on a combination of self-conception diversity and types of systems interdependence.

Interpersonal communication competence determines the range and types of joint actions which can be formed with diverse others. The range and types of joint action that can be formed with others limits individuals' capacities to develop, present, and validate their self-conceptions. This, in turn, determines the relative proportions of an individual's activities which take place within cultural, social organizational, and interpersonal communication systems.

A Program of Research

Finally, our discussion implies many important research problems. One group of questions flows from the analysis of role-taking levels. Perhaps the most profound of these is whether the *levels* are also developmental *stages.* At first glance, one is inclined to question whether a developmental progression should place seemingly egocentric behavior (the appropriative level) at a higher level of development than externally oriented behavior (the basic level). Flavell and his associates (1968), who treat role-taking in the context of general cognitive development, might raise such an objection. On the other hand, our analysis seems quite compatible with the description of *moral* development offered by Lickona (1974). Is it less reasonable to view interpersonal communication competence from the standpoint of moral development than from that of general cognitive development? We think not.

Several subsidiary questions may be raised in regard to the role-taking levels. Do individuals become "frozen" at low levels? What are the causes and consequences of such a state? What specific communication skills mark the transition to higher levels? What specific communication experiences facilitate the transition to higher levels?

A second group of research problems flows from the hypothesis that the self-conception is the generative mechanism for interpersonal communication. Most fundamentally, specific operations must be devised to carry out the general procedures that we have labeled content analysis, style analysis, and interaction analysis. The procedures developed, we expect, will not be unlike standard procedures that now go by those names. Modification of the standard procedures is needed to adapt them to our conceptualization. The necessary procedures having been developed, the general question can be investigated: Are role-taking levels reflected in *consistent* patterns of communication contents, styles, and relationships?

A third set of research questions ties the paradigm for inquiry back into the general analysis of communication systems. Here our focus shifts from the competency of the individual to the character of the system. Can we derive an empirically relevant typology of relationships from combinations of role-taking levels (somewhat in the fashion of the transactional analysts who derived such a typology from combinations of ego states)? The analysis into independent, counterdependent, dependent, and interdependent relationships is a foundation upon which we can build. Which specific sets of appropriative and synesic qualities are complementary and which are generative of interpersonal conflict? How do the several types of relationship structures evolve in response to stress? When and how do the cultural and social organizational system levels retard, facilitate, or shape the evolution of interpersonal relationships? Answers to these and related questions may lead to a theory of interpersonal communication appropriate to our contemporary era of diversity and interdependence.

NOTES

1. A more formal definition of the self-conception is given later in this paper.
2. The exposition in this section has been adapted from that of Cushman and Whiting (1969).
3. The typology that follows has been adapted from that of Dudley D. Cahn (1973).

REFERENCES

BLUMER, H. (1966). "Commentary and debate." American Journal of Sociology, 71:535-545.

BOGARDUS, E.S. (1967). Forty year racial distance study. Los Angeles: University of Southern California Press.

BYRNE, D. (1971). The attraction paradigm. New York: Academic Press.

CAHN, D.D. (1973). "A transactional model for interpersonal communication." Unpublished paper.

CURRY, T.J., and KENNY, D.A. (1974). "The effects of perceived and actual similarity in values and personality in the process of interpersonal attraction." Quality and Quantity, 8:27-43.

CUSHMAN, D., and WHITING, G. (1969). "Human action, self-conception and cybernetics." Paper presented at the convention of the International Communication Association, Phoenix.

--- (1972). "An approach to communication theory: Toward consensus on rules." Journal of Communication, 22:217-238.

FLAVELL, J.H., BOTKIN, P.T., FRY, C.L., WRIGHT, J.W., and JARVIS, P.E. (1968). The development of role-taking and communication skills in children. Huntington, N.Y.: Robert E. Krieger.

GOTTLIEB, G. (1968). The logic of choice. New York: Macmillan.

HARRE, H., and SECORD, P.F. (1973). The explanation of social behavior. Totowa, N.J.: Littlefield, Adams.

HALLER, A.O. (1970). "The Wisconsin Significant Other Battery." Final research report, U.S. Office of Education Grant 3-51170. Washington, D.C.: U.S. Department of Health, Education, and Welfare.

HUSTON, T.L. (ed., 1974). Foundations of interpersonal attraction. New York: Academic Press.

KUHN, M.H., and McPARTLAND, T. (1954). "An empirical investigation of self attitudes." American Sociological Review, 19:68-76.

LAUER, R.H., and BOARDMAN, L. (1971). "Role-taking: Theory, typology and propositions." Sociology and Social Research, 23:137-147.

LICKONA, T. (1974). "A cognitive-developmental approach to interpersonal attraction." In T.L. Huston (ed.), Foundations of interpersonal attraction. New York: Academic Press.

MAHONEY, E.R. (1973). "The processual characteristics of self-conception." Sociological Quarterly, 14:517-533.

McKEON, R. (1957). "Communication, truth and society." Ethics, 67:89-99.

MEAD, G.H. (1934). Mind, self and society. Chicago: University of Chicago Press.

MILLER, S., NUNNALLY, A.W., and WACKMAN, D. (1971). The Minnesota Couples Communication Training Program. Minneapolis: Interpersonal Communication Programs.

SPITZER, S., COUCH, C., and STRATTON, J. (1969). The assessment of the self. Iowa City: Sernoll.

SWENSEN, C.H., Jr. (1973). Introduction to interpersonal relations. Glenview, Ill.: Scott, Foresman.

TAYLOR, C. (1968). The explanation of behavior. New York: Humanities Press.

TURNER, R.H. (1956). "Role taking, role standpoint and reference-group behavior." American Journal of Sociology, 61:316-328.

Chapter 3

MODELING INTERPERSONAL COMMUNICATION SYSTEMS AS A PAIR OF MACHINES COUPLED THROUGH FEEDBACK

Joseph N. Cappella

TO USE THE TERMS "interpersonal" and "machine" together may seem inappropriate at best or perverted and inhumane at worst. The connotations of "machine" undoubtedly elicit "Brave New World" images which are incompatible with the visions of "communion" among humankind elicited by "interpersonal communications." By all ordinary definitions of machine, this terminological tension would be valid. However, the conception of machine to be pursued in this paper is not an ordinary one but rather is the conception suggested by Ashby (1963) in his *Introduction to Cybernetics.* I hope, then, that judgments of perversion and inhumanity can be suspended until at least the opportunity to demonstrate utility has been realized.

Ashby's conception of machine will be discussed in the section to follow but its implications may be summarized here. First, a machine is *not* to be confused with the reality under observation. It is but a formalization which represents that reality. In fact, the machine cannot be said to uniquely represent the behaviors being observed (Ashby, 1963:93). Many machines may represent the same "reality." Thus, to argue that a machine may not represent what is "really" happening is a truism which this paper will not deny.

Second, a machine is *not* an isomorphic (or one-to-one) representation of the reality but rather is a homomorphic (or partial) representation of an often complex situation. However, as Ashby (1963:104) puts it, "Knowledge can be partial and yet complete in itself" so that the "Scientific treatment of a complex

AUTHOR'S NOTE: The author wishes to acknowledge the contributions of Peter R. Monge of San Jose State University, John Hunter of Michigan State University, and Daniel Fogel of the University of Wisconsin-Madison to various aspects of this paper.

system does *not* demand that every possible distinction be made" (p. 105). Thus, to dismiss a machine as only a partial representation of the reality may be an accurate evaluation, but it will not alone invalidate the knowledge generated.

Finally, a machine is a list of variables which are juggled until a singleness of prediction is achieved. "Science simply refuses to study the other types [of systems] . . . dismissing them as 'chaotic' or 'nonsensical.' It is *we* who decide, ultimately, what we will accept as 'machine-like' and what we will reject" (Ashby, 1963:40). Thus, researchers single out for study that in interpersonal situations which is regular, recognizing full well that their representations will, of necessity, be partial ones and recognizing that their representations will constitute as much the observer's conception of what is real as what *is* real.

Given these caveats about machines and interpersonal communication, the remainder of this paper will present three substantive examples of machines representing aspects of interpersonal communication situations: (1) marital satisfaction and prediction of longevity as related to system stability; (2) mutual influence processes; and (3) two-person sound-silence patterns in informal conversations. Although these three situations seem to offer radically different partitions of interpersonal communication situations, I contend that a single type of machine, the *machine with input,* is at the heart of each situation. This contention, in turn, raises numerous questions. If each individual in a dyadic interpersonal situation is viewed as a machine with inputs and outputs, and if the output of each is the input of the other, then as qualitative differences in output emerge, are they accompanied by qualitative differences in the two-person machine? Furthermore, do the outputs of each individual regulate the system so that, if outputs were controllable, the system would be controllable? Put differently, if persons in dyads obey the same psychological processes but differ in their communication styles (either between individuals within a dyad or across dyads), are the dyads likely to give the appearance of being qualitatively different? I shall offer a tentative but affirmative response to this question in the subsequent sections.

THE MACHINE WITH INPUT

Ashby (1963:24) defines a determinate machine as "that which behaves in the same way as a closed, single-valued transformation." This definition is as simple to understand as its succinctness might suggest. Consider a machine with only two states, talking (T) or silence (S). T and S constitute a complete listing of all possible states of the system. Suppose that this machine behaves over time in such a way that T is always followed by S and that S is always followed by T. This statement specifies a closed, single-valued transformation on the states of the machine. The transformation is a rule or set of rules describing what each system state will become in the next time frame on the basis of where it was in the previous time frame. The transformation is closed because a system state (T or S) is always followed by a system state (T or S) and never anything else. Of course, behaviors other than talking or silence may be occurring but these are irrelevant to the behavior of the machine. The transformation is single-valued because each state is followed in time by one and only one state.

Since every machine is built from transformations which map states into states sequentially, the continued application of the transformation produces a sequence of states called the machine's *trajectory*. In the example above the trajectory is simply T, S, T, S, T, S, ... Thus a machine requires a clear and unequivocal specification of states and transformations (or rules) to map states into states, thereby producing an over-time pattern of state sequences.

Suppose that, when observing the T and S patterns of an individual, we observe a pair of transformations such that sometimes (1) T is followed by T and (2) S is followed by T, but at other times (1) T is followed by S and (2) S is followed by S. What is happening here? Are there two machines or still one, but one which is not single-valued? Suppose that we look further at what is occurring in the machine's environment. Assume that the first set of transformations operates when the only other person in the vicinity is silent (that is, S) and that the second set operates when the other person is talking (that is, T). Under these circumstances the machine is still determinate, but it is a *machine with input.* The input or "talk-silence" state of the other determines which pair of transformations will be applied. The trajectory for this machine also depends upon the input. If the input is S, then the trajectory will be either T, T, T, T, . . . or S, T, T, T, ... If the input is T, then the trajectory will be either T, S, S, S, . . . or S, S, S, S, ... Notice further that in this case the input *regulates* the machine since by controlling the input we can be assured that the machine will be in state T or state S regardless of the machine's starting state.

Ashby (1963, chapters 10-12) discusses regulation in terms of the blockage of information resulting from disturbances outside the system. Suppose that the system is following the stable trajectory T, T, T, T, . . . under input S and that some outside force (for example an interruption by a third party) either alters the trajectory directly by changing T to S or alters the input from S to T, thereby also altering the trajectory to a sequence of S's. If the input is also a good regulator, then it may either (1) anticipate the disturbance and continue to apply the input S thereby assuring a sequence of T's (Ashby, 1963:221) or (2) react to deviations from the desired sequence of T's by reapplying the input S when such errors are detected (Ashby, 1963:222). The former type is regulation by anticipation, and the latter is regulation by error. In either case, the effect of information associated with the disturbance is attenuated by the regulator, which in the simple case described is just the input.

The importance of regulation in machines cannot be overstated. If prescriptive statements about machines are to be made, then first "we must know what is important and what is wanted" (Ashby, 1963:219) (talk was the desired state above); second, we must know how the desired states are regulated; and, third, the mechanisms of regulation must be subject to control. The argument I am building maintains that in interpersonal communication the styles of interacting are the regulators of the system and that, since these styles are more subject to control than other aspects of the machine, system control is equivalent to control of style. If styles can be learned or unlearned, then desirable and undesirable outcomes can be controlled through appropriate manipulations of communication style.

Before substantive examples pertinent to the above thesis can be explored two further additions to the machine with input must be made: *feedback* and *probabilistic or multivalued transformations.* Instead of one machine with input, suppose there existed two machines with input such that the output of each machine was the input for the other. For example, suppose that the talk-silence machine with input is called machine A. If an identical machine, B, inputs a T or S from machine A, its transformations are determined by A. If machine B outputs a T or S to machine A, A's transformations are determined by B's input. The case of each machine affecting the other is called feedback (Ashby, 1963:53).

In the example, machine A and machine B are identical in their transformation rules and in the effects of input on the choice of transformation rules. The possible trajectories for these coupled machines are TT, SS, TT, SS, . . . or ST, ST, ST, . . . or TS, TS, TS, . . . depending upon where they start. Obviously, this machine is little aware of the norms surrounding turn-taking in conversation.

However, what if machine A is left alone but machine B is changed so that (1) if A is talking, then T goes to T and S goes to T, and (2) if A is silent, then T goes to S and S goes to S? (I have simply reversed the way A and B generate their talk and silence in response to input.) The two machines now have different communication "styles." If the reader follows the verbal transformation rules patiently, it is easy to see that the only trajectory for this machine is ST, SS, TS, TT, ST, SS, TS, TT, ... Thus, with a rather modest alteration in "style" of generating output, a rather substantial gain in adherence to turn-taking norms has been achieved. The point is that, while coupling two machines through feedback may be the fundamental paradigm for simulating two-person communication, the form of the feedback from each to the other could be crucial in determining the qualitative character of the system.

The final distinction to be made about machines in general is that the transformations need not be single-valued at all. Rather, it is quite legitimate for a machine to transform to more than one state but with different probabilities. For example, with machine A above, if B is silent, then T could go to T with probability 1.0 (which is a single-valued transformation). But with B silent, S could go to T with probability .50 and to S with probability .50. The machine A would then be stochastic rather than determinate, but all results for determinate machines would hold for the stochastic. Of course the probabilities must be stable or else stochastic becomes chaotic.

We are now ready to treat substantive examples of machines coupled through feedback. Each of the examples to be presented will differ in terms of the type of transformations applied, the character of the dynamics, the nature of the feedback, and the degree of regulation. In addition, each treats a substantively different aspect of two-person interactions. Nevertheless, each operates from the same logic which couples two machines so that each affects the other, exploring systematically the differences among machines as styles are modified.

STABILITY AND MARITAL SATISFACTION

Several years ago I sought to explain differences among married couples in satisfaction and predicted longevity of relationships. Two hunches guided my efforts. The first was that communication styles differed between the less satisfied and the more satisfied groups of partners; similarly, communication styles differed for those with a greater and those with a lesser likelihood of longevity. That these groupings (high and low satisfaction and high and low likelihood of longevity) differ in the *amount* of various types of communication is a commonplace in marriage research (Navran, 1967; Petersen, 1969). Granting this difference in mean scores, are there differences in the impact of communication on other important variables as a function of satisfaction and predicted longevity? In other words, does communication style, defined as the impact of communication on other variables (to be introduced below), differ systematically with satisfaction and predicted longevity?

My second hunch was derived from Ashby (1963:197) and links the concepts of "survival" and "stability." If a system is highly stable, then disturbances which affect the system (especially in its "desirable" states) affect it only in the short run, since a stable system brings the effects of disturbances under control. On the other hand, stability could be bad if the system continually returns to some state which is not desirable (Ashby, 1963:81). If the system is unstable, it will be affected permanently by every disturbance with which it is confronted. Since the survival of every biological system depends upon the stability of that system, might not the survival of various types of social systems depend upon how those systems handle disturbances? In short, are systematic differences in stability to be found in high versus low satisfaction and high versus low predicted longevity marriages?

As will be shown below, if there are systematic differences in stability among the various groupings of marriage partners, these differences *must* be due to differences in communication style. Furthermore, since stability and regulation go hand in hand (both block or attenuate the effects of disturbances), then communication styles (which determine stability) are the regulators of the system. These same ideas have been presented in a more naive form in papers by Cappella (1974a, 1974b) and Cappella and Monge (1974a, 1974b).[1] Let us examine them more fully.

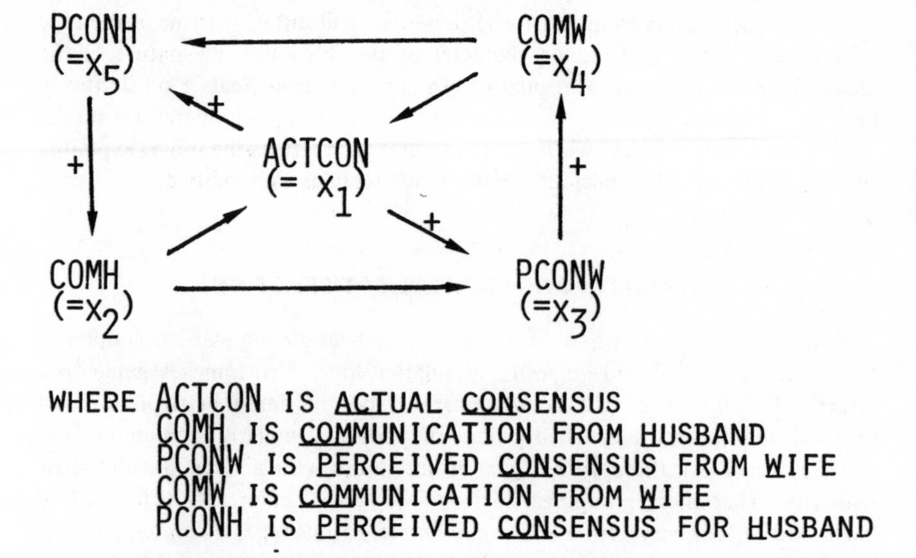

Figure 1: A CAUSAL DIAGRAM REPRESENTING PROPOSED RELATIONSHIPS AMONG ACTUAL CONSENSUS, PERCEIVED CONSENSUS, AND COMMUNICATION FOR A HUSBAND AND WIFE

The Model

A streamlined version of the model presented in more detail in Cappella (1974a:15) is offered in Figure 1. The patterning of effects in Figure 1 is derived from two fundamental presuppositions. The first is that, whatever differentiates types of interpersonal communication situations, they all have in common a characteristic interdependence of two or more persons. This interdependence is equivalent to a coordination of behavior and activities to solve problems, make decisions, and remove exigencies facing the system. The second presupposition recognizes that, in order to coordinate behaviors, individuals must be able to predict adequately the other's responses in various circumstances.

In order to measure the ability to predict another's response, I deserted the complexities of information theory and embraced the simplicities of the coorientation paradigm of Newcomb (1953), Laing et al. (1966), and Chaffee and McLeod (1968). In this scheme, each of three perceptions of some common object is a prediction of the other's perception, and a prediction of the other's prediction about your perception. From the six perceptions several interesting pairwise comparisons can be made. These are summarized in Table 1. The distinction between intrapersonal and interpersonal variables is an important one. In Figure 1, perceived consensus (which is just the sum of perceived agreement and perceived accuracy) is an intrapersonal variable. Actual consensus

TABLE 1

COORIENTATION VARIABLES DEFINED IN TERMS OF INDIVIDUAL PERCEPTIONS

Between Persons: Interpersonal

Agreement: my perception versus yours

Accuracy: my prediction of your perception versus your perception

Realization: my prediction of your prediction of my perception versus your prediction of my perception

Within a Person: Intrapersonal

Perceived Agreement: my prediction of your perception versus my perception

Perceived Accuracy: my prediction of your prediction of my perception versus my perception

(which is the sum of agreement, accuracy for both, and realization for both) is an interpersonal variable. However, high perceived consensus may or may not produce coordination since the predictions may be inaccurate, while high actual consensus ensures coordination since there is both agreement and the recognition of agreement.

Perhaps an analogy can help in arguing this claim. Suppose that a computer programmed to play chess is competing with a human opponent. In order for the human to win, he must correctly predict the next move or series of moves of his machine opponent and foil the machine's predictions of his own moves. Without knowledge of the programming instructions, including evaluation criteria, depth of search, etc., the human will probably be unsuccessful. However, if he has learned and stored the computer's programmed instructions, his chances improve. The reason is that, if the criteria for choice among alternative moves are the same for the human and the computer (that is, agreement) and if the human knows this (that is, accuracy), it is a simple task to predict the computer's next move. Furthermore, if the human knows the computer's prediction for his criteria for choice among alternatives (that is, realization), the human can foil the computer's predictions simply by violating his own criteria. Thus, in this competitive situation, success is contingent upon agreement, accuracy, and realization. In a cooperative situation, success is once again contingent on agreement, accuracy, and realization except that realization allows the *fulfillment, rather than the frustration,* of the other's expectations of self.

Granting that actual consensus produces coordination, Figure 1 shows actual consensus only as an antecedent to perceived consensus. The reasoning is that, as successful efforts at coordination increase, individuals will begin to perceive that they are more in agreement and more accurate than they had thought. While these observations may not be valid (for example, individuals at times undertake very similar actions, reach similar decisions, or solve problems in a similar way but for very different reasons), the *perception* of consensus should nonetheless increase.

In turn, Figure 1 shows that perceived consensus is the antecedent cause for communication to be generated toward the other. Interestingly, the literature is not consistent in describing the form of the relationship between perceived consensus and communication. Schachter's results (1951) favor a negative relationship, at least up to a point. Homans' (1950) theory and Byrne's (1971) research suggest a positive relationship, and recent work by Rosenfeld and Sullwold (1969) argues for a curvilinear relationship. These inconsistencies are more apparent than real, however, since each of the key studies above was carried out in a situation which placed different demands on subjects. In the present situation, which is quite macroscopic (as opposed to the microscopic group situations of Schachter and Rosenfeld and Sullwold), a positive relationship should, and in fact does, exist in the data.

Finally, the relationship between communication as antecedent to perceived consensus and communication as antecedent to actual consensus is permitted to vary. As was suggested earlier, we are investigating the possibility that the effect of communication on perceived consensus and on actual consensus will systematically vary with satisfaction and predicted longevity groupings. Style of communication, then, is the pattern of four regression coefficients linking communication with its consequent variables. The pattern could be the same or different for husbands and wives; it could be all positive, all negative, or a mixture of positive and negative. With two signs (+ and –) and four links there are 2^4 or 16 possible patterns of style, ignoring differences in magnitude of the coefficients. If, however, the different groupings of marital partners on satisfaction and predicted longevity do not show significant differences in style (that is, pattern of coefficients), then there cannot be differences in stability, and the approach to satisfaction and predicted longevity in terms of regulation is wrong. Let us take up the association between stability and style.

The Method

Stability is concerned with the dynamics of systems. The model of Figure 1 is a static one which has been described as if it were at equilibrium or rest. This equilibrium can be described mathematically in terms of a set of structural equations (Blalock, 1969, chapters 3, 4):

$$X_1 = b_{12}X_2 + b_{14}X_4 + a_1 \quad (1a)$$

$$X_2 = b_{25}X_5 + a_2 \quad (1b)$$

$$X_3 = b_{31}X_1 + b_{32}X_2 + a_3 \quad (1c)$$

$$X_4 = b_{43}X_3 + a_4 \quad (1d)$$

$$X_5 = b_{51}X_1 + b_{54}X_4 + a_5 \quad (1e)$$

where X_1 is actual consensus, X_2 is husband's communication, etc. The b's are coefficients indicating causal impact, and the a's are intercept values. In other words, the structural equations describe the interrelations among the variables after the system has "settled down" and stopped changing. The structural equation description can tell us nothing about the stability of the system and, in fact, is not a description of a machine at all since no dynamic character is involved. However, the static structural description can be replaced by its dynamic counterpart.

Following the lead of Blalock (1969) and Bonacich and Bailey (1971:225), the dynamic equivalent of equations (1a) – (1e) may be written: [2]

$$dX_1/dt = -X_1 + b_{12}X_2 + b_{14}X_4 + a_1 \quad (2a)$$

$$dX_2/dt = -X_2 + b_{25}X_5 + a_2 \quad (2b)$$

$$dX_3/dt = b_{31}X_1 + b_{32}X_2 - X_3 + a_3 \quad (2c)$$

$$dX_4/dt = b_{43}X_3 - X_4 + a_4 \quad (2d)$$

$$dX_5/dt = b_{51}X_1 + b_{54}X_4 - X_5 + a_5 \quad (2e)$$

Now the expression on the left may be read "the rate of change of" a particular variable, and the expressions (2a) – (2e) describe the dynamic, closed, and single-valued transformations necessary for a machine. Also, the system may be viewed as two machines coupled through feedback. The machine X_1, X_3, X_4 (actual consensus, wife's perceived consensus, and wife's communication) cannot be solved unless X_2 (husband's communication) is known, that is, unless the input is known. Similarly, X_1, X_2, X_5 needs X_4 (wife's communication) as input before it can be solved. To go back to the description of equations (1a) – (1e), notice that, when the rate of change is nonexistent, each term on the left hand side of (2a) – (2e) is zero. In this case (2a) – (2e) reduces back to (1a) – (1e).

In order to investigate the stability characteristics of a machine like (2a) – (2e) a certain amount of mathematical trickery and sophistication is needed. Let me try to talk around these prerequisites. Two methods of stability analysis are commonly used: the determinant procedure, which sets down necessary conditions (Blalock, 1969:107-125; Baumol, 1970), and the eigenvalue method, which sets down necessary and sufficient conditions for stability (Hirsch and Smale, 1974, chapters 3, 4; Bonacich and Bailey, 1971). Both methods use the matrix of coefficients (–1's, b's, and 0's) of the right hand side of (2a) – (2e). By the determinant procedure, if the determinant of this matrix of coefficients is positive, then the machine is unstable. If the determinant is negative, no general conclusions are possible, although the system is likely to be stable. By the eigenvalue technique, if the eigenvalues of this same matrix of coefficients are negative,[3] then the system is stable. In fact, if one sample has more negative eigenvalues than another, then that sample is "more stable" in the sense that it will return to normalcy in the face of disturbance more quickly than the other sample (with the less negative eigenvalues).

Recall that the object of our search is to discover if stability differences can help explain differences between high and low satisfaction and high and low predicted longevity partners. What could produce differences in stability values? Since stability depends on the coefficients in (2a) – (2e), differences in stability, say, between high and low satisfaction groups can only be due to different b values in the high satisfaction compared with the low satisfaction groups. But certain of the b's should not differ between groups—namely, b_{25}, b_{43}, b_{51}, and b_{31}. Thus, there should be no differences in stability due to these coefficients. However, we have assumed that the effects of husbands' and wives' communication on actual and perceived consensus (that is, b_{54}, b_{32}, b_{14}, and b_{12}) should differ between the satisfaction subgroups and predicted longevity subgroups. Consequently, differences in stability should be due solely to differences in communication style between subgroups. Because stability is associated with regulation and communication style determines stability, then the communication styles of husbands and wives regulate the behavior of the system. If these styles can be controlled (for example, through training—see Miller et al., 1971), the system can be regulated.

The relationship between stability and style can be carried a step further. If we assume that low satisfaction and low predicted longevity groups are more unstable than high satisfaction and high predicted longevity groups, not only must there be differences in style but these differences must yield eigenvalues for low groups which are more positive than eigenvalues for high groups. Unfortunately, there are equally good arguments for other types of stability patterns (Speer, 1970; Miller et al., 1971; Cappella and Monge, 1974b), but none is so compelling as to be preeminent. For example, it could be argued that excessive stability is as detrimental as instability since deviations from equilibrium can lead to creative insights and growth (Maruyama, 1963). Not all patterns of stability are possible, though, since no one has as yet argued that high satisfaction and high predicted longevity groups should be unstable and their low counterparts stable. Rather than try to settle the argument as to which type of stability is "best" in the face of equally powerful reasons but insufficient data, let us consider one set of results.

The Results

Self-report data from a self-selected sample of 32 married couples were gathered on communication (Navran, 1967), satisfaction (Locke and Wallace, 1959), predicted longevity (Locke and Wallace, 1959), and actual and perceived consensus on relationship rules (Cappella, 1973). In order to obtain estimates of the b_{ij}'s in equations (2a) – (2e) ordinary multiple regressions were carried out on the equations (1a) – (1e) separately for each of four groupings of the couples: high satisfaction, low satisfaction, high predicted longevity, and low predicted longevity.[4] The standardized regression coefficients for the groups are reported in Table 2.

Employing tests of equality between sets of coefficients in two linear

TABLE 2
STANDARDIZED REGRESSION COEFFICIENTS FOR HIGH AND LOW SATISFACTION AND HIGH AND LOW PREDICTED LONGEVITY GROUPS

	Satisfaction[a]		*Predicted Longevity*[b]	
	High (N = 16)	*Low (N = 16)*	*High (N = 16)*	*Low (N = 16)*
b_{12}:COMH → ACTCON	−.828	1.245	−.770	.686
b_{14}:COMW → ACTCON	.844	−.859	1.236	−.549
b_{25}:PCONH → COMH	−.012	.283	.143	.398
b_{31}:ACTCON → PCONW	.031	.111	.232	.205
b_{32}:COMH → PCONW	.087	−.022	.287	.073
b_{43}:PCONW → COMW	.230	.031	.539	.104
b_{51}:ACTCON → PCONH	.649	.411	.748	.511
b_{54}:COMW → PCONH	.209	−.013	.000	.220

a, b: The high and low satisfaction groups and the high and low predicted longevity groups are significantly different on mean satisfaction and mean predicted longevity respectively ($t = 7.52$ and 7.82, $df = 30$, $p < .01$).

regressions described by Fisher (1970), only b_{12} and b_{14} were found to be significantly different between high and low satisfaction and between high and low predicted longevity groups. The initial hypotheses were that (1) there would be no significant differences between subgroups on b_{25}, b_{31}, b_{43}, and b_{51} and (2) there would be significant differences in the effects of communication, that is, b_{12}, b_{14}, b_{32}, and b_{54}. The former hypothesis was supported but the latter was only partially confirmed since b_{32} and b_{54}, the effects of communication on perceived consensus, showed no significant pattern of differences. Therefore, the regressions for equations (1b) – (1e) were rerun using the entire sample. The results for high and low satisfaction groups only appear in Table 3 (predicted longevity groups produce essentially the same results and will be omitted from further discussion).

Overall the results of Tables 2 and 3 must be viewed as only partially encouraging. On the positive side, the relationships between perceived consensus and communication (b_{25} and b_{43}) and actual consensus and perceived consensus (b_{31} and b_{51}) are in the right direction and are the same across divisions of the sample. On the negative side, the relationship between communication and other's perceived consensus (b_{32} and b_{54}) is weak overall and does not exhibit the expected style differences. While the relationship between communication and actual consensus does exhibit the strong style differences hypothesized, these differences are somewhat difficult to interpret. The pattern of coefficients suggests that communication from wives in high satisfied groups and from husbands in low satisfied groups has a positive effect on actual consensus, whereas the communicative efforts from husbands in high satisfied groups and from wives in low satisfied groups has a negative effect on actual consensus. This result does not generate much "gut-level" confidence

TABLE 3
STANDARDIZED REGRESSION COEFFICIENTS, OVERALL F-RATIO, AND MULTIPLE R^2 FOR HIGH AND LOW SATISFACTION GROUPS MERGED FOR ALL BUT EQUATION (1a)

Coefficients		*Standardized Regressions*	*Overall F-Ratio*	*p*	R^2
b_{12}	High	−.828	.94	.415	.126
b_{14}	(N = 16)	.844			
b_{12}	Low	1.245	4.46	.033	.407
b_{14}	(N = 16)	−.859			
b_{25}		.345	4.05	.053	.119
b_{31}		.226	1.74	.192	.107
b_{32}		.161			
b_{43}		.281	2.57	.119	.079
b_{51}		.624	12.64	.0001	.446
b_{54}		.129			

because it is counterintuitive and bound so strongly to role differences. But precisely because it is not an obvious result it deserves further attention on different samples and with different instrumentation.

With regard to the relationships between style and stability both the determinant and eigenvalues methods are of interest. By the determinant method (only a necessary condition), all four groups exhibit a negative determinant, indicating that no group is unstable. However, the low satisfaction and low predicted longevity groups have determinant values which are more positive than their high counterparts (−.680 versus −1.22 for the satisfaction groups and −.82 versus −1.23 for the predicted longevity groups). I maintain that this difference is significant because the matrix system of equations (2a) – (2e) is biased in favor of stability results by virtue of placing −1's in the diagonal. Bonacich and Bailey (1971:225) justify this placement by assuming "that in the absence of system effect each variable would have equilibrium values for each combination of variables that effect it." Even granting this assumption, the magnitude of the diagonal elements is crucial. One can show, using a theorem by MacKenzie (1966:49), that, for the system (2a) – (2e) with the b's of Table 3, both the high and low satisfaction groups *must* be stable and that this result depends upon the magnitude of the diagonal elements. Thus, differences in determinant values between the high and low groups are due to differences in the off-diagonal scores with the diagonal scores tending to drive the overall determinant value negative. The point is that the difference in determinant values between high and low groups, with the low group more positive (that is, more in the direction of instability), may be more significant than at first meets the eye.

By the eigenvalue method (a necessary and sufficient condition) all groups (as expected by MacKenzie's theorem) exhibit negative eigenvalues on all five variables, thus ensuring complete stability. However, close examination of the differences in eigenvalues for those key system variables directly relevant to coordination (namely, perceived consensus for husband and wife and actual consensus) reveals an emergent pattern. (Recall that the more negative the eigenvalue the more quickly the variable returns to equilibrium when faced with a disturbance.) The eigenvalues for actual consensus are approximately equal between the high satisfaction (–.783) and the low satisfaction (–.852) groups. On both husbands' and wives' perceived consensus the high satisfaction group has more negative eigenvalues (–1.47 and –.765) than the low group (–1.29 and –.412). These differences in stability are due only to differences in style between the high and low satisfaction groups (essentially similar results obtain for the predicted longevity groups). *Thus, stability of the system, which appears to be related directly to satisfaction and predicted longevity, is controllable to the extent that communication style is controllable.* To be fair, this conclusion must be qualified by the limited sample size and its self-selected nature, self-report rather than observational data on communication, psuedodynamic rather than dynamic techniques, and some perhaps extreme assumptions in moving from the system (1a) – (1e) to (2a) – (2e). Let us take up some procedures which are not plagued by the last two of these qualifications.

MATHEMATICAL MODELS OF MUTUAL INFLUENCE

The dynamic character of the machine discussed in the previous section is only psuedodynamic since (1) the fundamental relationships between variables are static and (2) the move toward a dynamic formulation biases the model toward stability. In the mutual influence models of this section, the fundamental propositions will be change relationships of the form "A change in X depends upon Y." In other words, we begin with dynamics rather than artificially construct it. Second, the machine of Figure 1 is a kind of mutual influence model since it presumes that each person's communication will affect actual consensus and the other's perceived consensus. Presumably, the effects of communication on the complex variables of actual and perceived consensus occur through effects on the components of these variables, i.e., attitudes, perception of the other, etc. How communication is affecting these components cannot be determined in the previous model. In the models of this section the effects of two explicitly defined "styles" on attitudes, perceptions of the other's attitude, and attraction are explored in detail by employing mathematical tools.

A Paradigm for Mutual Influence

The framework for mutual influence is the now familiar coorientation or ABX model of Newcomb (1953). The beauty of Newcomb's structuring of ABX situations is found in the types of actions which an individual may undertake when individual strain is experienced. Specifically, when an individual acts to alter the situation, actions may be inner-directed toward changes in the individual system or they may be outer-directed toward inducing changes in the collective system. Changes in the individual system involve changes in attitude, attraction, or perception of the other. Actions directed toward the collective system take the form of communicative acts which would presumably have persuasive effect on the other. We shall focus solely on the collective system and the interactions which occur in its domain. Newcomb's approach to dyadic situations and dyadic influence isolates eight variables: A's and B's attractions for one another, A_a and A_b; A's and B's attitudes toward (perceptions of) the object X, P_a and P_b; A's and B's perception of the other's attitude, Q_a and Q_b; and the content of the messages which A and B transmit to one another (as measured on an attitude continuum), M_a and M_b. To begin to analyze the *dynamic* interrelation of these variables necessitates mathematical analysis.

While Newcomb's structuring of dyadic influence situations is useful, he does not specify in detail how attitudes, perceptions, and attractions should change as a function of the messages sent by the other. In order to do so, we may overlay any of the several attitude change models of the passive paradigm (Hunter and Cohen, 1974) on the Newcomb paradigm. As a first effort, we take up one of the simplest–information processing theory (Hovland et al., 1953; Hunter and Cohen, 1974).

In overlaying the assumptions of information processing theory on Newcomb's paradigm, we will be forced to consider not only changes in attitudes as a function of messages, but also changes in perception of the other, changes in attraction toward the other, strategies for generating message content, and the transmission of messages. In essence, we are taking the view that each individual is a subsystem of the collective system. Each subsystem is characterized by three variables: attitude, perception of the other's attitude, and attraction to the other. The two subsystems are linked only when there is transmission from A to B, N_a, or from B to A, N_b, or when both are transmitting. The effect that each subsystem has on the other depends upon the content of the messages sent, M_a or M_b, and their rate of transmission. Thus, the case of two machines coupled through feedback is once more at hand.

Change Propositions

Only the verbal form of the change propositions will be presented. More complete mathematical descriptions of these propositions are found in Cappella

(1974b, 1974c). As Hunter and Cohen (1974:10) point out, information-processing theory claims that the change in attitude is in the direction of the incoming message and is a linear function of difference between prior attitude and the position advocated by the message. Credibility factors, as measured by attraction, affect attitude change by forcing the change to be maximal for infinitely attractive others and to be minimal for infinitely disliked others. Finally, the amount of change increases directly with the number of messages sent by the speaker. These three factors are summarized in the equation for P_a in the appendix to this chapter.

The same factors that affect changes in attitude also affect changes in perception of the other, as a comparison of the form of the equations for P_a and Q_a in the appendix reveal. The only difference is that perceptions of the other are less resistant to change than are attitudes (Wackman and Beatty, cited in Wackman, 1973).

Changes in attraction should depend upon the degree of perceived similarity experienced (Byrne, 1971) and should exhibit both increases and decreases so that relationship continuation or dissolution is a possible outcome. In particular, attraction changes positively whenever incoming messages are within the hearer's latitude of acceptance (Sherif et al., 1965) and decreases whenever the messages are outside the acceptance region. Following Hunter and Cohen (1974:49) and Sherif et al. (1965:189), the width of the acceptance region expands as the source is seen as more attractive and shrinks as the source is seen as less attractive. Like the changes in attitude and in perception of the other, attraction is assumed to change more rapidly as the number of messages received increases. These factors produce the complex change function for A_a in the appendix.

Following Newcomb's idea that influence attempts directed toward the other were possible responses to individual system strain, a message transmission function was chosen such that (1) for a given level of attraction, the greater the perceived disagreement by A, the greater the transmission from A; (2) for a given level of perceived disagreement, the greater the attraction that A has for B, the greater the transmission from A; and (3) even when disliking is great, transmission is still positive and depends upon the amount of perceived disagreement. The first two characteristics have been well researched and validated by Festinger and his colleagues (Festinger, 1950; Back, 1951; Schachter, 1951; Festinger and Thibaut, 1951), and the third represents the fact that when individuals are constrained to remain in a dyadic situation (e.g., a work group), the social norm of reciprocal interaction outweighs the (negative) relationship between attraction and transmission.

In addition to the transmission of some message content, two decision rules for communicating attitudes by the speaker were employed. First, suppose the subject always speaks his or her mind; the message sent is then just the attitude that the speaker holds at that instant. This rule represents one style of generating messages and has been the one most commonly adopted in interactive models of attitude change (Abelson, 1964; Taylor, 1968). Let us call it the *veridical* style.

In the veridical style, the speaker says the same thing regardless of who the listener might be. But suppose that the speaker seeks to ingratiate his audience by shifting his message in the direction of his perception of the other's attitude. If we presume that individuals are more ingratiating for more attractive others and less ingratiating for less attractive others, then the degree of shift would be a function of attraction. When A thoroughly dislikes B, then he speaks his mind (that is, is veridical) and does not seek interpersonal rewards from B by ingratiating him. When A likes B a great deal, then he seeks to further the good graces of B by saying what he thinks B wishes to hear. We shall call this the *shift* style.

Having completed the detailed mathematical representation of the verbal propositions (summarized in the appendix), the goal is to understand the overall short-term and long-term behavior of this machine with a special eye to changes in machine behavior with changes in message style.

Some Selected Results: Style Differences and Mutual Influence

Because the full model is so intractable, an understanding of its complete characteristics was sought by a series of approximations. The simplest case (case I) is one in which both attraction and transmission are unchanging. Substantively, such a situation is equivalent to two long-standing friends informally discussing an issue while equally sharing the floor. With long-standing friends a minor disagreement (or agreement for that matter) is unlikely to affect appreciably their mutual attraction. Case II allows only transmission to vary and not attraction. Here, the long-standing friends may be more committed to resolving the perceived disagreement on the issue. Case III allows attraction to vary but transmission is held fixed. The substantive equivalent is an informal discussion among acquaintances in which sharing the floor is the conversational norm. Case IV is the full model with both attraction and transmission varying.

Case I: Fixed Attraction and Transmission. [5] As long as both persons are doing some talking and the disliking for the other is not extreme, then under both the veridical and shift styles the pair will converge to agreement and the perception of agreement regardless of the differences in initial attitudes or perceptions of the other. The actual point of final agreement differs for the two styles, however, with the veridical style producing an agreement point which is a weighted sum of (that is, a compromise involving) initial attitudes only and with the shift style producing an agreement point which is a weighted sum of initial attitudes *and* perceptions of the other (Cappella, 1974c). Finally, in the extreme case (for the shift style) in which a particularly quiet individual interacts with a talkative other, the quiet person ends up inaccurately perceiving agreement while there is actual disagreement. No such inaccuracies obtain when a quiet person and a talkative other interact veridically. The reason for this difference is that when the talkative person communicates veridically, the other changes his attitude toward the talkative friend's message which is the friend's actual attitude. With the talkative friend communicating in an ingratiating style, the quiet person still changes toward his friend's message, but now the message sent differs from the talkative person's actual attitude, producing disagreement.

Case II: Fixed Attraction and Varying Transmission. Under the assumptions of this case, the most probable final state for the interaction has one person perceiving agreement and being silent, the other person perceiving disagreement and transmitting, and the pair actually disagreeing. The system can go to states of agreement and accuracy for both, but such states are highly unlikely and, in fact, unstable (Cappella, 1974c:63-72). Both the veridical and shift styles exhibit the same behavior.

Case III: Fixed Transmission and Varying Attraction. In this case, the two-person system has no resting points but tends toward two qualitatively different directions: (1) toward agreement and perceived agreement with both A's and B's attractions increasing without limit and (2) toward both A and B disliking each other more and more as disagreement and perceived disagreement settle in for both. Whether the system heads toward the former or latter configuration depends upon the initial messages and the size of acceptance regions. Whenever A's and B's initial messages are within the other's acceptance region, when both initial messages are slightly outside the region, or when one message is within and the other message outside the other's acceptance, the system will change toward increasing mutual attraction and toward agreement and perceived agreement for both individuals. On the other hand, whenever both A's and B's initial messages are well outside the other's acceptance region, the system will change toward increasing mutual dislike and toward disagreement and perceived disagreement for both.

These conclusions hold for both the veridical and the shift models of message generation. However, their implications differ in significant ways. Suppose, first, that A and B disagree so that $P_a = P_b$ and both are well outside each other's acceptance region. If even one of the two persons is accurate (let us say $Q_a = P_b$) then with a shift style, A's initial message will be shifted in the direction of B's *actual position* and the likelihood that A's initial message will fall into B's acceptance region is increased. If the shift message does fall into B's acceptance region, the system will tend toward a qualitatively different state (mutual positive attraction and agreement) than the veridical model would predict (mutual dislike with disagreement). On the other hand, if A and B initially agreed but were both vastly *inaccurate,* then the veridical style would predict change toward mutual positive attraction and agreement and the shift style would predict mutual hostility and disagreement. Of course, this analysis does not cover all possibilities. But the two cases cited do point out that the choice of message style is crucial in predicting where the dyad is tending with varying attraction and constant transmission assumptions.

Case IV: The Full Model. The characteristics of this case tend to be an amalgamation of the results of cases II and III. In terms of differences in communication style, the conclusions are similar to those stated above for case III.

Summary and Implications

Consistent with the thesis of this paper, veridical dyads and shift dyads can exhibit behaviors which are qualitatively different from one another even if they start with the same attitudes, perceptions, and attractions. Thus, to the extent that styles are controllable, the qualitative behavior of the system is (at least in part) controllable. Of course, other styles need to be studied with the same attitude, attraction, and perception change propositions to determine if there are styles which are more powerful regulators than either the veridical or shift styles. Furthermore, no analyses have yet attempted to give each person in the situation a different style to determine if one machine will dominate the other as a function of style differences alone (Ashby, 1963:53). Such work is barely underway. Also, measurement procedures for assessing the evaluative component of messages (comparable to the evaluative component of attitudes) must be developed if styles of making attitudes known are to be studied empirically. Following work by Heise (1969) and Kintsch (1974), Cappella and Folger (1976) have begun to take some small steps in this direction.

Overall, the methods reported in this section are another (albeit sophisticated) tool for studying differences in machines due to communication style. While the methods are complex, they are also precise. They permit substantive conclusions under plausible assumptions *before* high risk research is undertaken.

MESHING STYLES AND STOCHASTIC MACHINES

Much theory and research in interpersonal relations have asked what kinds and degrees of compatibility or meshing are necessary to maximize satisfaction, attraction, task performance, rewards, etc. The work of Byrne (1971) on attitude similarity, of Carson (1969) on personality complementarity, of Schutz (1966) on interpersonal need complementarity, and of many others can be viewed in light of the question of meshing or compatibility. Why not view the meshing of communication styles in interaction as a predictor of attraction, satisfaction, and task performance? After all, how do we acquire information about another's attitudes, personality characteristics, and needs if it is not through the other's symbolic actions?

Although these questions are fundamental, a prior issue must first be settled. Is there any set of communication behaviors which are sufficiently predictable over time and across occasions that they can be said to represent a person's interaction style? Following the research of Jaffee and Feldstein (1970), our study begins with the most basic aspect of conversation–patterns of sound and silence. The results presented below are little more than an attempt to replicate Jaffee and Feldstein's results using the system for conversational analysis at the University of Wisconsin's Center for Communication Research.[6] The need for replication is important because other research (Hayes et al., 1970) failed to find results equivalent to the strong conclusions of Jaffee and Feldstein.

The Model

In a two-person conversation with each act coded as either talking (T) or silence (S), there are four possible states: SS, TT, TS, and ST, where TS means A is talking and B is silent, ST means A is silent and B is talking, etc. Following the evolution of these states over time is facilitated if the states are represented in matrix form such that the rows are the states at the previous time and the columns the states at the subsequent time of observation:

From/To	*SS*	*TT*	*TS*	*ST*
SS	P_{11}	P_{12}	P_{13}	P_{14}
TT	P_{21}	P_{22}	P_{23}	P_{24}
TS	P_{31}	P_{32}	P_{33}	P_{34}
ST	P_{41}	P_{42}	P_{43}	P_{44}

The P's in the matrix are probabilities of moving from some prior to some subsequent state. For example, P_{32} is the probability of the dyad moving from A talking and B silent to A talking and B talking. If a series of such matrices at different time points were observed and it was found that the probabilities did not change across the series, then we would have a machine and, in particular, the machine would be a Markov Chain (Ashby, 1963:165-186; Hewes, 1975). Jaffee and Feldstein (1970:72) term this model of two-person, sound-silence behavior the *single-source* model because the transition probabilities govern moves from dyadic states to dyadic states as if the dyad were a single machine.

On the other hand, the *separate-source* model (Jaffee and Feldstein, 1970:84-91) generates individual sound-silence parameters which can be used to reconstruct the dyadic transition matrices (like the one above). The parameters are defined (p. 86) as (1) the probability that A will talk given that the previous dyadic state was SS, or p(A = T/SS); (2) the probability that A will talk given that the previous dyadic state was TT, or p(A = T/TT), (3) p(A = T/TS), and (4) p(A = T/ST). Notice that the probability that A will be silent given that the previous state is SS is 1 – P(A = T/SS), and this same form holds for the other silence parameters. The same set of four independent parameters can be generated for B.

Now observe a most interesting advantage that has been gained by separating the individual parameters from the dyadic transition matrix. If both individuals make independent decisions as to when to talk, then (for example) the element P_{13} (which is the SS to TS transition) is just the probability that A will talk given that the previous state was SS–or p(A = T/SS)–*and* the probability that B will be silent given that the previous state was SS–or p(B = S/SS). But if they are independent choices, then P_{13} = P(A = T/SS) · P(B = S/SS), and the dyadic system can be built from two individual machines. If A and B interact on occasion 1 and C and D interact on occasion 1, then from A's parameters at occasion 1 and C's parameters at occasion 1, it should be possible to predict the transition matrix for A and C together at an occasion 2, even though the A-C pair had never been together.

A Replication

A sample of eight subjects–four males and four females–were randomly assigned to same-sex pairs to discuss informally a common set of issues which had been the object of an earlier questionnaire. The conversations were tape-recorded and lasted about 25 minutes. The conversations were automatically coded into sound and silence categories (see Note 5) with samples of each person's audio channel taken every 300 milliseconds (Jaffee and Feldstein, 1970:17). With the first five minutes of conversation ignored for warm-up, each 20-minute conversation yields 4,000 observations. Transition matrices and parameter values were constructed for each two-minute segment of the conversation yielding 10 transition matrices for each dyad and 10 sets of parameters for each person.[7]

On a second occasion the same subjects were randomly assigned to an opposite-sex partner for discussion of aspects of the same topic as on occasion 1. The data were analyzed as before. Finally, the same subjects returned on a third occasion to be paired with the same-sex partner with whom they had not yet conversed.[8] The data were treated as on the previous occasions.

Adopting the suggestions of Hewes and Evans-Hewes (1975) for handling time-series data, each of the four parameter values–P(T/SS), P(T/TT), P(T/TS), and P(T/ST)–were regressed separately as dependent variables on time, occasion, and sex of the dyad as a dummy variable *for the whole group.* The results in terms of variance explained were weak, with the *largest* multiple R^2 being .09. More importantly, even a glance at the residuals shows a strong and clear pattern of individual differences. Therefore, the same dependent variables were regressed on the same independent variables as above but *for each individual separately.* The variances explained improved dramatically. The average multiple R^2 was .291 for P(T/SS), .167 for P(T/TT), .551 for P(T/TS), and .187 for P(T/ST).

Since the independent variable of time within each occasion was significant ($p < .05$) in only two of the 32 regressions, and since the R^2's suggested a predictable process, a Markov Chain model was fit to the dyadic data within each occasion. In the present case, this involves comparing the tenth power of the initial two-minute transition matrix to the product of the 10 observed transition matrices for each dyad pair on each occasion.[9] The average of the absolute deviations between predicted and observed probability matrices is given by a matrix of average discrepancies:

.049	.019	.057	.047
.054	.036	.037	.042
.041	.021	.057	.041
.047	.018	.041	.051

No standard Chi-squared (Goodman, 1962) or Neyman Pierson (Jaffee and Feldstein, 1970) statistics were carried out since each dyad is based on 4,000 observations, almost ensuring a finding of significant difference. Rather, one only needs to "eyeball" the matrix of discrepancies to understand how well these data (when analyzed on an individual dyad basis) fit the assumptions of a Markovian machine.

Finally, individual parameters derived from the total time transition matrix for occasion 1 were used to predict the transition matrices for new dyadic conversations at occasions 2 and 3; similar predictions were made from occasion 2 to occasion 3. The average absolute discrepancy between predicted and observed transition matrices for each pair of dyads is:

.077	.019	.049	.052
.042	.068	.062	.052
.097	.036	.081	.010
.082	.016	.004	.091

As with the Markov matrix presented above, this represents an average deviation of the predicted probability of transition from the observed probabilities for each dyad. On the whole, predicting from occasion to occasion with changing partners does not fare quite as well as predicting within an occasion over time with the same partner. However, the average fit is rather pleasing to the eye since no predicted matrix element differs from an observed by even as much as .1 on the average.

Conclusions for the Sound-Silence Machine

Consistent with the results of Jaffee and Feldstein (1970:116), it seems that the patterning of sound and silence within dyadic conversations is quite regular and predictable, both within a conversation and across conversations, as long as the topic is held constant (although the partner need not be). As was pointed out earlier, this regularity is a fundamental prerequisite for any machine to be constructed. However, the regularity which has been described in this section represents nothing more than the observation that conversations have norms (reflected in the transition matrix) about *who* may speak *when.* The fact that the norms about who should speak next are weakest when both are talking or both are silent and strongest when one is talking and the other is silent is reflected by the very high variance explained for P(T/TS) and P(T/ST) and in the lower variances explained in P(T/TT) and P(T/SS). These smaller variances might be improved with a slightly different coding of the data which accounts for who is holding the floor when the SS and TT states occur (Jaffee and Feldstein, 1970:99-100). These results are not yet available.

What has been demonstrated in these data is (1) that Jaffee and Feldstein's results are replicable on a different automatic coding system and are not merely artifacts of their own system and (2) that individuals have styles of talk and silence which are unique to them and predictable at an individual level. What has not been demonstrated is *how* these individual style parameters may be *explained* in terms of other variables which can predict either the transition probabilities directly (Spilerman, 1973) or the parameter values. If this step can be achieved, then the Markov Chain would not merely describe the process but explain it, and predictions to new interactions would not necessitate prior interaction data.

What about regulation and style in the Markovian sound-silence machine? That there exist strong individual differences in the parameters P(T/SS), P(T/TT), P(T/TS), and P(T/ST) has already been pointed out. These differences produce differences in dyadic transition matrices, and these transition matrices determine the equilibrium values of the various dyadic states (SS, TT, TS, and ST). For example, the equilibrium probabilities for the four dyadic states could be (.1, .1, .4, .4), (.3, .3, .2, .2), or (.1, .1, .7, .1) depending directly upon the transition probabilities themselves. In the first case, most of the dyad's time is spent with one talking and the other silent, and this time is equally shared. In the last case the same is true except that the time with one talking and the other silent is not equally shared. In the middle case, about 60% of the dyad's time is spent in mutual silence or simultaneous talk (a very unlikely occurrence). The point is that these outcomes, which are equivalent to the probability distribution of the dyadic states, are determined (in this case by definition) by differences in the parameters P(T/SS), P(T/TT), P(T/TS), and P(T/ST). To say that differences in probabilities do control system outcomes is to state a now familiar refrain, "Communication style regulates the system!"

There are, however, two research questions that must be answered before the refrain can have important implications in the sound-silence context: (1) Is it possible to produce significant differences in the equilibrium distribution of dyadic sound-silence states? If this is not possible, then there is nothing to regulate. Thus far, research into sound-silence parameters has only randomly assigned individuals to partners and has not attempted to artificially assign persons to others based upon strong differences or similarities in talk-silence parameters. (2) If large differences in equilibrium distributions are observed, are they related to other interaction outcomes such as attraction, satisfaction, and talk performance? If an affirmative answer to this question is obtained, then not only does style regulate the system but prescriptions can then be offered as to the kinds of styles which produce the most desirable outcomes. Research is currently under way to answer these questions.

SUMMARY AND CONCLUSIONS

This paper has attempted to demonstrate two theses about interpersonal communication situations: (1) that interpersonal situations can be fruitfully conceptualized in the logic of cybernetics as two machines each taking in the other's output and providing input for the other; (2) that the kinds of input and output between machines (i.e., communication style) often regulate the behavior of the entire system so as to produce qualitatively different outcomes with different communication styles. Behind both these lies a set of beliefs. Even though communication styles are strongly personal, I believe that they are more subject to change through learning than are other psychological processes. Thus, where system outcomes differ and these differences are due to variations in communication style, then outcomes could be controlled through advice, training, and individual choice. Whether one approaches the study of human social behavior from a mechanistic or humanistic viewpoint, that viewpoint must have implications for the design and improvement of the social milieu. Cybernetics, a mechanistic world view if there ever was one, began as a pragmatic science aimed at design and regulation, not as an obscure and esoteric philosophy or mathematics. I hope that this essay's cybernetic view has remained true to this pragmatic orientation.

APPENDIX

With the credibility factor for person A given by $C_a = e^{A_a} / (1 + e^{A_a})$ and one-half the width of the acceptance region given by $t_a = e^{A_a}$, then the change propositions discussed in the text are given by

$$\Delta P_a = f\, C_a\, (M_b - P_a)\, N_b$$

$$\Delta Q_a = b\, C_a\, (M_b - Q_a)\, N_b$$

$$\Delta A_a = c \frac{t_a^2 - (M_b - P_a)^2}{1 + t_a^2} N_b$$

The transmission function has the form:

$$N_a = d \frac{|Q_a - P_a|}{\sqrt{1 + (Q_a - P_a)^2}} (1 + C_a).$$

Finally the two styles of sending messages are the veridical

$$M_a = P_a$$

and the shift style

$$M_a = P_a + C_a\, (Q_a - P_a).$$

The equations for person B can be obtained by changing all the subscripts above from a to b.

NOTES

1. The model, method, and results to be presented in the next three sections have benefited from much critical scrutiny and from interaction among data, propositions, and procedures. They are not identical with the model, method, and results of the previous papers. Where there are significant differences, I shall alert the reader.

2. Some very important assumptions are made in moving from the structural to the dynamic form. These will be discussed in a subsequent section.

3. Actually, only the real parts of the eigenvalues need to be negative.

4. The model of Figure 1 is underidentified, and, therefore, multiple regression coefficients are biased. However, in an article by Beaver (1974) the absolute bias in ordinary least squares (OLS) estimates for models with loop structures was not too excessive (in the vicinity of .2 to .4). Following Beaver's suggestions, I am currently developing an algorithm which will yield unbiased estimates for this model. Thus, the values for the b_{ij} presented in the test are biased, but not excessively.

5. Methods for generating results included standard techniques in linear systems theory for case I (Wiberg, 1971; Hirsch and Smale, 1974; Cappella, 1974c) and other mathematical and numerical techniques for cases II to IV (Cappella, 1974c).

6. The automated system consists of a PDP-12 computer and necessary software which converts analogue voice input to digital form. The input signal is smoothed, rectified, and sampled at 50 millisecond intervals and averaged in groups of six to yield a 300 millisecond sampling time. For futher details the interested reader may contact the author.

7. Daniel Fogel of the University of Wisconsin-Madison has constructed a FORTRAN program to facilitate this matter. Copies may be obtained from him at the Center for Communication Research.

8. One subject did not return for a third meeting, so a substitute was found. The substitute interacted for two of the three occasions, giving one subject two occasions and another four occasions.

9. Jaffee and Feldstein (1970:73) fit a Markov model to a *mean* transition matrix averaged over 50 individual matrices rather than fitting the Markov model to each individual dyad, as I have done.

REFERENCES

ABELSON, R.P. (1964). "Mathematical models of the distribution of attitudes under controversy." In N. Frederiksen and H. Gulliksen (eds.), Contributions to mathematical psychology. New York: Holt, Rinehart and Winston.

ASHBY, W.R. (1963). An introduction to cybernetics. New York: Wiley.

BACK, K.W. (1951). "Influence through social communication." Journal of Abnormal and Social Psychology, 46:9-23.

BAUMOL, W.J. (1970). Economic dynamics. London: Macmillan.

BEAVER, S. (1974). "The effects of causal feedback on ordinary least-squares estimators." Sociological Methods and Research, 3:189-208.

BLALOCK, H.M. (1969). Theory construction: From verbal to mathematical formulations. Englewood Cliffs, N.J.: Prentice-Hall.

BONACICH, P., and BAILEY, K.D. (1971). "Key variables." In H.L. Costner (ed.), Sociological methodology, 1971. San Francisco: Jossey-Bass.

BYRNE, D. (1971). The attraction paradigm. New York: Academic Press.

CAPPELLA, J.N. (1973). "A complex cybernetic model of interpersonal communication." Unpublished masters thesis, Michigan State University.

--- (1974a). "A derivation and test of a cybernetic, coorientation model of interpersonal communication." Paper presented at the convention of the International Communication Association, New Orleans.

--- (1974b). "A dynamic mathematical model of mutual influence according to information processing theory." Washington, D.C.: Proceedings of the American Cybernetics Conference on Communication and Social Processes.

--- (1974c). "Dynamic mathematical models of dyadic interaction based on information processing assumptions." Unpublished doctoral dissertation, Michigan State University.

CAPPELLA, J.N., and FOLGER, J.P. (1976). "An information processing explanation of the attitude-behavior inconsistency." Unpublished manuscript, University of Wisconsin-Madison.

CAPPELLA, J.N., and MONGE, P.R. (1974a). "A cybernetic model of growth in a system of interpersonal communication." Cybernetica, 7:559-575.

--- (1974b). "A general method for constructing communication models based on cybernetic systems analysis." Paper presented at the convention of the Speech Communication Association, Chicago.

CARSON, R.C. (1969). Interaction concepts of personality. Chicago: Aldine.

CHAFFEE, S., and McLEOD, J. (1968). "Sensitization in a panel design: A coorientation experiment." Journalism Quarterly, 45:661-669.

FESTINGER, L. (1950). "Informal social communication." Psychological Review, 17:271-282.

FESTINGER, L., and THIBAUT, J. (1951). "Interpersonal communication in small groups." Journal of Abnormal and Social Psychology, 44:92-99.

FISHER, F.M. (1970). "Tests of equality between sets of coefficients in two linear regressions." Econometrica, 38:361-365.

GOODMAN, L.A. (1962). "Statistical methods for analyzing processes of change." American Journal of Sociology, 68:57-78.

HAYES, D.P., MELTZER, L., and WOLF, G. (1970). "Substantive conclusions are dependent upon techniques of measurement." Behavioral Science, 15:265-268.

HEISE, D.R. (1969). "Affectual dynamics in simple sentences." Journal of Personality and Social Psychology, 11:204-213.

HEWES, D.E. (1975). "Finite stochastic modeling of communication processes: An introduction and some basic readings." Human Communication Research, 1:271-283.

HEWES, D.E., and EVANS-HEWES, D. (1975). "Toward a process model of social interaction." Paper presented at the convention of the Speech Communication Association, Houston.

HIRSCH, M.W., and SMALE, S. (1974). Differential equations, dynamical systems, and linear algebra. New York: Academic Press.

HOMANS, G.C. (1950). The human group. New York: Harcourt, Brace, and World.

HOVLAND, C.I., JANIS, I.L., and KELLEY, H.H. (1953). Communication and persuasion. New Haven, Conn.: Yale University Press.

HUNTER, J.E., and COHEN, S.H. (1974). "Mathematical models of attitude change in the passive communication context." Unpublished manuscript, Michigan State University.

JAFFEE, J., and FELDSTEIN, S. (1970). Rhythms of dialogue. New York: Academic Press.

KINTSCH, W. (1974). The representation of meaning in memory. New York: Halstead.

LAING, R.D., PHILLIPSON, H., and LEE, A.R. (1966). Interpersonal perception: A theory and a method of research. New York: Springer.

LOCKE, H.J., and WALLACE, K.M. (1959). "Short marital adjustment and prediction tests: Their reliability and validity." Marriage and Family Living, 21:251-255.

MacKENZIE, L. (1966). "Matrices with dominant diagonals and economic theory." In K.J. Arrow, S. Karlin, and P. Suppes (eds.), Mathematical models in the social sciences. Stanford, Calif.: Stanford University Press.

MARUYAMA, M. (1963). "The second cybernetics: Deviation amplifying mutual causal processes." American Scientist, 51:164-179.

MILLER, S., NUNNALLY, E.W., and WACKMAN, D.B. (1971). The Minnesota Couples Communication Training Program. Minneapolis: Marital Resource Center.

NAVRAN, L. (1967). "Communication and adjustment in marriage." Family Process, 6:173-184.

NEWCOMB, T. (1953). "An approach to the study of communicative acts." Psychological Review, 60:393-404.

PETERSEN, D.M. (1969). "Husband-wife communication and family problems." Sociology and Social Research, 53:375-384.

ROSENFELD, H.M., and SULLWOLD, V.L. (1969). "Optimal information discrepancies for persistent communication." Behavioral Science, 14:303-315.

SCHACHTER, S. (1951). "Deviation, rejection, and communication." Journal of Abnormal and Social Psychology, 46:190-207.

SCHUTZ, W.C. (1966). The interpersonal underworld. Palo Alto, Calif.: Science and Behavior Books.

SHERIF, C.W., SHERIF, M., and NEBERGALL, R.E. (1965). Attitude and attitude change: The social judgment-involvement approach. Philadelphia: Saunders.

SPEER, D.C. (1970). "Family systems: Morphastasis and morphogenesis or 'Is homeostasis enough?' " Family Process, 9:259-278.

SPILERMAN, S. (1973). "The analysis of mobility processes by the introduction of independent variables into a Markov Chain." American Sociological Review, 37:277-294.

TAYLOR, M. (1968). "Towards a mathematical theory of influence and attitude change." Human Relations, 21:121-140.

WACKMAN, D.B. (1973). "Interpersonal communication and coorientation." American Behavioral Scientist, 16:537-550.

WIBERG, D.M. (1971). State space and linear systems. New York: McGraw-Hill.

Chapter 4

A RELATIONAL APPROACH TO INTERPERSONAL COMMUNICATION

Frank E. Millar and L. Edna Rogers

PEOPLE BECOME AWARE OF THEMSELVES only within the context of their social relationships. These relationships, whether primarily interpersonal or role specific, are bestowed, sustained, and transformed through communicative behaviors. With increasing frequency, social scientists are accepting Bateson's (1958) notion that all message exchanges have both *content* and *relational* characteristics. Roughly, the former refers to the object or referent specified in the message, and the latter refers to the reciprocal rules of interdependence that combine the persons into an interactive system. The rules that bind people together distinguish the type of social relationship. If the same rule structure is applicable to a larger number of interactive systems in particular situations, then the relationship is considered to be more role bound, more "social," and less individualized. The more any given relationship is characterized by a relatively unique rule structure, the more individualized, the more "interpersonal" the relationship.

This paper is concerned with the combinatorial rules that characterize interpersonal relationships and relational level measurements of these rules. Specifically, this paper outlines (1) a conceptual development of basic relational dimensions which characterize interactive systems, (2) a relational level measurement technique, and (3) initial research findings utilizing this measurement technique.

Before moving to the conceptual development, we should mention the assumptions behind the approach advocated. Following the symbolic interactionists, we assume that people's interactions with their environments are mediated through a linguistic system. Humans have the ability to "know that they know" because they are both the creators and prisoners of the symbols used to categorize their realities. Furthermore, we assume that humans are purposeful systems. Ackoff and Emery (1972:31) define a purposeful system as "one that can change its goals in constant environmental conditions: it selects goals as well as the means by which to pursue them." In other words, people are intentional agents who actively create their environments. Purposeful systems require both positive and negative feedback in order to assess progress toward goals and for the validity of the goals to be reasserted. In sum, since a person's "reality" is largely a function of his or her own making, choice and change (and hence the information upon which decisions are delineated and rationalized) are two crucial themes that must be emphasized in any communication theory of human behavior.

Given that people are symbolic, purposeful systems, it follows that through the exchange of messages they become aware of their various alternatives and choose among them. Functionally, the communication process is largely a negotiation process whereby persons reciprocally define their relationships and themselves. Much of our co-present behavior is intended to produce relationships within which each can be the self-desired and each is the desired-other for the other participant (Laing et al., 1966). Assuming the above picture of social behavior, the question becomes what parts of this ongoing process are to be set out for analysis and how are they to be studied.

CONCEPTUAL ORIENTATION TOWARD SOCIAL RELATIONSHIPS

A variety of classifications have been offered to categorize social relationships. These efforts have varied from simple enumeration of noun-pairs (e.g., husband-wife, teacher-student, employer-employee, doctor-nurse), to psychologically oriented concepts (dominant-submissive, managerial-self-effacing), to supposedly one-dimensional classifications (voluntary-nonvoluntary, primary-secondary, fleeting-repetitious), to more societal level typologies (Gemeinshaft-Gesellshaft, sacred-secular, mechanical solidarity-organic solidarity). While several insights and guides for delineating relationships are contained within these a priori schemes, relatively little work has used the message exchange process as a basis for classification. Avoidance of the significance of communicative processes, as well as relational distinctions, is due, in part, to the fallacious but implicit assumption that a group is a group (Argyle, 1969). Regardless of a group's history or lack of one, its current external situation, its immediate task concerns, its size,[1] and/or its typical information exchange patterns, researchers have tended to assume that what is true for one group is likewise true for another. The failure to take into account these and other distinctions has resulted in much of the noncomparability and nonadditiveness of small group research (Golembiewski, 1962) and has left the "types of social relationships that characterize human interaction . . . largely unconceptualized" (Denzin, 1970:67).

Another contribution to the inadequate conceptualizations of relationships has been the consistent refusal to include time and developmental factors. The quest for explanatory variables independent of temporal and processual effects may provide adequate conceptualizations of reactive systems, but not of purposeful systems.

To criticize what is primarily a sociological tradition for not emphasizing the explanatory potential of message-exchange variables is probably unfair. But why have communicologists not been more concerned with creating these types of theoretical perspectives? Communicologists, at a minimum, must share the view that communicative behavior is not just the mechanism through which predetermined actions are exhibited, but that it is a "formative process in its own right" (Blumer, 1969:53). To paraphrase Duncan (1967:249) people do not relate and then talk, but they simultaneously relate *in* talk. To deny or deemphasize that the message-exchange process modifies expectations and behavioral performances negates communication as a social science; it negates the symbolic, purposeful characteristics of human systems, as well as a large number of everyday observations and insights.

A further reason for the lack of adequate conceptualizations in the interpersonal communication area has been the virtual monopoly of the traditional monadic level of analysis. While it would seem apparent that primarily personal, individual concepts would be inadequate for studying *inter*personal relations, the movement to the dyadic or relational level of analysis has been a slow and difficult one. Jackson (1965:4), focusing on family systems, expresses the difficulty when he states:

> It is only when we attend to *transactions* between individuals as primary data that a qualitative shift in conceptual framework can be achieved. Yet our grasp of such data seems ephemeral; despite our best intentions, clear observations of interaction process fade into the old, individual vocabulary, there to be lost, indistinguishable and heuristically useless. To put the problem another way, we need measures which do not sum up individuals into a family unit; we need to measure the characteristics of the supra-individual family unit, characteristics for which we have almost no terminology.

The "qualitative shift" in conceptual frameworks and operational measures is "not a simple extension of the action or the interaction models"; rather, it is a shift away "from the individual as the unit of analysis to *the relationship as the unit of analysis*" (Parks and Wilmot, 1975:9). A relation is a "property or properties of a set of objects and/or events that they do not have taken separately" (Ackoff and Emery, 1972:225). The unit of analysis in a transactional perspective is a minimum of two, a dyad; and the focus of analysis is on the systemic properties that the participants have collectively, not individually. The system is viewed as a joint product of behavior, a product admittedly made up of individual actions, but one that has a "life" of its own which goes beyond the sum of its constituent parts.

A transactional perspective of communication behavior tries to look directly at the combinatorial rules characterizing the system's message-exchange process and not at the individual characteristics brought to the situation by the individual participants. A relational view requires the development of variables that describe the system's structure. On the basis of system variables, predictions are made of relationally bound social behavior, rather than individual behavior irrespective of particular social relationships and environmental conditions.

This transactional perspective emphasizes a dynamic, emergent, holistic approach to the study of social behavior. It requires social scientists to look for multiple causes and multiplicative effects, rather than unidimensional and additive cause-effect sequences. It necessitates the development of reciprocal or nonrecursive, as well as recursive models of behavior. Further, if social science is not to get lost in a sea of isolated studies for which no linking vocabulary exists, it requires the use of variables that can describe and differentiate behavior across situations so that situations can be compared and contrasted.

THREE TRANSACTIONAL DIMENSIONS OF RELATIONSHIPS

The following transactional dimensions are proposed in an effort to stimulate dialogue about how to conceive of interpersonal relationships. This conceptual framework is quite literally "in process" and is suggestive rather than definitive. The particular dimensions suggested have grown out of an attempt to synthesize what we believe are three interrelated but conceptually distinct themes found in the literature on social relationships. These dimensions of *control, trust,* and *intimacy* are not intended to be an exhaustive list of relational variables.[2] They are intended to be viewed as three basic joint products of behavior that emerge, have "life," and fluctuate through the exchange of messages–basic products in the sense that, given the advent of precise operations, all social relationships can be usefully described and differentiated over time and situations.

In proposing these three dimensions we have kept several points in mind. First, all relationships take on a "supra-individual quality, and membership in them provides a source of labels and directives for action by both the insider and outsider" (Denzin, 1970:76). The larger the number of people involved in the system, the more cognizant people are of these "supra-individual" relationships. Conversely, the smaller the number, the less aware members are of this quality, so that in a dyad, the participants are almost exclusively aware only of the other, and not of their relationship (Simmel, 1950). Second, relational rules, although conceptually abstract, are directly concerned with, and manifested in, behavior.

Behaviorally, these joint products are "neither situationally nor personally abstract" (Denzin, 1970:72) but have relevance *only* within the context of a specific relationship and the behavior of its members. The task of the social scientist attempting to describe these relational rules is to categorize various bits of behavior which appear to work together to maintain and change particular rule structures. The proposed dimensions are three rule structures of all social relationships that should be discernible through careful observation of verbal and nonverbal behaviors.

Control

In an ongoing message exchange, definitions of self vis-à-vis the other are continually offered or "given-off" (Goffman, 1959). These definitions refer to the participants' "expected acts of deference and demeanor" (Denzin, 1970:71) regarding how the two participants are going to, and should, behave in each other's presence. The control dimension is concerned with who has the right to direct, delimit, and define the actions of the interpersonal system in the presently experienced spatial-temporal situation. The time relevancy of this dimension is always the *present,* since the right to define will vary over situations and content areas. In this temporal sense, the control dimension is the most basic and dynamic of the three, for the question of definitional rights must be continually negotiated according to changing internal and external conditions.

The more one person asserts relational definitions (i.e., makes one-up movements) that are accepted, the more dominant that person is said to be in that system. The more one-up moves offered but not accepted by a one-down response, the more domineering that person. But notice, to equate dominance with control is a mistake in interpretation—a frequent confusion of content and relational levels of analysis. The control pattern is defined by both parties and a one-down movement may be just as directing (though often called submissive) as a one-up statement.

Of the three dimensions to be presented, the most work has been done on the control dimension. An extended discussion of this work will be pursued in a later section of this paper. For the moment, it is sufficient to state that there are at least two continua that characterize this transactional dimension (Millar, 1973). The first, a *rigid-flexible* continuum, refers to the frequency with which the assertion and acceptance of definitional rights alternate between the members of the system. The more one individual defines the system's actions within and across situations, the more rigid the control pattern. The more alternation in who delimits the dyad's action, the more flexible.

A second characteristic continuum, *stable-unstable,* refers to the system's own consistency in asserting and accepting definitional rights to the dyad's own norm concerning the predictability and appropriateness with which control maneuvers are transmitted. The more consistent the pattern in the timing and direction of one-up and one-down strategies, the more stable the control pattern. The more seemingly unrelated that each relational move to its immediately preceding movement is, the more unstable the control pattern.

Trust

The second proposed dimension concerns both the inherent uncertainty of the behaviors of symbolic, purposeful systems and the system members' attempts to seek and develop dependable sources of rewards (McCall and Simmons, 1966:170). Given that people can choose and change, there is no certainty that desired behavior will, in fact, occur. Reactive systems which cannot choose their responses to external conditions can, in principle, be predicted with certainty; purposeful systems cannot. The best that can be done is to establish constraints (i.e., commitments, rules, norms, laws, agreements, etc.) on behavior and then make probability estimates about the likelihood that a particular other will behave congruently with those expectations in a given situation. However, every acknowledged constraint implies an obligation that the constraint will actually be followed. These concerns with another's predictability and the obligatory nature of any constraint on choice are the ingredients of this relational dimension. The temporal relevancy of trust, then, is the *future,* although the probability estimates of another are obviously based in the past.

Trust is said to exist in a relationship if both participants have manifested trusting and trustworthy behaviors (Millar, 1972; Millar and Millar, 1976). In the same way that a one-up move is assumed to be an assertion of the right to define and a one-down move is an acceptance of the other's definition, so trusting behaviors are an admission of one's vulnerability and dependence on another and trustworthy behaviors are a recognition of that vulnerability and the obligation not to exploit it.

Given this notion of trust as a relational variable, several comparisons can be made between ego's and alter's behavior to describe and differentiate the degree of trust in dyads. One such characteristic continuum is called the *vulnerability pattern.* This score reflects the combined frequency with which the members have placed themselves in a vulnerable position relative to the other. A vulnerable position is one where the outcome, which is a function of alter's behavior, is potentially less rewarding to ego than the potential costs. This score could run from zero to infinity with lower scores indicating a suspicious or distrusting relationship, middle-range scores a trusting one, and larger frequencies a risky transactional pattern.

A second continuum for discriminating between relationships on trust is the *reward dependability* pattern. This measure is based on the difference between the frequencies, weighted by their subjective reward value, with which ego and alter have each been rewarded for their positions of vulnerability. The greater the difference score, the more one person is dependent on the other and the more potentially exploitative the relationship; the smaller the difference, the more interdependent the participants, the more trust in their relationship.

A third continuum to characterize the degree of trust is labeled the *confidence* pattern. A suggested measurement of this variable is the absolute difference between ego's and alter's probability estimates of betrayal, multiplied by the number of relevant situations' scores. The larger the difference, the more unilateral the relationship; the smaller the difference, the more cooperative the relationship, the more mutual confidence, and the more trust in the transactional pattern.

Intimacy

As previously stated, it is assumed that social relationships are at least partially "built" on the perceptions and metaperceptions of self and other (Laing et al., 1966). These perceptions occur through the exchange of behavior. This third transactional dimension, intimacy, is concerned with our "attachments" (McCall and Simmons, 1966:172), the degree to which each person uses the other as a source of self-confirmation and the affective evaluation of the self-confirmation. This dimension is crucial to defining more individualized versus more role-bound relationships.

The characteristic variables of the previous dimensions were particular types of observable behaviors. The primary variables of concern here are perceptions. Since these are inherently "black box" (although hopefully measurable by such schemes as Laing et al.'s (1966) IPM and/or indicated by a variety of nonverbal behaviors), this dimension is considered to be the most subjective and interpretative of the three. This subjectivity creates serious measurement problems which, unfortunately, encourage a monadic rather than a dyadic analysis.

Intimacy is not based on the content of the relationship (Simmel, 1950:126-127),[3] but on the degree to which ego's view of alter's view of ego (ego's alter's ego) acts as a limiting factor on ego's behavior. The more frequently that ego's alter's ego acts as a constraint on the respective behaviors, the more intimate the relationship.

The feeling of intimacy, the strength of our "attachments," and the affect of love stem from the positiveness that ego has for ego's alter's ego.[4] The positiveness or negativeness of this perception is assumed to be related to its similarity with ego's view of ego (ego's ego). The more that ego exclusively shares and/or experiences his desired self with alter, and vice versa, the stronger the affect that ego has for alter and alter for ego. Intimacy rests on the reciprocal dependence and affectivity of ego on alter as a source of self-confirmation.

Given this notion of intimacy, the following two continua are suggested as ways of describing and differentiating interpersonal relationships. One, the *transferable-nontransferable* continuum, refers to the difference between the number of situations, weighted by their frequency, within which ego's alter's ego is equivalent to ego's ego for both participants. The smaller the difference, the more unique the relationship and the less transferable (McCall, 1970); the greater this difference score, the less unique, the more transferable (i.e., the larger the number of alters that ego has with whom he can be the self he desires to perceive himself to be), and the less intimate the relationship.

The *degree of attachment* continuum is measured by the difference between the number of situations, weighted by their frequency,[5] within which ego's alter's ego and alter's ego's alter act as a limiting factor on ego's and alter's behavior respectively. The more equivalent this difference score, the more interdependent the relationship. The more each person is said to "need" the other, the more "attached" the dyad. The larger the difference in these limiting frequencies, the more asymmetrical the pattern of interdependence, the less the mutual attachment, and the less intimate the relationship.

These three dimensions–control, trust, and intimacy–form a conceptual framework by which to chart social relationships. The framework and the suggested measurements will hopefully serve to stimulate a relational level analysis of interpersonal communication systems.

RELATIONAL LEVEL RESEARCH

At this point in the development of a relational approach, the control dimension has been the most adequately researched. A full conceptualization of this dimension and the basic operational procedures will be discussed in the following section. This approach will provide an extended illustration of the relational approach and serve as a procedural guide for the development of other relational level dimensions.

Development of a Methodology

The conceptual base for the relational control analysis stems from the application of the systems approach to human interaction. This is notably the accumulative efforts of Bateson (1958), Jackson (1959, 1965), Haley (1963), and Watzlawick et al. (1967). Sluzki and Beavin (1965) have provided the most influential work at the operational level.

The relational control analysis incorporates the assumption that messages contain both report (content) and command (relational) aspects. Message exchange involves the reciprocal offerings of relation definitions with the control pattern residing in the exchange, not in the message. Moreover, if message exchange is ongoing, transactional systems are ever evolving, with communication patterns continually changing and new relational rules emerging. Thus, "steady states" may be evident at a given point in time but not necessarily over time.

The relational control coding system to be discussed here focuses on (1) indexing *relational control* rather than content of messages, (2) defining *message sequences,* rather than individual message units, and (3) mapping *transactional patterns* as they unfold over time.

Only a general outline of the coding scheme will be presented, since its full details are given elsewhere (Ericson and Rogers, 1973; Rogers and Farace, 1975). In this system, which reflects the work of Sluzki and Beavin (1965) and Mark (1971), each message is viewed as a stimulus for the following message and as a definer of the preceding message. In a series of two-message exchanges, it is the second of the pair that defines the transaction type. Each message is categorized according to a three digit code. The first digit designates the speaker, the second refers to the grammatical form, and the third indicates the response mode of the message relative to the previous message. The coding scheme is based on the idea that the control definition is rooted in both the grammatical form of a message and its response form. In this manner, any communicative exchange can be represented by a series of sequentially ordered, three digit codes. The code categories used are as follows:

1st Digit	*2nd Digit*	*3rd Digit*
1. Speaker A	1. Assertion	1. Support
2. Speaker B	2. Question	2. Nonsupport
	3. Talk-over	3. Extension
	4. Noncomplete	4. Answer
	5. Other	5. Instruction
		6. Order
		7. Disconfirmation
		8. Topic Change
		9. Initiation-Termination
		0. Other

The three digital coding represents the first step toward indexing relational structure. The next step is to translate these message codes into control codes, i.e., to specify the control direction among three mutually exclusive possibilities. These assignments are made on the basis of whether a message is (a) an attempt to assert definitional rights, which is designated as one-up (↑), (b) a request or an acceptance of the other's definition of the relationship, designated as one-down (↓), or (c) a nondemanding, nonaccepting, leveling movement, which is designated as one-across (→).

The control directions of message types are given in Figure 1. The five grammatical forms (second digit) and the 10 response modes (third digit) represent 50 different combinations, each with its own control designation.

This control matrix forms the basis for obtaining transactional information. The theoretical concepts of symmetry, complementarity, and transition are

	1 Support	2 Nonsupport	3 Extension	4 Answer	5 Instruction	6 Order	7 Disconfirmation	8 Topic Change	9 Initiation Termination	0 Other
Assertion 1	↓	↑	→	↑	↑	↑	↑	↑	↑	→
Question 2	↓	↑	↓	↑	↑	↑	↑	↑	↑	↓
Talk-over 3	↓	↑	↑	↑	↑	↑	↑	↑	↑	↓
Noncomplete 4	↓	↑	→	↑	↑	↑	↑	↑	→	→
Other 5	↓	↑	→	↑	↑	↑	↑	↑	↑	→

Figure 1: CONTROL DIRECTIONS OF MESSAGE TYPES

operationalized by combining the control direction of one message with the control direction of a contiguous message. The similarities or differences between the paired control directions are used to define the three basic types of control patterns: (1) *complementarity,* where the control directions are different and directionally opposite; (2) *symmetry,* where the control directions are the same; and (3) *transition,* where the paired directions are different but not opposite. In a complementary transaction, the interactors' behaviors are fully differential, and the definition of the relationship offered by one is accepted by the other. A symmetrical transaction involves one interactor behaving toward the other as the other has behaved toward him; thus, there is a similarity of definition by the two individuals. In a transitory transaction, one of the interactor's behaviors minimizes the issue of control. In this type of exchange one interactor offers or responds with a neutralized control definition. Each transactional unit is structural information and provides a measure of the speakers' relationship.

By combining the three control directions, nine transactional or relational units are developed. These transactional units are given in Figure 2. Complementary types are those combining one-up and one-down control dimensions and are shown in cells 2 and 4 of the matrix. Symmetrical transactional units are shown in cells 1, 5, and 9 of the matrix. Cell 1 is termed *competitive symmetry* and refers to the escalating symmetrical style of Watzlawick et al. (1970:107). Cell 5 is labeled *submissive symmetry* and depicts one-down definitions by both members. Cell 9 is called *neutralized symmetry* and characterizes reciprocal messages neither accepting nor asserting relational definitions.

Control Direction of Speaker B's Message	Control Direction of Speaker A's Message		
	One-up (↑)	One-down (↓)	One Across (→)
One-up (↑)	1. (↑↑) Competitive Symmetry	4. (↑↓) Complementarity	7. (↑→) Transition
One-down (↓)	2. (↓↑) Complementarity	5. (↓↓) Submissive Symmetry	8. (↓→) Transition
One-across (→)	3. (→↑) Transition	6. (→↓) Transition	9. (→→) Neutralized Symmetry

Figure 2: CONTROL CONFIGURATIONS OF THE NINE TYPES OF TRANSACTIONAL UNITS

Previously, the control-defining nature of messages has been conceptualized as having only two directions, either one-up or one-down, and transactional units have been conceptualized as either symmetrical or complementary. The addition of a third direction, one-across, which represents an attempt to sensitize the control measure, produces an additional type of symmetry and third type of transactional exchange—the transitory category.

Transitory transactions refer to paired messages in which one of the statements is one-across. Cells 3, 6, 7, and 8 represent the four transitory transactional types. Cells 3 and 7 refer, respectively, to neutralized toward one-up and one-up toward neutralized transactional units. Cells 6 and 8 refer, respectively, to movements of neutralized toward one-down and one-down toward neutralized patterns.

The three types of symmetry, the four types of transition, and the two types of complementarity offer a more complete set of structural concepts by which to describe ongoing conversations.[6] These transactional units can be summed across a dyad's message exchange to obtain its predominant transactional pattern. Likewise, a stochastic analysis, or other time-series analysis, of the dyad's interchange can be performed to discover what message types tend to follow and precede given transactional units both within and between transactional types.

In brief, the coding procedure has three basic steps. First, each message is given a three digit code category representing the speaker, the grammatical form, and the response mode of the message. Second, control directions are assigned to each message according to a set of rules based on the combination of the form and response mode categories. Third, the designation of the transactional types results from the combined control directions of sequentially paired messages. In the initial study utilizing this three digit code, the reliability figures ranged from

.68 to 1.00. The average reliability across all comparisons was .86 (Ericson and Rogers, 1973).[7] Thus, the coding procedure seems to give expanded relational level conceptualizations and is operationally workable.

Relational Control Findings

The research to be reported here is based on the interactional data from a random sample of 65 husband and wife dyads.[8] In the discussion of four topics, these dyads produced a data base of nearly 14,000 messages. Transitory units accounted for almost 60% of all transactions coded. There were about 8% more one-down transitory exchanges than one-up. Approximately 30% of the transactions were symmetrical with neutralized symmetry accounting for the largest proportion (20%). Submissive symmetry and competitive symmetry were the least frequently occurring types of transactions (about 5% each). Complementary units made up a little more than 10% of the total transactions.

Utilizing these data, Rogers (1972) compared the transactional communication patterns of marital pairs exhibiting different levels of role discrepancy. "Role discrepancy" refers to the degree of inequity perceived to be present in the dyadic system. Duration of the marriage, or history, was utilized as a control variable.

Communication differences were found to be related to role discrepancy level. These differences were particularly evident in the short history dyads (married 11 years or less) as compared to long history dyads (married 12 to 26 years). Dyads with higher role discrepancy tended to have more competitive symmetrical transactions and had significantly more neutralized symmetry observed in their conversations.[9]

An analysis of transitory transactions by discrepancy level found one-down transitory transacts, particularly with the husband one-down, to be significantly more characteristic of low discrepant dyads. This corresponds with several other findings of the study. Message control direction also correlated with discrepancy level. High discrepant couples had more one-up and fewer one-down statements in their conversations than low discrepant dyads. Wives in the higher discrepancy pairs sent more one-up messages and their husbands transmitted fewer one-down statements than their respective low discrepancy counterparts. In addition to these differences, it was found that low discrepant dyads expressed more support statements and more unsuccessful talk-overs and tended to have more speaker turnover (as evidenced by more transactions and fewer silences in their discussions) than high discrepant dyads.[10]

An overall view of the relational patterns indicates that in the high discrepant dyads' interaction the general flow of control was one-across toward one-up and that in the low discrepant dyads it was one-across toward one-down with considerably less one-across symmetry.

Ericson (1972) used dominance-submission scores as predictors of transaction types and found no relationship between this psychologically oriented variable and the presence of complementary or symmetrical transactions. However, utilizing a deviation-from-randomness score, Ericson found a general indication of nonrandomness in the use of transaction types; more specifically, the marital dyads used fewer transactional types when discussing a family situation topic than an emergency situation topic.

Millar (1973) used the rigid-flexible and stable-unstable continua of the control dimension as the independent variables in his analysis of the marital pairs. "Rigidity" refers to a lack of alternation in the transactional pattern and "stability" refers to the predictability of the pattern. Scores on these two variables were found to be independent (r = .02) and differentiated the couples on several indices.

Looking at these two continua separately, we found the following main effects. Couples classified as rigid had (a) more transitory transactions in their discussions, (b) a higher frequency of husband one-down type of transitory exchange, and (c) more one-across symmetrical transactions than did the flexible couples. Flexible dyads, on the other hand, had a larger proportion of (d) complementary transactions, (e) transitory transactions with the husband one-up, and (f) competitive and (g) submissive symmetrical configurations in their discussions than did the rigid couples.

Marital pairs classified as stable reported more satisfaction with their interspousal communication and discussed more topics more frequently than did the unstable partners. Stable couples seemed to have more dynamic conversations than the unstable pairs, as they exchanged more messages in comparable lengths of time. Furthermore, stable partners had more transitory and fewer complementary transacts in their discussions than the unstable dyads.

By combining the scores on the two continua, the couples were classified into four structural types. Each of these four groups had some communicative characteristics that uniquely distinguished them.

The single most frequently observed transaction for the stable-rigid dyads was the transitory unit with the husband one-down. These couples were the only ones where the complementary transact with the husband one-down was less frequently used than the reverse with the husband one-up. Wives in the stable-rigid pairs were the only group of wives to make more one-up statements than their husbands, and they were also the only wives who challenged (i.e., gave a one-up response to) their husbands' one-up assertions more often than the husbands challenged their one-up statements. In other words, the wives in the stable-rigid groups were the only wives who seemed to dominate the couples' conversational patterns. Interestingly, these couples also reported the most overall satisfaction with their interspousal communication.

The unstable-rigid couples spent the longest time discussing the four topics, but had the fewest number of transactions coded. More than any other group, their conversational style seemed to be less of an exchange and more a series of relatively long, individual messages stated in each other's presence. The neutralized symmetrical transaction was their single most frequently observed structural pattern. Husbands in this group challenged their wives' one-up moves less than any other group of husbands and were the only husbands to respond with a one-across statement to their wives' preceding one-up message more than their wives responded in this way to them.

The stable-flexible couples manifested the most interaction in their discussion, as they had the largest number of transactions coded. These dyads were most frequently observed in the transitory unit with the wife one-down. This was the only group where the husbands made significantly more one-up moves than their wives.

Of the four types of couples, the unstable-flexible had the most complementary and the fewest transitory units observed in their discussions. Their coded conversations also contained the lowest proportion of one-down transitory units. Even though their single most frequently coded transaction was neutralized symmetry, they were observed in this pattern significantly less often than the rigid couples. These findings suggest that these couples were not likely to use the one-across movement in a nondemanding way, but were more likely to use one-across statements in an avoiding "holding pattern" with neither member willing to assert or submit definitional rights.[11] Of the four groups, the unstable-flexible husbands were the most likely to give a one-up response to their wives' one-down messages and to respond submissively to their wives' one-down movements. Similarly, the unstable-flexible wives were the most likely to respond with a one-up move to their husbands' one-down messages and were the least likely to respond to one-down messages with a one-across statement. This pattern of responses gives the impression of a defensive and/or punitive style of verbal exchange, an impression that is not suggested by the structural patterns of the other three dyadic types.

In all of the research efforts, pattern recognition has been an overriding goal. A more recent attempt to expand the ability to explicate transactional patterns over time involves the application of stochastic models. Parks et al. (1975) utilized Markov Chain analysis in an initial step toward describing the patterning of relational control. Examination of first-order (paired messages) and second-order (two sets of paired messages) transaction matrices verified previously noted patterns, namely the centrality of the one-down transitory exchange. While both first and second order system states had fairly high levels of entropy, indicating a substantial amount of uncertainty, once the system reached one of the two one-down types of transitory transactions (either →↓ or ↓→), the system was most likely to remain there.

Neutralized symmetry was another frequent system state; however, the system was unlikely to retain this structure and was most likely to move to one of the two transitory states described above. Neither competitive nor submissive symmetry had their state as the most probable transition nor probable incoming transitional state. With a marital dyad data base, competitive and submissive symmetrical transactions were relatively infrequent occurrences and were rarely maintained as an ongoing pattern. The most frequent control direction following a one-up or one-down movement was one-across.

In a second paper (Parks et al., 1976), longer transactional sequences have been analyzed with the Markov procedures. In addition, relational control patterns of dyads exhibiting differing levels of role discrepancy, history, and communication satisfaction are compared. The goal of the stochastic analyses is more precise pattern identification.

CONCLUSION

The orientation, concepts, and operations discussed in this chapter are in various formative stages of development. The relational approach presented tries to capture the co-defining nature of the interaction process. The assumptions and goals of this approach and the research work reported are clearly reflected in the following quotation from Blumer (1969:53):

> In setting up studies of human group life and social action there is need to take social interaction seriously. It is necessary to view the given sphere of life under study as a moving process in which the participants are defining and interpreting each other's acts. It is important to see how this process of designation and interpretation is sustaining, undercutting, redirecting, and transforming the ways in which the participants are fitting together their lines of action. Such a necessary type of study cannot be done if it operates with the premise that group life is but the result of determining factors working through the interaction of people. Further, approaches organized on this latter premise are not equipped to study the process of social interaction. A different perspective, a different set of categories, and a different procedure of inquiry are necessary.

With continuing conceptual development and research on relational dimensions of message exchange, considerable progress will be made in understanding interpersonal communication processes.

NOTES

1. It is frequently assumed that what is true of dyads is equally valid for larger groupings. Simmel (1950) seriously questioned the validity of this assumption and it is denied in this article.

2. We are not that satisfied with the labels themselves since the terms have been extensively used to reflect the more monadic, unidirectional, and attitudinal perspectives. Perhaps they would better have been labeled I, II, and III.

3. Various behaviors like openness, self-disclosure, sexual contact, and frequency of touch may be necessary but not sufficient for claiming that a particular relationship is intimate.

4. Hate would have the same perceptual condition but a negative valence.

5. This is probably an exponential rather than an arithmetic weighting factor, but for illustrative purposes the latter will be assumed.

6. Ways of improving the coding system are presently under consideration: namely, (1) adding an intensity measure to the control movements, (2) incorporating a time measure of the duration of control, and (3) analyzing the possible multifunctional aspects of the one-across messages.

7. Reliability figures based on the control directions, the second step of the coding procedures, were practically at the 1.00 level.

8. The couples were randomly selected from a telephone listing of a Midwest metropolitan and suburban area. They all had at least one child under 12 years of age. The interactional data base was tape-recorded conversations of each pair discussing four topics—two topics concerning family situations and two concerning family behavior in emergency situations. Self-report data were also obtained from each husband and wife separately.

9. No variations in complementary exchanges were noted by discrepancy level.

10. A comparison of dyads differentiated by role discrepancy level also showed significant differences on the self-report data. Compared to high role discrepant dyads, lower role discrepancy dyads spent more time together, talked with one another more, talked about more topics, particularly more personal topics, and were more satisfied with their communication relationship and with their marriage.

11. One-across messages seem to have multiple relational functions. In the one-down, one-across exchange, the one-across message appears to be a low level assertion of relational definition. In the one-up, one-across transaction, it appears to function as an attempt to curb the assertion of control. Instead of submitting to or directly challenging the assertion, a less demanding, but not accepting response is transmitted. With neutralized symmetry, one-across messages seem to indicate an avoidance of definitional rights.

REFERENCES

ACKOFF, R.L., and EMERY, F.E. (1972). On purposeful systems. Chicago: Aldine-Atherton.

ARGYLE, M. (1969). Social interaction. New York: Atherton.

BATESON, G. (1958). Naven (2nd ed.). Stanford, Calif.: Stanford University Press.

BLUMER, H. (1969). Symbolic interactionism, perspective and method. Englewood Cliffs, N.J.: Prentice-Hall.

DENZIN, N.K. (1970). "Rules of conduct and the study of deviant behavior: Some notes on the social relationships." In G.J. McCall, M.M. McCall, N.K. Denzin, G.D. Suttles, and S.B. Kurth (eds.), Social relationships. Chicago: Aldine.

DUNCAN, H.D. (1967). "The search for a social theory of communication in American sociology." In F. Dance (ed.), Human communication theory. New York: Holt, Rinehart and Winston.

ERICSON, P.M. (1972). "Relational communication: Complementarity and symmetry and their relation to dominance-submission." Unpublished doctoral dissertation, Michigan State University.

ERICSON, P.M., and ROGERS, L.E. (1973). "New procedures for analyzing relational communication." Family Process, 12:245-267.

GOFFMAN, E. (1959). The presentation of self in everyday life. Garden City, N.Y.: Doubleday.

GOLEMBIEWSKI, R.T. (1962). The small group. Chicago: University of Chicago Press.

HALEY, J. (1963). "Marriage therapy." Archives of General Psychiatry, 8:213-224.

JACKSON, D.D. (1959). "Family interaction, family homeostatis and some implications for conjoint family psychotherapy." In J.H. Masserman (ed.), Individual and family dynamics. New York: Grune and Stratton.

--- (1965). "The study of the family." Family Process, 4:1-20.

LAING, R.D., PHILLIPSON, H., and LEE, A.R. (1966). Interpersonal perception: A theory and a method of research. New York: Harper and Row.

MARK, R.A. (1971). "Coding communication at the relationship level." Journal of Communication, 21:221-232.

McCALL, G.J. (1970). "The social organization of relationships." In G.J. McCall, M.M. McCall, N.K. Denzin, G.D. Suttles, and S.B. Kurth (eds.), Social relationships. Chicago: Aldine.

McCALL, G.J., and SIMMONS, J.L. (1966). Identities and interactions. New York: Free Press.

MILLAR, D.P., and MILLAR, F.E. (1976). Messages and myths. Port Washington, N.Y.: Alfred Publishing.

MILLAR, F.E. (1972). "Towards a new conceptualization of trust." Unpublished paper, Michigan State University.

--- (1973). "A transactional analysis of marital communication patterns: An exploratory study." Unpublished doctoral dissertation, Michigan State University.

PARKS, M.R., FARACE, R.V., and ROGERS, L.E. (1975). "A stochastic description of relational communication systems." Paper presented at the convention of the Speech Communication Association, Houston.

PARKS, M.R., FARACE, R.V., ROGERS, L.E., ALBRECHT, T., and ABBOTT, R. (1976). "Markov process analysis of relational communication in marital dyads." Paper presented at the convention of the International Communication Association, Portland.

PARKS, M.R., and WILMOT, W.W. (1975). "Three research models of communication: Action, interaction and transaction." Paper presented at the convention of the Western Speech Communication Association, Seattle.

ROGERS, L.E. (1972). "Dyadic systems and transactional communication in a family context." Unpublished doctoral dissertation, Michigan State University.

ROGERS, L.E., and FARACE, R.V. (1975). "Analysis of relational communication in dyads: New measurement procedures." Human Communication Research, 1:222-239.

SIMMEL, G. (1950). The sociology of Georg Simmel (K.H. Wolff, trans.). Glencoe, Ill.: Free Press.

SLUZKI, C.E., and BEAVIN, J. (1965). "Simetria y complementaridad: Una definicion operacional y una tipologia de parejas." Acta Psiquiatrica y Psicologica de America Latina, 11:321-330.

WATZLAWICK, P., BEAVIN, J., and JACKSON, D.D. (1967). Pragmatics of human communication. New York: Norton.

Chapter 5

COMMUNICATION AND RELATIONSHIP DEFINITION

Teru L. Morton, James F. Alexander, and Irwin Altman

THEORISTS AND RESEARCHERS in the social sciences and humanities have long viewed communication as an important aspect of interpersonal behavior. Wide variation exists, however, in the ways in which the relationship between communication and interpersonal behavior has been conceptualized. Using the familiar one-way effect model of source-channel-receiver, for example, behavioral scientists have greatly increased our understanding of communication in laboratory and field settings. Examples of well-developed areas include social psychological studies of persuasion and attitude change, in which either source variables or motivational states of receivers are manipulated. Research on these topics seems to demonstrate that the impact or meaning of communication can be influenced by changing the characteristics of the source or the receiver. In other fields, communication has been studied as an indicator of the nature and quality of relationships; theories of personality and abnormal behavior have both contributed to, and grown out of, analyses of communication in different types of relationships, such as therapists-clients, happily married versus divorcing couples, and supervisors-trainees.

Recently, a new view of communication as a vehicle for interpersonal control has emerged, which goes beyond traditional approaches. For example, in an analysis of schizophrenia and other clinical phenomena, Haley (1963) and Bateson et al. (1956) suggested that communication is an attempt to define a relationship. In a similar vein, the communication theorists Miller and Steinberg (1975) proposed that communication reflects an attempt to influence another's behavior to produce physical, social, or economic rewards. Furthermore, social learning clinicians have addressed the control properties of "tact" and "mand" communications (Patterson and Reid, 1970), and Goffman (1961, 1967) is among the sociologists and social psychologists who have described socially accepted rules of interaction related to interpersonal control. Similarly, numerous researchers concerned with self-disclosure as a communication process (Altman and Taylor, 1973; Cozby, 1973) imply an interest in *mutuality* of disclosure. However, while many writers have gone beyond earlier input-channel-output models by acknowledging that communication as control is a transactional process, they have continued to employ individually oriented levels of analysis, rather than explicitly focus on *mutual* communication between people.

As these approaches stimulate increasing research on communication, a need is emerging for integrative constructs and propositions. Specifically, researchers presently lack a suitable framework for treating the interpersonal relationship itself as an appropriate unit of analysis. Such a level of analysis not only addresses properties of sources and receivers as individuals, but focuses on the two-way communication that flows between participants to a relationship. In this paper, communication is treated as a vehicle for interpersonal control, but the analysis is extended to the mutual control inherent in social relationships. We will offer the proposition that "mutuality of relationship definition" is central to the viability of interpersonal relationships. Simply put, this theme states that consensual rules and modes of communication between people are the bedrock of social bonding. This idea, seemingly obvious, rests on the assumption that the key ingredient to understanding social ties between people is reflected in the properties of their relationship to a degree equal to or greater than in their characteristics as separately functioning individuals. In pursuing this thesis, we will demonstrate that using the *social relationship,* not the actors taken separately, as the central unit of analysis permits integration of previous approaches, and also offers new arenas of interest and investigation.

The next section offers several key propositions about social relationships, which are presented as generic, universal aspects of relationship forms and stages, each centering on interpersonal control processes. The second part of the paper illustrates how these basic propositions can be applied to the analysis of a variety of relationship forms.

BASIC THEMES AND DEFINITIONS

I. Every Viable Social Relationship Requires Mutuality of Control Between Participants. The major themes of this section are that (a) interpersonal communication is the primary vehicle through which individuals define relationships and (b) every viable social relationship requires mutuality or consensus of relationship definition. Conversely, a relationship crisis involves nonmutuality of relationship definition.

Theorists and laymen alike would agree with the general idea that in "good" relationships people agree and that in "bad" relationships they disagree. Beyond easy acceptance of this truism, however, there are widely divergent views about the reasons for consensus between people, or lack of consensus. Husbands complain that wives won't support their decisions (and vice versa); sociologists point to incompatibility of values as a source of conflict; traditional psychologists emphasize lack of congruence between interactants' needs; and comedians joke about divorces occurring over burnt toast and uncapped toothpaste tubes.

Unfortunately, consensus or lack of consensus about single aspects of a relationship seems to be a poor predictor of social bonding or relationship viability. The Bunkers in TV's *All in the Family,* for example, seem to disagree on just about everything, including religion, politics, food preference, and dress style. Yet their relationships persist and even grow. Why? From our theoretical perspective we assert that all participants, in spite of their bickering, *mutually agree on the definition of their relationships,* part of which includes the fact that they agree that they can disagree about a number of specific issues. So it is that we hypothesize that mutuality of relationship definition is the fundamental prerequisite for relationship viability. As such, the issues of compatibility and viability are elevated beyond the realm of additive properties of actors to the relationship per se as the unit of analysis.

This conceptual framework is not restricted to particular content areas of the relationship, but includes the structural dynamics of the relationship itself. The distinction between *content* and *relationship* aspects of communication is critical, and often overlooked or confused. That is, every communication contains simultaneous expressions of content and relationship. While consensus about content of a communication (agreement about some topical issue) is certainly important to the maintenance of a relationship, we propose that consensus about the *form* or *definition of the relationship* is even more critical. For example, a teenager might request, "May I have the car?" or assert, "I am taking the car." In these two statements, the content (acquisition of car) is the same, but the *relationship definition* between the teenager and the parent differs in the balance of influence and resource control recognized. In response to the latter assertive demand, a parent might respond, "Have fun," thereby accepting both content and a particular relationship definition (the teenager's option to control resources). Or the parent might respond with, "Have you finished your homework?"–in this case countering the teenager's attempt to redefine the relationship with a re-redefinition entailing parental control of resources, with the teenager's access to those resources based on an acceptable response to clear parental control. Because each member in the relationship is both a sender and a receiver of communications, mutuality of relationship definition–not so much content of communication–is a vital necessity. In our terms, mutuality or agreement about how the relationship is to be defined is tantamount to a good "fit" between people.

To summarize, we hypothesize that mutuality among parties to a relationship exists when there is consensus about the definition of that relationship, and that mutuality is a generic characteristic of the interpersonal relationship itself, rather than a property of individuals. However, it is important to examine how communication mediates mutuality of relationship definition. In the following discussion, we will describe certain dynamics underlying relationship definition, in terms of the multimodal nature of mutuality processes and in terms of the concept of influence potential.

II. Mutuality of Relationship Definition Is a Multimodal, Multilevel Communication Process. Communications, or attempts to define relationships, may be sent or received at various levels of intimacy and in qualitatively different forms, such as verbal, nonverbal, and environmental modes (Altman and Taylor, 1973; Altman, 1975). Furthermore, communication can occur in a single mode or in a combination of modes. Given this proposition, we can derive two implications. First, mutuality of relationship definition need not occur within a single form of communication between people, but can be manifested in a variety of ways. Second, mutuality does not necessarily involve simplistic reciprocity or matching of responses or involve topical similarity of communication exchange. People may establish mutuality by identical reciprocity of verbal content (Altman, 1973) or by dissimilar mixes of verbal disclosure, nonverbal behaviors, and environmental action. Naturally, however, mutuality can occur only at those levels and modes of communication where both interactants can perceive the definitional impact of communication. Thus, while a mother may both cuddle and talk to her infant, the newborn may be capable of responding only to the nonverbal mode of communication. Consequently, the mother's early attempts at relationship definition will be effective (i.e., "accepted" by the infant) only in the nonverbal mode.

To illustrate the multimodal, multilevel quality of mutality, consider the process of privacy regulation. Altman (1975) has viewed intimacy and privacy as a dialectic process involving openness-closedness or accessibility-inaccessibility of the self to others. As such, intimacy and privacy may be regulated by environmental mechanisms (personal space, territorial behavior), nonverbal mechanisms (body language), and verbal mechanisms, primarily through selectivity of self-disclosure. These three modes of communication operate in an integrated and systemic fashion, compensating for one another, amplifying one another, and occurring in different combinations.

Self-disclosure has attracted much attention for its central role in the early development of social relationships. Within the framework provided here, however, it represents only one modality of communication in relationships, albeit a crucial one. That is, the verbal mode of regulating intimacy and privacy is only one of several major vehicles for attaining mutuality of relationship definition, and its use varies as a function of the particular relationship form and the degree to which the interactants accept it as a vehicle for relationship definition.

A second point regarding self-disclosure is that it is best viewed as a property of relationships, and not solely as a property of individuals. To anticipate a later section in the chapter, acquainting dyads appear to depend heavily on tit-for-tat reciprocity of self-disclosure to attain mutuality, while well-acquainted dyads appear to substitute a much wider range of behaviors to maintain mutuality and are less apt to display point-for-point disclosure reciprocity (Altman, 1973; Morton, 1976). Thus, by considering self-disclosure at the level of the social relationship as well as at the level of the individual, we can better understand the dynamics of mutuality of relationship definition.

In summary, understanding the process of relationship definition highlights the importance of considering communication as a multimodal and multilevel process. Mutual responses in any social relationship operate in a systemic and unified fashion and may be examined in their own right as a coherent process. Even if one considers only a single communication mode, such as self-disclosure, focus on the *social relationship* as the unit of analysis vastly enhances understanding of the reciprocal and conjoint quality of communication between parties to the relationship.

III. As Relationships Develop, Modes of Exchange Tend to Expand and Diversify. An important challenge to the study of interpersonal communication is the need for an organizational schema general enough to apply to classes of relationships, yet specific enough to differentiate between distinctly different relationship forms. Historically, researchers have had most success in developing such schema in the highly restrictive environment of the laboratory where communication dimensions have been studied one at a time. But those who work in naturalistic settings and have tried to capture the richness of naturally occurring communication processes have encountered much greater difficulty in developing such schema.

This difficulty emerges from an inherent process in interpersonal relationships, namely, the expansion and diversification of modes of exchange. As described in the preceding section, interpersonal communication is a multimodal, multilevel process. Even that principle, however, fails to account for the dynamic quality of interpersonal exchanges because, as relationships develop, they necessarily include greater and greater domains of interaction. Early interaction in the parent-child relationship, for example, is primarily restricted to the domain of biological states, i.e., hunger, pain, physical stimulation, and the like. In later years, however, interactions concern a wide range of domains, including language development, moral judgments, sibling relationships, and many more. Because these domains are so varied, greatly expanded repertoires of communication modes and levels are required to attain mutuality of relationship definition. Thus, as the scope of a relationship expands, the modes and levels of communication processes correspondingly expand and diversify.

The implications of this process are important, both for interactants in the relationship and for scientists observing it. For interactants, their ability to develop mutuality of interpersonal relationships may be a result of constitutional, historical, and environmental variables. A person's inability, constitutional or otherwise, to generate or perceive communication in one or more modes may limit the prospect of attaining mutuality of relationship definition with another person. A person's biological and/or social history may seriously limit his or her ability to develop long-term relationships. A child, for example, restricted to only a narrow band of interpersonal exchange modes in order to attain mutuality at home, may later be seriously hampered in generating and perceiving the subtle but wide range of multimodal exchange necessary to develop enduring adult relationships. Thus, as we will see in a later section, the parent-child relationship is not only a major relationship form in which interactants must attain mutuality, it is also a stage which strongly influences the nature of subsequent relationship forms.

As mentioned above, the multimodal nature of relationship mutuality and its expansion as relationships develop also creates difficulty for the researcher. While we will argue that well-developed relationships possess certain common *generic* qualities, the *particular* modes of exchange in any one relationship may be so idiosyncratic and complex as to defy simple description.

IV. Relationship Crises Entail Nonmutuality of Relationship Definition. The dynamic quality of social relationships has important implications for the attainment and maintenance of mutuality. Because both new and established relationships are characterized by expanding domains of interaction and diversification of exchange modes, frequent relationship redefinition may occur resulting in temporary or longer periods of nonmutuality of relationship crisis.

Nonmutuality exists when there is disagreement about either the form of a relationship or the particular "mix" of exchange processes used to define the relationship. The resulting relationship crisis may be as "ordinary" as the parent's refusal to continue allowing the child to grunt and point in order to produce a desired object, or it may be as tragic as a teenage runaway, designed to severely restrict parental influence. In all instances, however, participants must struggle to reestablish consensus, which can occur in one of two ways: a return to previously accepted interaction modes and/or relationship forms, or a recalibration involving consensus about new interaction modes or relationship forms. If mutuality is not eventually attained the relationship is likely to terminate.

Relationship crisis, then, is a *transitional* process associated with dynamic changes involved in the formation, expansion, and dissolution of social bonding. The importance of the principle of relationship crises is that like the principle of mutuality, it highlights the idea that social interaction is not just a function of the properties of individuals, but is inherently a generic characteristic of the interpersonal relationship itself.

V. Consensus About Relationship Influence Potential Determines the Characteristics and Social Bonding of a Relationship. Thus far we have advanced the thesis that relationships can be maintained only if there is mutuality, consensus, or "fit" between the respective relationship definitions of the interactants. We have further suggested that multimodal, multilevel communication is the major vehicle for establishing mutuality of relationship definition.

Here we wish to introduce another concept, *influence potential,* as a crucial dynamic related to the level of intimacy and the intensity of social relationships. Consider an individual's relationships with a car-pool partner on the one hand and with a spouse of 20 years on the other. While both relationships may be characterized by complete agreement concerning relationship definition, they will almost certainly differ in terms of their intensity, or degree of "social bonding." Thus, while mutuality of relationship definition may account for the basic existence of a relationship, it is not sufficient to explain the range and variety of relationships. We propose the concept of *influence potential* as a dynamic determining this variation in the nature of relationships. Briefly, we hypothesize that degree of social bonding is a function of the consensus by both parties about the degree and distribution of their *relationship influence potential,* which is, in turn, a function of their individual influence potentials.

Individual influence potential consists of any combination of the following: (1) reward, such as monetary gain, political advantage, and liking, (2) withdrawal of reward, such as the loss of money or love or a demotion, (3) punishment, including physical and psychological forms, (4) coercion, including the threat of punishment or withdrawal of reward. Such notions of rewards and costs, power, influence, etc. are common enough in the existing social and behavioral science literature. In extending these traditional concepts, however, we make individual influence potential a *relational* concept involving mutual perception and acceptance by both parties to the relationship. Thus, for example, blackmail operates as a control strategy only if the blackmailer informs the victim of his influence potential and the victim "accepts." Individual influence potential, then, is an individual's ability to influence the other's behavior, as *mutually recognized* by both members of the relationship.

Where the level of analysis centers on the interpersonal relationship itself, information about one person's influence potential is most meaningful when related to information about the other's influence potential. In the present paradigm, therefore, we will discuss *relationship influence potential,* or the combination or pooling of both individual influence potentials. Consensus about relationship influence potential is a critical component of mutual relationship definition. Mutual perception and acceptance of the degree and distribution of influence potential in the relationship represents, we submit, a major dynamic determining the nature of a relationship.

The degree of relationship influence potential is tantamount to the degree of social bonding or pervasiveness of the relationship. Thus, the greater the influence potential in the relationship, the more pervasive, encompassing, and broad is the social bond. Returning to an earlier example, car poolers attain consensus to the effect that each has some minimal influence over the other. But because this influence extends over only a small aspect of their lives, the social bonding in the relationship is low. In contrast, both members of a long-term married couple typically influence large segments of each other's lives–by mutual consensus. Therefore, this latter relationship involves high social bonding and high relationship influence potential.

We are now ready to introduce still another concept–*distribution of relationship influence potential.* The earlier examples implied relatively equal amounts of individual influence potential, but relationships also exist where participants possess markedly different influence potential with respect to one another. Thus, relationships vary not only in overall degree of influence potential, or strength of social bonding, but also in the distribution of influence potential. Consider a somewhat oversimplified example: If both spouses in a "traditional" marriage agree that the husband does and should possess greater influence potential, then the relationship "happily" endures. If, perhaps as a result of the feminist movement, one or both participants reject the traditional definition of marriage as including disparity in the distribution of influence potential, the relationship may undergo a crisis of nonmutuality. Despite the oversimplified rhetoric of both traditional and new models of marriage relationships, neither a disparate nor an egalitarian distribution of relationship influence potential necessarily ensures a viable social bond. Rather, viability exists when there is mutuality, including consensus by the partners concerning degree and distribution of influence potential.

FOUR PROTOTYPE RELATIONSHIP FORMS

In the preceding sections we described major principles associated with the viability of any social relationship. With the exception of occasional examples, however, the principles have been quite abstract and not applied to the myriad subtleties involved in all social relationships. No single paper, of course, can hope to describe the specifics of each and every relationship, because the particular types of communication exchanges involved in a social bond depend upon the unique mixture of contextual variables, individual learning histories, biological constraints, and cultural norms. Nevertheless, sufficient communality exists within and across certain major relationship forms that they can be compared. In this part of the chapter we will consider four major relationship forms, demonstrating how the generic processes of mutuality of relationship definition and relationship influence potential are common to all, yet how and why each form represents a unique blend of these generic processes.

The Parent-Child Relationship

The relationship between a mother and a child is one of the most powerful bonds in our society—psychologically, physically, sociologically, and legally—and it is also one of the most difficult relationships to terminate. Explanations for this bonding usually include reference to the child's dependency and some mixture of "mother instinct," social norms, and role expectations. Interestingly, however, this bond is essentially thrust upon two strangers with the expectation that it will remain viable and produce a socialized member of adult society.

The task of mothering or parenting is a rather awesome one, for it requires rapid attainment of mutuality of relationship definition even though the participants begin with extraordinarily divergent behavioral repertoires. The newborn has only a few primitive but powerful behaviors to influence parental behavior: crying, cooing, throwing up, etc. The parent, on the other hand, has a potentially wide range of behaviors but quickly learns that only a restricted set will influence child behavior. Stated differently, although a wide range of interactive behaviors or communications are physically possible, only a very few can be used to produce mutuality of relationship definition.

Mutuality of relationship definition in the new parent-infant relationship is usually attained in a unimodal fashion, that is nonverbally. Crying, for example, is initially a simple reflex, becoming a communication (or relationship definition) as the infant comes to recognize that feeding follows. Where mutuality of relationship definition at this primitive level is attained, increasing socialization is made possible. Clinical evidence suggests that neglected or abandoned infants, deprived of opportunities to establish a relationship at this level, experience serious difficulties in establishing other kinds of interpersonal relationships (Mussen et al., 1969:228-236). Correspondingly, autistic children must first learn mutuality of control through the nonverbal mode before they can acquire verbal skills through modeling (Lovaas et al., 1966). Once this initial relationship between infant and parent is mutually established, as it almost always is, the relationship influence potential in this relationship form is high. With successive stages of maturation, however, the distribution of this influence potential becomes somewhat skewed, with the parent usually having much greater capacity to limit the older child's behavior. That is, the parent has resources such as milk and toys and can send and receive communication in many more ways. Furthermore, she or he has a strong cultural-social-legal mandate to employ these resources and capabilities in socializing the child.

At successive stages of socialization, then, a continual interfacing of the child's biological maturation with increasingly more complex patterns of communication and control occurs within the parent-child relationship. One of the major features of this ongoing relationship is the expansion of mutuality to the verbal mode and to multiple levels within this mode. The child's repertoire of control strategies, initially limited to smiling, crying, and grunting, increasingly expands with the acquisition of more complex verbalizations. Thus, the grunt and pointed finger of a very young child may suffice to define both content ("I want a cookie") and relationship ("You are in control of resources") in an acceptable way. Later, however, the parent responds only to a verbalization ("May I have a cookie?"). Thus, the distribution of influence potential remains constant and in favor of the parent, while the modes of exchange proliferate. It should be noted that, while increasing verbal skills of the child may be learned through intentional prompting and reinforcing on the part of the parent, and also less planfully through modeling and trial-and-error sequences, much of this early learning occurs for instrumental ends toward attaining a specific desired goal (e.g., a cookie).

Initially, children's verbalizations are comparatively more directive than those of their parents (Turk and Bell, 1972). Over time, however, the growing child develops increasingly indirect control strategies, as evidenced in the progression from crying to "Give me," to "Please may I?" to "I think we should." Within this progression lies also the rudiments of self-disclosure, a critical kind of communicative control which blossoms in later relationship forms. Even in the early stages of this first relationship form, however, the child begins to learn the control function of this kind of communication. The replacement of a morning tantrum with "I don't like the school lunch" represents an improved procedure for attaining a homemade lunch. And the barter, "If you read me a story I'll tell you a secret," reflects an emerging ability to use and withhold personal information to exercise control over others.

While certain control procedures are learned as instrumental behaviors, considerable generalization occurs such that the child develops control strategies or styles. These may be evidenced at various levels or modes, based on biology (large children are more likely to develop aggression, attractive ones cuteness), culture (males are usually allowed to control more through physical force), and already existent family patterns (an overinvolved mother may respond only to explicit verbalizations, or even to dramatic physical activities). Even very young children can be observed with particular talents in one or more of such basic control strategies as giving, requesting, taking, and withholding on both verbal and nonverbal levels. These primitive privacy regulation tactics are often described by parents and others as central personality traits (bully, shy, talkative, cute, stubborn, etc.). Where such procedures enable mutuality of control, maturation may prompt a shift in behavioral topology, but the functional strategy—e.g., coercion—may be sustained (Patterson and Reid, 1970).

Obviously, there are innumerable crises during all stages of childhood, each of which involves an attempt by one party or the other (usually the child) to alter the definition of the relationship and the distribution of relationship influence potential. A two-year-old may test limits by seemingly deliberate misbehavior, a five-year-old may demand increasingly lengthy rituals before going to bed, and an eight-year-old may insist on doing things without assistance. All these acts represent attempts at altering the definition of a relationship with parents, especially in regard to the distribution of influence potential. Sometimes these crises are solved by parental reassertion of control by means of sanctions; sometimes the result is a slight redistribution of relationship influence potential in the direction of the child. In most cases, mutuality is soon restored and mutual control strategies are agreed upon, largely because the child recognizes and reaccepts the parental definition of the relationship.

In summary, the parent-child relationship is characterized by mutuality of control, which expands from a single mode and a primitive level to multiple modes and levels. The increasing complexity of verbal control strategies represents the rudimentary development of self-disclosure as a major vehicle of relationship definition. The development of a generalized "style" of relationship control bridging several modes and levels may occur to the extent that it allows mutuality of control. Finally, the parent-child bond is characterized by a high amount of relationship influence potential and interdependence and by a skewed distribution of influence potential, with the parent employing his or her greater control capability to continually redefine the modes of exchange prescribed by the relationship form.

The Parent-Adolescent Relationship

Mutuality of relationship definition is as necessary for the maintenance of the parent-adolescent relationship as it is for the preceding developmental one. But attaining this mutuality is often considerably more difficult, for a drastic redefinition of the relationship usually occurs, and the transition from the parent-child to the parent-adolescent relationship form is often characterized by substantial nonmutuality. Indeed, puberty, with its explosive biological basis, is perhaps the greatest developmental crisis in our society. The adolescent's accelerated hormonal and muscular development combine with enhanced cognitive abilities to yield drastically increased interpersonal control capabilities. At the same time, sexual drives combine with social norms to create a quantitative, if not qualitative, increase of interest in peer activities and a concomitant decrease in family activities. These forces, often defined as "independence," entail major changes in both the amount and distribution of influence potential in the parent-adolescent relationship and also in the modes of exchange which are used in the relationship. This redefinitional period occurs as a normative crisis, and it is usually resolved as mutuality is restored through a new relationship definition.

The adolescent invests an increasing amount of time and interest in peer relationships which, in striking contrast to his relationship with parents, are characterized by relatively even distributions of influence potential. That is, adolescents have few legal, social-cultural, and economic resources available to control each other, and thus they are much more restricted to such processes as the reciprocity of self-disclosure to attain mutual relationship definition. It is also within peer relationships that the adolescent learns that self-disclosure begets self-disclosure, and he or she comes to employ this kind of communication in a relational fashion, rather than as an instrumental act to attain a specific immediate goal.

As the adolescent divines the utility of reciprocal exchange and the regulation of intimacy and privacy, he or she devalues the existing relationship with parents, who also experience nonmutuality with respect to issues of child discipline (Blood and Wolfe, 1960; Aldous and Hill, 1969; Burr, 1970). The resulting reduction of parental influence potential is clearly evident in the area of resource possession and management. In the adolescent culture, possession of one's own goods is a mark of status and in turn an augmentation of control strategies. An allowance and a job are valued as a means to a car, clothes, dates, and the other trappings of a middle-class teenage lifestyle. Also important to the teenager is time away from home and self-management of that time. This increasing autonomy, or independence in time, space, and resource management, reflects a reduction in parental influence potential in conjunction with an increase in adolescent influence potential.

Another feature of this stage is the adolescent's possession of a large repertoire of potential influence strategies. Once again, these capabilities exist in many modes and in a complex and diversified schema. The teenager's verbal skills are well developed; he or she may argue, console, advise, and criticize. Nonverbal control skills have also expanded to approximate those of parents, including the use of complex facial and body expressions to create a desired impact. The adolescent's use of the environment also expands to include increasingly autonomous exit from and entry to the home. Thus, the adolescent's large repertoire of potential control strategies rivals that of parents, with the exception of a few strategies which remain the exclusive prerogative of the parent (e.g., the granting of an allowance or a private bedroom or the threat of legal action for extreme misbehaviors).

It is within this newly emerging relationship form that the teenager comes to recognize and extensively employ nondisclosure as an interpersonal control strategy. Privacy regulation on an environmental level can be observed in the form of clubhouses, closed bedroom doors, and the keeping of a diary. Privacy regulation on a verbal level occurs (often to the exasperation of parents) through such strategies as evasiveness, noncommitalness, and precipitous withdrawal from family exchanges. The control value of secrets is usually learned as a preteenager, but secrecy greatly increases as a control strategy during this period, as exemplified in the dialogue: "Where did you go, Johnnie?" . . . "Out." . . . "What did you do?" . . . "Nothing." The teenager can now regulate accessibility and privacy just like the parent, and nondisclosure, once solely available to the parents, now becomes a powerful strategy which limits the control options of the parent.

The great changes in the amount and distribution of influence potential represent a period of nonmutuality as parents and the adolescent endeavor to reach consensus about the redefinition of their relationship. But it is also the case that successful redefinition of the parent-adolescent relationship does occur, albeit through a lengthy process of relationship redefinition. Consensus must be attained about the modes of exchange of the newly emerging relationship–and at multiple levels of the relationship. For example, mutual privacy regulation in the environmental mode may require renegotiation of home territories–open or closed doors, private space, and bathroom use. The adolescent's new skills at both sending and recognizing nonverbal communications of fatigue, anxiety, depression, or disapproval may also require greater sensitivity to this mode as a vehicle for reestablishing mutuality of relationship definition. In the verbal mode, the teenager may offer self-disclosures about activities outside the home or about personal feelings which, if appropriately reciprocated, may also facilitate mutual redefinition of the relationship form and modes of exchange.

Recent family interaction research has viewed adolescence as involving a changing definition of relationships between parents and children and the resolution of this "crisis" through mutual redefinition. This research reveals that adolescence is, in fact, characterized by decreasing parental dominance and increasing child dominance (Alexander, 1970, 1973), and occurs through a shift in the distribution of relationship influence potential in favor of the adolescent (Mischler and Waxler, 1968; Jacob, 1974), although the parent retains greater influence potential throughout. Alexander (1973) suggests, however, that if the adolescent's "acceptable" dominant communications (e.g., suggestions, self-disclosures) meet with parental response of greater submission and less dominance (e.g., agreement, compliance, or reciprocal self-disclosure), then the redistribution of influence potential within the relationship is accepted by both parties and the more dramatic and unfortunate consequences of adolescent change are avoided. If, in contrast, parents attempt to maintain the modes of exchange and unequal distribution of influence potential characterizing the earlier parent-child relationship, then nonmutuality may be sustained, resulting in continued conflict and even runaway or ungovernable delinquency.

To summarize, the parent-adolescent relationship is characterized by a drastic shift in relationship definition which results in a kind of "crisis." As the world of peers becomes increasingly influential for the adolescent, the parent-adolescent relationship undergoes major changes in influence potential; the overall amount of interdependence is reduced, and the distribution approaches greater equity, with individual influence potential increasing for the adolescent and decreasing for the parent. The nonmutuality of this period is exacerbated by the rapid biological changes of puberty and the social and cultural standards bestowing new freedoms upon the adolescent. Where the relationship is eventually successful, as it usually is, we hypothesize that it is characterized by a shift in the distribution of mutual influence potential in the direction of the adolescent.

The Relationship of Acquainting Pairs

Like the parent-child relationship, acquainting pairs consist of two strangers who must develop mutuality to establish and maintain a relationship. Beyond this point, however, the similarity ends. Unlike the parent-child form, acquainting pairs have very few formal constraints, nor does society demand that any particular pair establish a long-term viable relationship. Interactants can, relatively speaking, "take it or leave it," so that relationship crises resulting from nonmutuality tend to be easily resolved, or the relationship may be terminated with little anguish to either party. As a result of this low social bonding, participants tend to engage in limited and predictable interactions as they struggle with the interpersonal issues of mutuality, influence potential, and modes of exchange.

The most striking characteristic of acquainting relationships is the relatively low amount and equal distribution of influence potential. Unlike parents, for example, strangers can rarely give or take away resources such as money, food, clothes, and access to and from home; nor can they invoke legal sanctions to influence behavior. And, having no shared history, they have no knowledge of the unique mixtures of verbal, nonverbal, and environmental communication strategies that can provide a basis for mutuality of relationship definition. As a result, acquainting pairs must use a relatively narrow band of culturally accepted communication modes, such as self-disclosure of superficial information, to undertake a preliminary exploration of the potential mutuality of their relationship.

The relatively superficial, stylized verbal and nonverbal communication of strangers has been well documented (Levin and Gergen, 1969; Altman and Taylor, 1973; Cozby, 1973). During the early stages of this relationship, both the content and form of exchange are quite selective and are characterized by reciprocity or a "tit-for-tat" alternation of essentially similar responses. Reciprocity in the acquainting relationship is a pervasive phenomenon (Altman, 1973) and represents a simple form of dealing with strangers. That is, as a stylized strategy, reciprocity of exchange allows each individual to employ a nearly identical amount and distribution of influence or control, and it provides the best assurance for egalitarianism and easy sharing of a mutual relationship definition. Thus, in a superficial reciprocity exchange, neither party "puts all his cards out," and both exhibit stylized and homogenous relationship definitions and thereby avoid novel interactions which could result in nonmutuality. In conjunction with guarded intimacy and positive self-presentation, reciprocity assures rewarding contacts, equity of influence potential, and a sensitive and fluid calibration of the acquainting relationship.

As implied above, the range of communication modalities in the early acquainting relationship is quite narrow, with verbal self-disclosure playing a dominant role. While nonverbal and environmental behaviors are undoubtedly involved in early acquaintance interactions, research indicates that not only is the repertoire of responses relatively narrow but also the nature of the communications is stereotyped and culturally normative (Altman and Taylor, 1973).

Where there is a poor fit of relationship definitions during the acquaintance stage, the relationship is easily terminated, since there is relatively little commitment by the parties to one another. If mutuality is attained through reciprocity of exchange in superficial areas, however, an incremental increase in intimacy of self-disclosure occurs (Altman and Taylor, 1973). This gradual rise in intimacy level is associated with a concomitant elevation of relationship influence potential which is reflected in stronger social bonding. As bonding increases, research and theory on the acquaintance process indicates that the active search for mutuality not only continues to focus on present ongoing interactions, but also involves a "forecasting" or future-oriented perspective (Altman and Taylor, 1973). Thus, young adults evaluate one another in terms of acceptability of attitudes toward religion, education, sex roles, child rearing, etc. (Rubin, 1973:194-208). Such issues represent potential areas of mutuality or nonmutuality which need to be explored, and they usually represent topics which bear on the eventual amount and distribution of influence potential. Because of projected or actual nonmutuality in certain of these areas, many dating couples terminate their relationship. Eventually, of course, most young adults find themselves in one or more relationships characterized by mutuality of relationship definition, coupled with acceptable amounts and distribution of influence potential. Some of these relationships develop into the form of an established mate relationship.

In summary, the acquaintance relationship, like all other relationship forms, is characterized by mutuality of definition by participants, usually through a very limited set of culturally normative communication transactions, guarded intimacy, positive self-presentations, and reciprocity of exchange, predominantly by means of self-disclosure. These characteristics of the acquainting relationship facilitate preservation of an equal distribution and low amount of influence potential as the parties engage in a preliminary mutual exploration of their relationship. Where mutuality of relationship definition is not easily achieved, or where future nonmutuality is predicted, the relationship is easily terminated. To the extent that the relationship achieves an acceptable level of consensus regarding relationship definition, the stage is set for a more intimate degree of social bonding. Again, while the particular details of the acquainting relationship are unique to that form, the underlying generic properties of mutuality of relationship definition, the multimodal quality of communication, and the key ingredients of influence potential can be used to portray this relationship within the generic framework of this chapter.

The Diversified Mate Relationship

Mutuality of relationship definition is critical for a viable marriage or other long-term relationship, but the high rates of divorce and reported marital dissatisfaction attest to the difficulties of attaining or maintaining such mutuality. The marriage relationship is (or was until the 1960s and until the rise of the feminist movement) shrouded with romantic myths suggesting an indefinitely extended courtship, an unending mirrorlike reciprocity or "happily ever after," and a stable division of sex roles which seemingly operates in a simple and mutually agreeable fashion. In contrast, we shall describe the marriage relationship as dynamic rather than static and as involving recurring nonmutuality of relationship definition and occasional crises and redefinitions of mutuality. Indeed, the complexity, expansion, and diversification of communication processes in a long-term mate relationship bear testimony to the need for repeated relationship definitions, modifications, and recalibrations of the distribution of influence potential among parties as the degree of social bonding increases.

We have already noted that as a couple progresses from dating to mating the intimacy of mutual disclosure increases, which corresponds to a rise in relationship influence potential. This heightened social bonding is also associated with a wider ranger of mutual influence and control strategies. With a greater shared history, partners gain increased knowledge about what influence strategies and communication modes work best in what situations for them, and they gradually develop idiosyncratic and unique-to-the-dyad mechanisms for establishing mutual definition of their relationship and for acceptable distribution of influence potential.

As part of this process, positive self-presentations of the earlier acquainting relationship become less necessary in advanced stages of bonding. The parties are more willing to share increasingly intimate information, including vulnerabilities and other negative disclosures. Such private and often socially undesirable information functions to greatly increase the overall amount and distribution of relationship influence potential and draws the parties into a situation involving "intimate blackmail" (Simmel, 1964), where each knows some central things about the other, strengthening their interdependence. In addition, in advanced relationships, earlier reciprocity becomes increasingly unnecessary, and even insufficient as a primary mutual influence mechanism. As the relationship advances, increasingly well-tailored and unique patterns of communication are conjointly determined (Altman, 1973; Morton, 1976).

Another feature of the advanced relationship is an increase in the use of a variety of modes of communication. Verbal disclosure is accompanied by, and substituted for, a growing repertoire of private, nonverbal, "shorthand" expressions. These shorthand expressions include such behaviors as a glance, a facial expression, a postural shift, mutual touching, and physical proximity and allow participants to substitute preferred modes of exchange to facilitate continued mutuality of relationship definition.

The conjugal pair also has a shared history and usually anticipates a shared future in regard to activities, friends, material possessions, and parental roles. This intense level and scope of social bonding requires that the partners have an acceptable level and distribution of relationship influence potential with respect to one another and with those with whom they deal. Because of the complexity and scope of their involvement with one another, it is likely that they will undergo crises about the mutuality of their relationship definition. Thus, if the relationship is to remain viable, there will be a recurring need to establish new levels of mutuality and distributions of influence potential. Assuming successful redefinition of their relationship, it is likely that new strategies of mutual control will evolve but also that old forms will be partly retained, so that their shared repertoire of communication modes and mutuality of influence will cumulate, rather than being completely reestablished following each redefinition. Thus, while mutuality of communication occurs primarily through the verbal mode of self-disclosure in the early acquainting process, and later expands to other communication modes, self-disclosure will always continue to be a necessary vehicle for maintaining mutuality of relationship definition. Indeed, one of the most common sources of friction in marriages is one spouse desiring more self-disclosure and reciprocity than the other (Rausch, 1974). Similarly, the high rate of positive verbal exchange in the early acquainting process may be reduced as other modes of communication are evolved, but when a reduction in communication of positive affect becomes too drastic, marital discord is likely (Birchler et al., 1972). Finally, while overall "point-for-point" reciprocity is relaxed in the advanced relationship, at least within a short time frame, different reciprocity rates will probably develop for different kinds of situations and exchanges.

Naturally, just as in more superficial bonds, consensus about the degree and distribution of influence potential must be achieved if the advanced relationship is to be sustained. However, couples undoubtedly vary considerably on these dimensions. While the amount of interdependence within a typical marriage is generally high, some marriages are characterized by a higher level of relationship potential than others. And, while the distribution of influence potential among partners must be mutually defined, and is equal in some instances, many partners mutually agree to an unequal distribution of control capabilities. In fact, it is often the case that one person in a pair may be recognized and accepted by both participants as having greater control capabilities in one situation (e.g., financial decisions), while the other may have more influence potential in another domain of their lives (e.g., child rearing).

In summary, the mate relationship is characterized by mutual control in a highly diversified combination of verbal, nonverbal, and environmental modes. The degree of relationship influence potential in a marriage is typically high, and this interdependence extends over a large range of issues and life areas. The need for mutuality of relationship definition is crucial if the bond is to be a viable one, but temporary nonmutuality usually occurs as new areas of the relationship are uncovered. As mutuality is restored and/or redefined at new levels, an increasing variegation and expansion in communication and control patterns occurs, and there may also be an elaboration and a new realignment of the distribution of influence potential in the relationship. Unfortunately, as mentioned earlier, many couples cannot attain new levels of mutuality and ultimately terminate the relationship.

A CONCLUDING COMMENT

We had several goals in writing this paper on interpersonal communication. First, we wished to emphasize the importance of the "social relationship" itself as an appropriate unit of analysis. While many speak of interpersonal and social processes, the literature in this field has really focused on the individual participant as the unit of analysis and then only inferred to the level of the mutual relationship between people. Second, we wished to emphasize the "systemlike" quality of social interaction, which includes many interlocking modes of communication, mutuality of relationship definition, and the crucial role of mutual influence processes. Third, we hoped to set the stage for a parsimonious analysis of four major relationship forms—parent-child, parent-adolescent, acquainting pairs, and intimates—within a common theoretical framework. While many others have dealt with each of these relationship forms, one rarely finds a conceptual system which systematically contrasts and compares them in common terms.

As we wrote and rewrote this chapter, we often wondered whether anything new was being said. After all, the topics addressed have been, in one form or another, examined for many years by many researchers. But the value of this chapter resides not only in the content but in the extent to which old ideas and research findings have been integrated in a new way, as well as in the degree to which we have been able to set the stage for new theoretical, empirical, and pragmatic work as a result of this formulation.

At a theoretical and empirical level, the framework proposed in this chapter suggests some needed directions of research. For example, the framework highlights the importance of continued research on "reciprocity" of self-disclosure, since this line of analysis clearly implies a social relationship as an important unit of study. But it also suggests that we closely examine "intact" relationships, along with laboratory contrived arrangements where confederates respond in a fixed way. That is, we need to examine "real" couples (Morton, 1976), parents and their children, and a host of other relationship forms. Second, the framework of this chapter emphasizes the importance of adopting a multimodal approach to understanding reciprocity. Within the context of single studies, we need to consider communication at verbal, nonverbal, and environmental levels simultaneously, as a system of communication. By restricting their focus to only a single mode of communication, most prior research studies obscure the understanding of the dynamics of social relationships, particularly those that have moved beyond the simple exchanges of strangers. Third, by virtue of the generic communality of all relationships, we emphasize the need to sample broadly and to apply the same logic of theory and research not only to different relationship forms but to the same relationship at different stages of its history, including crises. For too long research has restricted itself to cross-sectional, short-term analyses of relationships. We now need to adopt a more longitudinal perspective to better track the ebb and flow of individual relationship histories as they progress through formation, stability, and crisis.

Beyond these few examples of theorizing and research which are suggested by the framework of this chapter, there are several important implications for the "real world." Our emphasis on understanding interpersonal relationships beyond the properties of individual interactants has considerable implications for educational, counseling, and therapeutic services of all kinds. For example, the framework of the present chapter implies that parent education programs include training to heighten awareness and ways to cope with the issue of mutuality of relationship definition, and thereby move beyond the simple guidelines currently available regarding such specific and individualized behaviors as thumb-sucking, temper tantrums, and learning alphabets. Or one might extend the logic of this chapter to premarital counseling programs. Here, not only does our framework emphasize the importance of understanding mutuality regarding religion, sex, child-rearing attitudes, and the like, it also suggests that couples begin to understand and develop strategies for resolving the inevitable relationship crises which will result from increased bonding and the diversification and expansion of relationship domains and modes of exchange.

The ideas expressed in this chapter further suggest, and even demand, that we leave behind all the rhetoric involving what relationships "should be" to obtain viability. The issue is not, for example, that marriages should be egalitarian, patriarchal, or matriarchal in order to develop, but that they can take any of these forms as long as mutuality of definition is perceived and accepted by the parties. Similarly, parents of adolescents in educational and therapeutic settings can be educated on the critical role of mutuality of relationship definition, the inevitable impact of changing relationship influence potential at different stages in a child's life, and the changing mixtures of verbal, nonverbal, and environmental communication modes.

These few examples of the application of the proposed framework to theoretical, empirical, and pragmatic activities illustrate the heuristic value of the model we have proposed. Future activities, we hope, will add precision and comprehensiveness to the proposed principles, which in turn should vastly expand our knowledge of the dynamics of interpersonal relationships.

REFERENCES

ALDOUS, J., and HILL, R. (1969). "Breaking the poverty cycle: Strategic points for intervention." Social Work, 14:3-12.

ALEXANDER, J.F. (1970). "Videotape recorded family interaction: A systems approach." Paper presented at the convention of the Western Psychological Association, Los Angeles.

--- (1973). "Defensive and supportive communications in normal and deviant families." Journal of Consulting and Clinical Psychology, 40:223-231.

ALTMAN, I. (1973). "Reciprocity of interpersonal exchange." Journal of the Theory of Social Behavior, 3:249-261.

--- (1975). The environment and social behavior. Monterey, Calif.: Brooks/Cole.

ALTMAN, I., and TAYLOR, D.A. (1973). Social penetration: The development of interpersonal relationships. New York: Holt, Rinehart and Winston.

BATESON, G., JACKSON, D.D., HALEY, J., and WEAKLAND, J. (1956). "Toward a theory of schizophrenia." Behavioral Science, 1:251-264.

BIRCHLER, G.R., WEISS, R.L., and WAMPLER, L.P. (1972). "Differential patterns of social reinforcement as a function of degree of marital distress and level of intimacy." Paper presented at the convention of the Western Psychological Association, Portland.

BLOOD, R.O., Jr., and WOLFE, D.M. (1960). Husbands and wives. New York: Free Press.

BURR, W.R. (1970). "Satisfaction with various aspects of marriage over the life cycle: A random middle class sample." Journal of Marriage and the Family, 32:29-37.

COZBY, P.C. (1973). "Self-disclosure: A literature review." Psychological Bulletin, 79:73-91.

GOFFMAN, E. (1961). Encounters. Indianapolis: Bobbs-Merrill.

--- (1967). Interaction ritual. New York: Doubleday.

HALEY, J. (1963). Strategies of psychotherapy. New York: Grune and Stratton.

JACOB, T. (1974). "Patterns of family conflict and dominance as a function of child age and social class." Developmental Psychology, 10:1-12.

LEVIN, F.M., and GERGEN, K.J. (1969). "Revealingness, ingratiation and the disclosure of the self." Proceedings of the 77th Annual Convention of the American Psychological Association, 4(1):447-448.

LOVAAS, O.I., BERBERICH, J.P., PERLOFF, B.F., and SCHEFFER, B. (1966). "Acquisition of imitative speech in schizophrenic children." Science, 151:705-707.

MILLER, G.R., and STEINBERG, M. (1975). Between people: A new analysis of interpersonal communication. Palo Alto, Calif.: Science Research Associates.

MISCHLER, E.G., and WAXLER, N.E. (1968). Interaction in families: An experimental study of family processes and schizophrenia. New York: Wiley.

MORTON, T.L. (1976). "The effects of acquaintance and distance on intimacy and reciprocity." Unpublished Ph.D. dissertation, University of Utah.

MUSSEN, P.H., CONGER, J.J., and KAGAN, J. (1969). Child development and personality. New York: Harper and Row.

PATTERSON, G.R., and REID, S.B. (1970). "Reciprocity and coercion: Two facets of social systems." Pp. 133-177 in C. Neuringer and J.L. Michael (eds.), Behavior modification in clinical psychology. New York: Meredith.

RAUSCH, H.K. (1974). Communication, conflict, and marriage. San Francisco: Jossey-Bass.

RUBIN, Z. (1973). Liking and loving: An invitation to social psychology. New York: Holt, Rinehart and Winston.

SIMMEL, G. (1964). "The secret and the secret society." Pp. 307-316 in K. Wolff (trans. and ed.), The sociology of Georg Simmel. New York: Free Press.

TURK, J.L., and BELL, N.W. (1972). "Measuring power in families." Journal of Marriage and the Family, 34:215-222.

Chapter 6

INTERPERSONAL COMMUNICATION IN DEVELOPING ACQUAINTANCE

Steve Duck

CONSIDERABLE RESEARCH has recently been devoted to the information aspects of acquaintance (e.g., combination rules about how pieces of information are treated) and the affective side of attraction (e.g., conditioned responses to certain types of information stimuli), with debate centering on whether the two aspects are contrasting or complementary (Kaplan and Anderson, 1973). The present paper concerns the *content* involved in communication during acquaintance and how its operations relate to other social psychological processes. I shall thus examine acquaintance and *forming* friendships as an information-based communication process and attempt to cut through the controversy and make confrontation or reconciliation logically unnecessary by showing the different conceptual levels at which the communication phenomena can be placed.

My analysis centers on the types and statuses of information communicated at various points in acquaintance (e.g., initial encounter, forming friendship, established choice), an approach based on a cognitive perspective derived from the personality theory of George Kelly (1955; Duck, 1973b). Against this theoretical backcloth, recent empirical work will be reported which suggests, broadly, that acquaintance is a communication process whereby an individual transmits (consciously) or conveys (sometimes unintentionally) information *about his personality structure and content* to potential friends, using subtly different means at different stages of the friendship's development. The two individuals involved in the acquaintance are thus enabled in several ways to make a series of guesses or assessments of the potential level of similarity between their personalities: the higher the implied similarity level at a given point, the more likely a subsequent positive relationship between the two individuals.

In broad terms, any claim that developing acquaintance derives its affective, evaluative, or emotional component from communicative exchanges assumes that acquaintance involves the transmission and reception of information. The bulk of this discussion thus concerns the *types* of information and what others *do* with it. My position, in turn, assumes that one individual is primarily a transmitter, one a receiver, and that information flows from one to the other. Although hopelessly simplistic in a number of ways, such simplification is necessary for analytic purposes, and the complexities involved can be more firmly reattached to the basic concepts as the analysis proceeds. For example, the above statements suggest that information flow occurs; I shall go on to argue that it occurs in different important and psychologically significant ways at different points of acquaintance.

Again, the above outline is simplistic because it assumes that an individual is *either* a transmitter *or* a receiver. Yet in social transactions individuals usually serve both functions simultaneously. Although it is sometimes convenient to *assume* that people do not, or that they are primarily one or the other, social-psychological work too often bases theories of attraction on a one-sided analysis of the processes involved (Duck, forthcoming b). Furthermore, it is simplistic to assume that individuals always consciously transmit the information that is received by another person. Some cues not under their conscious control (class or race, for example) nevertheless count as useful information to others in attraction contexts. Moreover, it is an oversimplification to assume that all "messages" are understood by the receiver, that he is always able to distinguish signal from noise, that he always pays attention to what the transmitter *wants* him to observe, or that he *only* pays attention to it. Human receivers are active processors of information just as human transmitters are; they vary sharply in their abilities to tune into the right "bandwidth" of cues and to detect accurately cues of different types (Cook, forthcoming). Consequently, it is unrealistic to assume that there is *a* message: in real-life contexts, information about others is available to interactors at hundreds of levels simultaneously, ranging from the olfactory to the philosophical! Research on information in acquaintance has been hindered by the fact that, for necessary reasons of control in experiments, researchers have often been forced to assume that only a few pieces of information are tranmitted at a time, that subjects treat such information mechanistically and make no idiosyncratic inferences from it, and that they all detect its significance to an equal extent (Ajzen, forthcoming).

PERSPECTIVES ON INFORMATION IN ACQUAINTANCE

Much recent work on information and initial attraction to strangers has attempted to establish why information is attractive—specifically, whether its informational aspects or conditioned affective component is most influential in determining attraction responses (Kaplan and Anderson, 1973; Ajzen, 1974; Byrne et al., 1974). Some of this research, for wholly understandable experimental reasons, has suffered from the reductionist simplifications noted above, but a more serious criticism is that there has been little analysis of the different ways that the term "information" is used in such research. Such differences become especially important in the context of a view based on long term development of relationships which sees different sorts of information as influential at different times.

Information

In examining the various assertions about the attractiveness ratings resulting from information, it is important to clarify the varied ways in which the concept of "information" has been used in research on attraction and the differing beliefs that investigators have about information. Previous work may then be synthesized by use of a concept of *hierarchical levels of information,* for it is clear that in other contexts we distinguish between the terms "Shorthorns," "cattle," "ungulates," and "mammals" in terms of the inclusiveness of the label, the level of description, or the hierarchy of meaning and significance. Information about others can be likewise conceived. It is one thing–albeit, the primary thing–to argue that different types of information have different and unequal status in the context of acquaintance (e.g., information about physical characteristics, information about attitudes, information about personality), quite another to claim that each type can carry significant implications about another type (e.g., that subjects infer about attitudes on the basis of other people's physical characteristics), and still another to propose that the various types of information about someone are conceptually, significantly, and functionally related (e.g., that the level where we describe someone as an extrovert–gross label though it is–might exert a contextual influence on how we interpret his subsequent behavior). Finally, most important of all is the step which argues that the different types of information may be *hierarchically* related in terms of level.

By distinguishing the different conceptual levels at which certain kinds of information *inform* about an individual, however, it is possible to make a plausible case that some of these levels of information are typically suited to interacting individuals at some points of interaction and not others, but that their linkage in hierarchical fashion means that individuals can see a piece of information at one level and form related expectancies about what will be found at other levels of the hierarchy.

To substantiate this point, I shall argue that investigators studying isolated or "pure" bits of information (e.g., traits) are justified in concluding that these bits have both evaluative and affective overtones (which implies that even apparently specific information has more than a surface meaning), that all information behaves differently when presented in a context (as *always* occurs in real life), that individuals combine information in ways which are predictable from the values of the context and of the individual bits of information, that subjects add something of their own and infer to information not available directly, and that information about another person's cognitive structure is gradually built up by this means. Some readers may feel that this last point is simply arguing that individuals in acquaintance merely proceed by self-disclosure, but this misses the point. A self-disclosure perspective examines primarily the behavior of the transmitter (i.e., how he reveals himself to the others, whether this depends on reciprocity from the other, how it influences attraction; La Gaipa, forthcoming). I am further arguing that the most important effects on acquaintance stem from what the receiver *does* with such information (how he judges what is revealed, how he interprets the revelation) not from the fact that the transmitter makes such information available, although that is important. In short I follow Kelvin (forthcoming) in looking *both* at attraction as a response of the attracted individual *and* at attraction in terms of the stimuli which make someone attract*ive,* rather than concentrating on just one side of things.

Information and Affect. A crucial feature of my analysis is an examination of the ways in which the term "information" has been used. From an *information processing* viewpoint, an individual's attraction to another person is a function of his or her information about the other person and what he or she makes of it. Thus, individuals may operate by attaching evaluative scale weightings to all pieces of information and combining them in various ways (e.g., summing, averaging) to arrive at overall judgments (Ajzen, forthcoming). Innumerable studies have been completed on impression formation and person perception where subjects are presented with information (e.g., a list of traits) and form judgments on the basis of this information. As part of this work, studies have established the evaluative weightings which individual instances of trait terms habitually are assigned within our own cultural context (Anderson, 1968). Quickly it was recognized (Bohac and Reboussin, 1967) that there are many affinities between such a task and the task involved in most research where judgments of attractiveness are involved. Clearly, impressions are sometimes formed in this way in real life (e.g., from letters of reference) but in acquaintances where a judgment of *liking* rather than suitability for a job is involved the task involves a heavier affective or emotional component. Could it be argued that there is, therefore, a difference between the two situations as a function of the likelihood of conditioned affect attaching to information in an attraction context?

Most work in the area of attraction has concerned the reinforcement properties of information about attitude statements (usually, but not exclusively measured in terms of similarity; Clore, forthcoming). The subject is exposed to an attitude profile purportedly derived from another experimental subject but actually rigged by the experimenter to reflect the subject's own attitudes to a precisely measurable degree (Byrne, 1971). Such studies have invariably shown that the amount of attraction to "the stranger" is related to the amount of reinforcement obtained by the subject from the attitudes endorsed by the stranger–e.g., more reinforcement is obtained if the attitudes are regarded as important by the subject or if the attitudes cannot be verified except by comparison with the attitudes of others. However, Kaplan and Anderson (1973) have argued that the observed effects can be better explained within the information processing framework noted above: namely, that individuals take account of scale weightings attaching to the pieces of information about others and arrive at attraction judgments by weighted averaging of these information values. Byrne's work uses attitude statements allegedly endorsed by a stranger, while Anderson's research uses personality trait descriptions applied to the stranger; nevertheless, Kaplan and Anderson (1973) do not consider that the differences between these types of information are significant conceptually.

Against this, Byrne et al. (1974) argue that information and affect (reinforcement) are not orthogonal concepts and that each has a place in attraction. Many cues have both informational and affective components (e.g., attitudes) while others can be characterized as primarily informational (e.g., adjectival descriptions of others) or primarily affective (e.g., personal evaluations of subject by other). In a study which manipulated both informational and affective components of attitudes simultaneously, Byrne et al. (1974) were able to show that, though perceived similarity was affected by only the informational component of the stimulus variables, interpersonal attraction was influenced by both informational and affective components.

It is easy, however, to be captivated by the similarities between the two methodologies (both of which involve some form of judgment about others on the basis of some form of information about them) and to overlook the different logical and epistemological statuses of the information used in the two contrasting (or reconcilable) methodologies. In the case of attitudes, subjects usually believe that they are dealing with information supplied by another subject under experimental conditions: in the case of trait descriptions, they typically believe that they are dealing with information supplied by the experimenter or someone else about a third party. In the one case they appear to receive *direct* access to the cognition of another individual; in the other, they seem to receive *indirect* access to the other's cognition by means of descriptions which seem appropriate to some judge (who is, after all, as external to the other's cognition as is the subject himself!). This difference of status is empirically important, for it can be translated into a hypothesis about acquaintance processes and the different information about other that an individual has available at varying times.

Again, attitude studies usually measure similarity or dissimilarity between subject and some others; trait studies usually stop short at measuring operations with simple descriptions, without assessing similarity. But perception of similarity to someone on a descriptive dimension and simple perception that a dimension applies to other are two logically and psychologically different operations, and it is implausible that the two processes are as comparable as has been claimed. To observe that a given description applies to other is one informative act; to observe that the description also applies to self (i.e., to detect similarity between self and other on that dimension) is another, with the latter perhaps leading to the initiation of other types of evaluative or affective responses. For one thing, each act provides a different context for assessing information, and it is clear that such a context influences the information which is presented and affects the information's status or the way it is treated, even in the laboratory (Clore, forthcoming). In real life, where contexts are much richer, the receiver of information in the interpersonal communication process has a difficult task sorting out and responding to different statuses of information as appropriate within a given context. This is a particularly important point when personality itself is viewed as an active information processing mechanism (Kelly, 1955), and in this context the discovery of how such an information processing mechanism affects the interpretation of the information is particularly crucial.

Information and Context. Several aspects of the context in which an interaction takes place influence the interpersonal communication process. First, *context* applies to the *receivers* of the information insofar as they perceive similarities or differences between the present interaction and others within their experience; second, it affects the *transmitters* insofar as they may choose to transmit different sorts of information depending upon the circumstances in which they perceive themselves to be; third, it affects the behavior of the stimulus information presented in its background.

No one enters an interaction with a mind totally free from past history. Individuals do not communicate with others with completely neutral feelings about everyone and everything (Wright, 1965), as so many studies assume by their designs. Instead, people have a history of experiences in similar circumstances and a background of reinforcements or of judgments or personal weightings for certain sorts of information or input. Thus, it is not surprising that individuals' beliefs about an interaction actually influence the way they behave in it and the way they treat the other person involved (Harré, forthcoming).

Nor are the transmitters in a stimulus vacuum; they present information in ways which serve their present purposes. Thus, Cooper and Jones (1969) found that subjects chose to conceal their true opinions in the presence of authority figures when obnoxious others uttered statements that reflected the subjects' true opinions, and Kleck et al. (1966) found that individuals interacting with disabled others were more likely to express opinions not representative of their actual beliefs.

Similarly, Stroebe et al. (forthcoming) showed that level of self-esteem influenced how persons interpreted negative or positive evaluations from others and whether they attributed their judgments to sincerity or role playing. Low self-esteem subjects took positive evaluations as role play and negative ones as sincere, while high self-esteem subjects responded contrarily. Thus, the history and past experiences of both receiver and transmitter probably influence not only how each chooses to deal with his or her side of the interpersonal communication process but also the outcomes of the interaction for each. One way that this occurs is clearly a function of the information provided by context and the way it affects inferential processes.

Information and Inferences. Ajzen (forthcoming) distinguishes two approaches (mechanistic and constructive) to the ways in which individuals process information, of which context is a part. A *mechanistic* approach assumes that receivers are passive recipients of information and operate according to combination rules attaching to normative weights associated with information items (Anderson, 1968). Receivers deal with information as they find it and operate upon it as an adding machine, simply calculating the necessary weighted average resulting from all the inputs. Evaluative or attraction judgments can be completely understood in terms of the information about someone that the subjects are given. In this respect, the mechanistic model differs from the *constructive* model, which centers on salient beliefs.

Information and Belief. Evidently, one problem about presenting subjects with information about others is that they are likely to use it! Ajzen (1974; forthcoming) has argued that providing subjects with information about some characteristics of another person also permits them the opportunity to draw inferences from that information to other likely characteristics. Ajzen (1974) contends that similarity is usually found to be related to attraction because of the empirical relationship between similarity and affective value: it is the desirability of traits rather than their similarity to those of self which increases the attractiveness of the stranger.

Clearly, information about a stranger's opinions can be used to form beliefs about the stranger's cognitive structure or value system. For Ajzen (1974), attraction scores are simple products of the subjective probability that the stranger has a particular attribute and the subjective value attaching to that attribute. This suggestion imports an extra complexity to the concept of "information" as used in the controversy sketched in the preceding section, for it indicates that subjects may not simply be using information as experimenters think they are. Ajzen (forthcoming) opts for a *perceived attributes* model in which individuals use provided information as a means of inferring to other traits and base their attraction responses on the inferred traits rather than the presented ones. In terms of the previous argument, any affect associated with information attaches to the *inferred* information rather than the *presented* information. Although Ajzen himself does not go this far, it could be maintained that cues give rise to inferences from which individuals are further able to infer similarity between themselves and the other, and this presumed level of similarity may be what influences attraction rating.

Ajzen's (forthcoming) perceived attributes model certainly raises questions about the status of "information" presented to subjects by experimenters, even in its simplest form of adjectival descriptions. Do subjects take the information as fact and work with it? Do they infer from it and evaluate the inferences for attractiveness? Do they infer from it and use the inferences as a context for evaluating the original information? Do they evaluate both original and inferred information? In any case, the original information probably changes in value as a function of subjects' tendencies to infer, but this reflects the complexity of real-life interpersonal communication, which is by its nature a sequential and inferential process. The psychological significance of these processes will occupy the rest of this discussion.

Information and Cognitive Organization. I have already argued that information and judgments about people can be conceived hierarchically; I have also contended that personality is an information processing mechanism; and I have assumed that personality disclosure takes place in acquaintance. These three points are related in several ways, particularly in light of the fact that self-disclosure involves "exhibition" of personality, which can be conceived as an information processing mechanism with several levels, related to the different levels of information about others. For example, Kelly's Personal Construct Theory (1955) measures personality in terms of the hypotheses (constructs) that individuals make about life, including events and people: several systems for classifying constructs have been devised, based in essence on the level of analysis in each case. Thus, constructs about others can be factual (objective but nonphysical, e.g., "married-unmarried"), physical ("tall-short"), interactional (referring to habitual behavior, e.g., "talks a lot-is usually quiet"), role-based (referring to habitual roles fulfilled or jobs done, e.g., "is a teacher-is a policeman"), or psychological (referring to motivational states, character, etc., e.g., "confident-shy"). However, it is possible to find several categories and levels of analysis through which this latter category can be subdivided (Duck, 1973b; forthcoming b).

Information about an individual's personality can be revealed in self-disclosure through any of these levels, and it plays a part in the development of acquaintance because it gives access to his or her thought processes at several levels and in relation to several different sorts of phenomena. This information itself constitutes a different *level* of information (information about cognitive organization as opposed to information about, say, external appearance; information about how the individual *assesses* external appearance as opposed to information about what his own external appearance is like, if you will).

This argument has two facets: first, the transmitter transmits information about himself in various ways and at various levels (e.g., by his external appearance, interactional cues, or his personality structure, seen in terms of how he processes information about others); second, the receiver processes this information in various characteristic ways and *in doing so* simultaneously transmits back to the original transmitter information about *how* he processes information. Consequently in processing information from another person, the receiver himself begins to act as a cue to the transmitter in terms of what the receiver's processes reveal about the receiver. Stated differently, individuals process certain information about others (e.g., their external appearance) *before* they process other information (e.g., their personality). But this is a sequential theory of acquaintance based on information processing and interpersonal communication.

Acquaintance

Parallel to the analysis of information in terms of levels is the analysis of acquaintance in terms of sequence. Acquaintance or friendship formation is a *process* of interpersonal communication that has different manifestations and different parts. The argument is *not* that in acquaintance individuals transmit information; that is obvious and trivial. Rather, the claim is that they transmit different types of information at temporally appropriate times. In other words, acquaintance is a developmental process involving stages and characteristically different mechanisms at each stage, and the cues precipitating initial choices are *not* those that protend and maintain the acquaintance once it has begun. This position removes the emphasis of attraction research from the traditional question of what stimuli are attractive and focuses it on the questions of *how* does acquaintance develop and what *causes* the development. Thus, the view posits a special relationship between acquaintance and the layers or levels of information discussed above.

The Acquaintance Process. Empirical work on friendship has concentrated predominantly on the initial part of the process: encounter with a stranger, reactions to a stranger, impressions of a stranger (Byrne, 1971). Although it is clear that, where friendship develops, there is a point at which initial attraction must *become* friendship, it is unclear whether or not the cues promoting attraction are those that promote long-term relationships. Moreover, there is a paucity of research on such questions. There are some studies of marital choice (e.g., Murstein, forthcoming), some studies of friendship (e.g., McCarthy and Duck, forthcoming), and a few relating to choices made at different times (e.g., Duck, 1973a). But longitudinal studies are rare, perhaps because of the methodological or conceptual problems associated with carrying them out. (One such study is reported in detail below.) Such studies as have been done (Izard, 1960; Newcomb, 1961; Levinger et al., 1970; Duck and Spencer, 1972) and such analyses as have been made of recent developments (Duck, 1973b; Levinger, 1974; La Gaipa, forthcoming) suggest strongly that there are changes of *process* as relationships develop that are not predictable merely from the study of initial encounter. Importing of temporal elements to the analysis of information and acquaintance entails important differences in the way that information is conceived.

Some of the points in the previous section can lead to the prediction of certain testable differences. For example, it was argued that direct and indirect accesses to others' cognitions are importantly different statuses of information inadequately distinguished in previous empirical work. Which type of information, direct or indirect, most accurately reflects the development of real-life acquaintance? The answer is: neither and both. In real-life interaction individuals are normally able to make some general, indirect judgment about another person *before* they have any direct access to that person's actual cognitive apparatus (e.g., they can assess race, height, hair color, etc. from considerable distance and without any interaction taking place). If this is the *only* information available, it is understandable if individuals place much reliance on it (witness the studies of prejudice and stereotyping). It is also plausible in the context of attraction that individuals use such information to make evaluative inferences—witness studies by Dion et al. (1972) indicating that physical attractiveness provokes observers to assume attractive personality characteristics in physically attractive individuals. This also places in the context of *developing* acquaintance the fact that individuals make evaluative responses to such information *before* they look at the deeper, less accessible, but ultimately more important cognitive information.

The preceding analysis leads to the hypothesis that any laboratory comparison of the relative influence of simple descriptive information and of cognitive information will show that *at the initial stage of encounter,* information about external or physical characteristics exerts more influence on attraction scores. In reporting this very finding, Duck and Craig (1975) argued that, in real-life acquainting, such "external" information normally provided an important context within which the other's cognitive apparatus could subsequently be assessed (e.g., pugnacious behavior from 112-pound weaklings and from musclemen may be differently interpreted) and that, accordingly, the different *logical* statuses of the information involved are mirrored by their different *temporal* statuses in the acquaintance process.

A similar argument applies to the different *logical* status of *similarity to* someone and simple *description* of someone. What happens in real life? Presumably individuals are able to *describe* others before they can make any sensible or accurate judgments about the similarity level existing between themselves and the others. It is not, however, too early to make possibly inaccurate judgments or sheer guesses, and a wealth of literature suggests that subjects *assume* similarity or overestimate similarity levels whenever there is insufficient evidence for them to know with any certainty whether they are or are not similar to the other person (Newcomb, 1961; Byrne and Griffit, 1969). It follows that evaluative assessments of others, rather than simple similarity, should have more influence on attraction scores at the earliest points of acquaintance. There are complications here; both similarity and description can have informational and affective components as Byrne et al. (1974) and Clore (forthcoming) have shown. Also, the informational or affective components of similarity in a given piece of evidence clearly depend in part on the descriptive context in which the evidence is embedded: e.g., similarity with a mentally disturbed other is *not* attractive to subjects (see Clore, forthcoming, for a discussion).

Thus, acquaintance is here conceptualized as a process whereby individuals gather information about others at different levels—the ultimate level being information about personality. This is a filtering process on similar but more expanded lines as those suggested by Kerckhoff and Davis (1962). These authors argue that value consensus promotes short-term relationships while need complementarity promotes longer ones, and they suggest that individuals operate filters (i.e., successive, sequential criteria) by which they assess the value or viability of relationships. Levinger et al. (1970) were unable to replicate these findings at this level of abstraction, but Duck (1973b) has proposed that information about personality (needs, values, etc.) is only one of a series of filters. The layers of filters that concern personality are related to acquaintance only after some time has elapsed, simply because that is their proper place in a sequence of correspondences between levels of acquaintance and levels of information. Previous searches for a relationship between personality similarity and acquaintance are thus confounded by temporal inappropriateness (Duck, 1973a).

Acquaintance and Information. Once it is proposed that acquaintance is a process with different emphases and stages, it is both necessary and easier to show the nature and focus of the stages. Initially, it can be done on an intuitive basis by examining acquaintance from the point of view of the information available to subjects during early encounters (Duck, forthcoming a; forthcoming b). This perspective can be combined with the one discussed earlier, since it can be argued that individuals seek information about others in a hierarchical fashion, *not* seeking the higher levels immediately since this is a meaningless quest when the context is missing. Such higher levels of information can be acquired only through a slower process of building up from different bits, styles, and levels of information. Therefore, individuals value information at different levels at different times as a function of the likelihood that it will combine with present information to cast further light on others (i.e., not simply as a function of evaluative loading).

Duck (1973b) hypothesized that the filtering process goes something like this: broadly, individuals assess the general population of those encountered against a distinct and sequentially ordered set of criteria, filtering them down to a few who become firm friends. If any individuals fail to satisfy the first criterion then they are rejected as potential friends, although, where circumstances subsequently enforce interaction—e.g., in a closed field (Murstein, forthcoming)–rejection can be rescinded if new evidence comes to light. Individuals who satisfy the first filtering criterion are allowed to pass on to the next, and so forth.

In the most recent version of this filtering theory (Duck, forthcoming a; forthcoming b), the filters are arranged in sequence starting with such sociological or incidental cues as proximity of dwelling, frequency of meeting, or expectancy of future interactions. Once two individuals know that they are destined to meet again and do so often enough for acquaintance to be feasible, then the individuals can pay attention to other cues and filters. From a perspective based on the development of acquaintance, the next set of filters would be cues observable not only from a distance but before interaction itself occurs (e.g., physical and external cues such as height, hair color, and physique) which may indicate social status or imply general suitability as an acquaintance. Thus, clothing may act as a filter cue insofar as it suggests not only status but also cleanliness and style of life. Given this viewpoint, some findings can be reinterpreted; e.g., the many findings reported by Stroebe (forthcoming) on the matching of individuals on intelligence, social position, and economic status can be taken to show the operation of filters at early points in acquaintance rather than show such cues as final causes of friendship. Such cues operate to filter the acceptable from the unpromising. Not only do they have an inherent affective value, they may also *suggest* to subjects likely topics in any conversations with the other, where the other's interests and emphases lie,and what the other thinks of himself or herself.

From a developmental perspective, once two persons have seen each other, the next likely stage is interaction, where a whole range of cues becomes available to them. From gestures, eye movements, and other nonverbal cues the observer can gather information in order to assess the other or form a more particular picture of the other in terms of attractiveness (Cook, forthcoming). Such behavioral cues have been suggested (Duck, 1973b) to act as filters at stages of acquaintance where interaction occurs. Subsequent filters relate to more cognitive attributes such as attitudes or personality. Thus, on the basis of directly available information, the first filters eliminate from potential interactions those on whom, for whatever reason, it would be wasteful to spend time forming friendships. It simply is not *possible* to form a close friendship with every conductor, shop assistant, librarian, or secretary that one encounters in the everyday commerce of life. But there is no claim that the filters operate slowly; several may pass in a fleeting moment, particularly those that apply earlier (Duck, 1973b).

The above suggestions make it clear that relationships grow in a way that reflects the level of information available to interacting individuals at different points of acquaintance. Therefore, since acquaintance grows as a function of information, it is primarily a communication process where different levels of information are exchanged at relevant points.

COMMUNICATION IN ACQUAINTANCE

When arguing the above case, one complication arises from the fact that in a complex social situation such as acquaintance, information can serve many functions simultaneously. Thus, the present case assumes that items of information can be assessed in terms of their properties (affect, evaluation, or saliency), in terms of what they say (informative qualities), and in terms of what they suggest (i.e., the implications they carry for other levels of the hierarchy and the light they shed on other aspects of the person being observed). Furthermore, individuals will often be faced with decisions between conflicting items of information (e.g., physically attractive individuals with unpleasant habits).

Since both information and acquaintance are very complex phenomena, and since other chapters in this volume address some of the logical, empirical, and theoretical issues involved, the present section looks at four broad levels of information that are relevant to acquaintance. For this purpose, it is necessary to view the individual and the other, respectively, as receiver and transmitter and (although the other transmits at several levels simultaneously) to look at the appropriate level of transmission for the receiver to sample in any given circumstances.

Clearly, since all information is, in a sense, available at any given time, the receiver must select that level which is relevant to his purposes, but needs to be able to identify the levels when observed. For this reason, acquaintance may be a skilled process on the receiver's part as he or she selects the correct cues and deals with them properly. On the other hand, the transmitter must also select information to transmit or to emphasize at given points, and impression management is possible in many ways during acquaintance (Harré, forthcoming; Kelvin, forthcoming). Consequently, acquaintance may also be a skilled process on the transmitter's part, as he or she selects the correct behaviors and presents them properly. Since in real life the two individuals occupy both roles simultaneously, both skills are required simultaneously, though the ability to perform one well does not necessarily imply comparable skill in performing the other. Future research might well examine the extent to which acquaintance is a skilled performance in ways comparable to other social behavior. Cook (forthcoming) has shown how regulation of social behavior is required for acquaintance to occur; the present argument extends this point and claims that actual processes of acquaintance, rather than the behaviors which expedite it, may amount to a skilled strategic performance. Certainly in each case both encoding and decoding of desired cues is required (Cook, forthcoming), as well as a smooth performance where each interactor acquires and releases information at "correct" rates of speed at correct levels at correct times. For the purposes of this analysis, it is convenient to assume that one interactor is a receiver and the other is a stimulus and to start at the level where no interaction takes place but where information is still transferred.

Information From Others as Stimulus Objects

Although, as argued above, the most basic stimulus cue that an individual takes into an *interaction* is his physical appearance, most work on attraction has looked at physical attractiveness rather than physical characteristics per se (Duck and Craig, 1975). While physical characteristics are presumably usually assessed willy-nilly in terms of attractiveness, the strong experimental manipulation of physical attractiveness may help to obscure the *other* implications that observers may draw from physical cues. Nor is it yet clear how physical information interacts with other information available in attraction circumstances, although presumably it normally provides strong context in real life (Dion et al., 1972). But these studies show that physical attractiveness is taken by subjects to imply other forms of attractiveness, indicating the possible weakness of studies that manipulate attractiveness alone and fail to seek the meaning of physical cues in themselves.

Accordingly, Duck and Craig (1975) examined the relative effects of external information (physical information and factual information) and psychological information (trait attributes) on attractiveness. External information and psychological information items were chosen with evaluative weightings which placed them close to the middle of the normative ranges for psychological traits and for other terms. In two experiments, it was found not only that external information exerted more influence on attractiveness scores but also that a similarity-dissimilarity manipulation was most potent in the case of external information. Thus, external information apparently has more influence on attraction than psychological information; this is a surprising finding from the conventional perspective but not startling when acquaintance is viewed "sequentially" and when it is realized (1) that the bogus stranger method used by Duck and Craig represents the most basic informational standpoint from which to observe others and thus reflects a very early point of acquaintance and (2) that in this experiment the statuses of the two sorts of information are equivalent (i.e., both originate from judges external to the other) and differ only in terms of meaning relative to context. The results might have been very different had we used "direct" access to psychological traits (for example, by representing the traits as self-ratings by the other).

A further study tested this possibility (Duck and Craig, in preparation c). In this second study, external information and attitude information were manipulated where external and psychological information had been used before. Recall that it was argued earlier that psychological traits are indirect information about another person, that attitudes are direct information (as used in the bogus stranger paradigm), and that attitude information therefore has higher status. Despite the above findings, then, it was not surprising to discover that external information exercised *less* influence on attraction than attitude similarity; indeed, this result suggests the cogency of the previous analysis.

Even more significant, however, are the findings of Duck and Craig (in preparation a) where all three levels of information (external, psychological, and attitudinal) were manipulated in order to confirm their relative statuses. Because the manipulation involved giving subjects information about strangers' qualities in each of the three categories, it was predicted and found that the previous findings were replicated (i.e., attitude $>$ external $>$ psychological). This outcome reflects the relative positions of these judgments in terms of status (direct access to cognition is higher status information than external, "objective" description which, in turn, is of higher status than the judgments of cognition made by another outside judge or observer). The resounding influence of attitudes on attraction thus derives from their status as information about a part of an individual's cognition and thought structure. However, a more complete grasp of another person's cognition requires an understanding of more than just attitudes, and for this reason I suspect that direct access to psychological information that includes self-ratings of character, personality, and needs has the highest status of all in this context. This belief rests on the assumption that acquainting individuals are less concerned with the properties of each other as stimulus *objects* and more concerned with them as stimulus *persons* having minds, characters, cognitions, and psychological properties. However, studies testing this question need to be clear about the different levels at which such information can be assessed (see below).

Information From Others as Stimulus Persons

Although individuals' characteristics have certain informational or affective value, part of their significance in attraction contexts lies in the implicative value that they have in terms of the other, as yet unobserved, characteristics that they suggest. Harré (forthcoming) has argued that individuals with certain characteristics are presumed to be able to *do* certain things. To use a trivial example, a person in overalls is presumed to be able to do things with car engines. In the context of attraction and acquaintance, from particular external cues there follow certain implications that have a bearing on what individuals get out of an interaction. Thus, discovery of an individual's socioeconomic status may be attractive not only because such similarity is attractive (Byrne, 1971) but also because certain socioeconomic statuses imply that someone has a specific range and fund of knowledge, skills, and techniques. Similarity of socioeconomic status may thus even imply similarity of Weltanschauung or attitudes. Certainly it is statistically likely that someone from a comparable level will have a more similar framework than someone from an entirely different background.

Kerckhoff (1974) has examined the way in which such tendencies may be emphasized. Most cultures have rules about permissible relationships, and there are usually norms about who "may" associate with whom. In general, individuals of the same race within a culture tend to associate, with similar economic and intelligence levels exerting like influences. Though this could be due to pressures to stay within a given class or social grouping for its own sake, there is nothing inconsistent between such observations and the findings of attitude or personality attraction studies, since similarity of class and social origin may trigger expectations of similar values, beliefs, and attitudes. Consequently, if one accepts the inferential nature of individuals, it could be argued that the presentation of such cues as intelligence level simply permits subjects to jump inferentially to assumptions of similarity of attitudes–assumptions they respond to according to the empirical generalizations previously discovered in attitude attraction research (Byrne, 1971). Like the external cues discussed above, these cues have at least three levels of influence on attraction: (1) their own evaluative or affective weights, (2) the evaluative or affective weights of the properties they imply, and (3) the attractiveness of the implied levels of attitude or personality *similarity* derivable from the cues and their implications.

The receiver and observer, by actively processing any information presented by the other, may be able to make shaky but supportable assumptions about the other's personality and attitude structure on the basis of cues which, on the face of it, have nothing at all to do with attitudes or cognition. Duck (1973b) found that subjects who gave physical descriptions of others nevertheless suggested primarily psychological implications of these descriptions. Such a process of inference–of assumption about the invisible on the basis of the visible–could clearly be a motive force in the progression from one level of information to another in acquaintance. However, this inference process interacts psychologically with the structure of the receiver's personality, his accuracy and skill as an observer, his judgmental confidence, and the consistency that he is able to detect and label in the transmitter during interactions–a consistency that provides a basis for making attributions about the transmitter's personality.

Information From Others as Interactors

It is fairly well established that both personality and current motivational states can influence what observers make of the outside world. For example, Mitchell and Byrne (1973) reported a relationship between authoritarianism and reactions to physically attractive defendants in trials, and the literature provides many examples of the influence of style of thought on impression formation (Craig and Duck, forthcoming). Furthermore, Robbins (1975) has shown how personality style affects detection of, and reaction to, consistency in others. Subjects were given conflicting information about others. Dogmatic subjects took in less information before passing final judgment, gave more extreme stability ratings, and demonstrated a greater tendency to explain away impression-discrepant information rather than to withhold judgment.

In view of these findings, it is surprising that work on attraction has often ignored the influence of personality on reactions to information. However, Craig and Duck (forthcoming) have argued that discovery of how individual personalities react to degrees of similarity-dissimilarity on different sorts and statuses of information, particularly when conflicting sorts are available in real life interactions, has important implications for attraction research. Two important ways in which interpersonal attitudes can be similar or dissimilar stem from a distinction between evaluative and descriptive aspects of attitudes about others. Therefore, Craig and Duck (forthcoming) tested two predictions: (1) that the relative effects of the two types of information on attraction are different (this prediction was confirmed, with the main influence stemming from evaluative similarity) and (2) that cognitively complex subjects are less likely than cognitively simple subjects to rate strangers as unattractive when they manifest descriptive *dis*similarity. Indeed, cognitive complexity did interact with descriptive similarity, and complex subjects were more accepting of strangers who used different descriptions—a finding of particular relevance to this discussion.

Clearly, such contrasting types of information are freely available in real-life encounters, and the effects of sequences of such information are not clearly understood (Clore, forthcoming). Indeed, work in attraction has too often attended solely to "set piece" studies and has overlooked the fact that, in real life, individuals learn much from such sequences of communication. One variety of sequence lies in the comparison of the other's behavior toward self with the other's behavior toward third parties. Thus, if I find the other pleasant, but suspect that he or she is an ingratiator, I can observe his or her interactions with various parties of different status. Others can inform me about his or her personality without his or her behavior being addressed directly or exclusively toward me. As yet, this area is little researched and it is not clear how the influence of such knowledge interacts with other forms of information from the other.

Information About Personality

One primary function of acquaintance is to gain information about the other's personality in order to establish the extent to which it is similar to one's own and therefore validates it (Duck, 1973b). But there are many levels at which "a personality" may be conceptually analyzed (e.g., needs, gross traits like extrovert-introvert, subtler analysis in terms of several trait dimensions, such as dominance, femininity, psychological mindedness, as on the CPI). Therefore, since one can be similar in needs, similar in level of extroversion, or similar on several other dimensions, it follows that there are several hierarchical levels at which personality similarity can be analyzed (Duck, 1973a, forthcoming a, forthcoming b). It is plausible that each hierarchical level of similarity analysis is appropriate to only some levels of friendship development (Duck, 1973a). This latter point has been often overlooked, even where research has concentrated not just on the ways in which cues give indirect information about personality, but in the majority of research that has dealt with the effects of direct access to the other's personality and particularly with the effects of knowledge about the level of similarity between other's personality and one's own (Byrne and Griffit, 1969; Duck 1973a). Accordingly, most work on personality similarity is equivocal since investigators have not recognized the different levels at which they were analyzing the relevant concepts (Duck, forthcoming a). Thus, some studies show that communication about personality promotes attraction (Byrne and Griffit, 1969), some that natural populations of friends manifest personality similarity (Izard, 1960), and some that there are no effects of personality similarity on attraction ratings (Hoffman and Maier, 1966).

In attempting to clarify this state of affairs, Duck and Craig (in preparation b) argued that different levels of personality similarity are related to acquaintance at different temporal points of development, with "gross" ones related initially and "finer" ones later. The grounds for this position stem from Duck (1973a), who showed similarity on the CPI predicted sociometric choices by newly acquainted individuals but not by well-acquainted ones, while Kelly's (1955) Reptest predicted choices of well-acquainted persons but not newly acquainted ones. In a longitudinal study where friendship choices were tapped at three different points of developing acquaintance (one month, three months, and eight months), Duck and Craig (in preparation b) gave an unacquainted pool of subjects three different personality tests. To deal with the hypothesis of interest, personality tests that measure personality at different *levels* and in ways that correspond to the level available to observers at different points of acquaintance must be selected. Thus, it is necessary *ex hypothesi* to have one test that measures at a gross trait-dimensional level, one that measures personal value systems, and one that measures the fine shades of personal semantic and cognitive space. The tests selected were the CPI, which categorizes subjects' answers to about 400 questions in terms of 18 dimensions (e.g., dominance and tolerance), the Allport-Vernon Study of Values, which assesses values of six sorts (e.g., religious, economic, and political), and the Reptest, which measures subjects' hypotheses about all manner of events, things, and people.

While similarity on the CPI predicted sociometric choices at none of the three points of time, similarity on the AVSV predicted choices at Time 2 ($p < .01$), and the Reptest predicted choices only at Time 3 ($p < .01$), although similarity of "style" of construing also predicted choices nonsignificantly at earlier points ($0.1 > p > .05$). Since these results showed that none of the measures of personality correlated with sociometric choice at Time 1, had the study not been longitudinal the authors would have erroneously appeared justified in concluding that personality similarity was *not* related to attraction. As it turned out, different measures, tapping different levels of conceptualization of personality, were differently and exclusively able to predict sociometric choices at the various times chosen for measurement. This study thus underlines the importance of the temporal appropriateness of measures predicting attraction rather than simply the importance of the level of analysis on its own; i.e., both level of personality similarity and level of acquaintance must be considered together.

In this empirical context, therefore, it is imperative to distinguish between simply communicating about a certain level or depth of information and determining the appropriateness of that level of information to the development of acquaintance. In a similar vein, but with a different theoretical thrust, Kaplan et al. (1974) have found that intimate probing questions were appropriate and attractive only in informal interpersonal settings, whereas such questions were unattractive in highly formal circumstances. Thus, any model which predicts that intimacy is a direct function of the amount of self-disclosure may be misleading. It appears more reasonable to argue that intimacy is a function of the amount of disclosure made at the appropriate level, in the appropriate circumstances, and at the appropriate time. But is "appropriateness" the only limiting factor and how is the formation of friendships to be conceived in such a process?

INFORMATION FOR WHAT?

The basic relationship between *information* and *acquaintance* is the relationship between a hierarchy of knowledge and a sequence of attraction behavior. Individuals gather information at different levels or at different times as a means of filtering their acquaintances so that they end up with a small pool of close friends who support their personality structure in various ways (Duck, 1973b; forthcoming a). Not only do they assess their own affective reactions to information presented by the other, they also infer from what they observe and gauge the attractiveness of inferred attributes. In addition, they determine the level of *similarity* to themselves that is implied by the inferred attributes.

There is one additional feature: individuals assess another person's value as a source of reinforcement-through-similarity *before* they calculate the similarity level that actually exists between themselves and the other (Duck and Craig, 1975). The observed habit (Newcomb, 1961) of assuming similarity could thus have a *function* in acquaintance that follows directly from the context of the information available. Specifically, as individuals evaluate others in terms of descriptive categories—but before they assess actual similarity—they are able to make guesses or assumptions about the quantity of similarity that they may experience at the next relevant level of information. Simultaneously, individuals determine, by means of information available, whether they would value the discovered or expected similarity—i.e., whether the other is the kind of person who provides a positive model for social comparison. If so, the individuals look for similarity; if not, they filter the person out.

While the above analysis can integrate findings which have appeared to be in conflict, it also raises several intriguing empirical questions for subsequent research. Its main advantage, however, seems to lie in its simultaneous contribution to several of the mini-issues that occur in the attraction literature. To such questions as "What is the relative status of similarity and complementarity in attraction?" "Why do attitudes influence attraction so clearly, when the effects of personality are so ambiguous?" and "Why do some studies show that similarity of needs causes attraction and some not?" it offers one single answer; define the level of information being communicated and relate it to a sequential model of acquaintance.

REFERENCES

AJZEN, I. (1974). "Effects of information on interpersonal attraction: Similarity versus affective value." Journal of Personality and Social Psychology, 29:374-380.

--- (forthcoming). "Information processing approaches to interpersonal attraction."

ANDERSON, N. (1968). "Likableness ratings of 555 personality-trait words." Journal of Personality and Social Psychology, 9:272-279.

BOHAC, N.C., and REBOUSSIN, R. (1967). "Effects of varying ratios of favourable to unfavourable adjectives on the primacy effect in forming impressions of personality." Paper presented at the convention of the Midwestern Psychological Association, Chicago.

BYRNE, D. (1971). The attraction paradigm. New York: Academic Press.

BYRNE, D., and GRIFFIT, W. (1969). "Similarity and awareness of similarity of personality characteristics as determinants of attraction." Journal of Experimental Research in Personality, 3:179-186.

BYRNE, D., RASCHE, L., and KELLEY, K. (1974). "When 'I like you' indicates disagreement: An experimental differentiation of information and affect." Journal of Experimental Research in Personality, 8:207-217.

CLORE, G. (forthcoming). "Reinforcement and affect in attraction."

COOK, M. (forthcoming). "The social skill model and interpersonal attraction."

COOPER, J., and JONES, E.E. (1969). "Opinion divergence as a strategy to avoid being miscast." Journal of Personality and Social Psychology, 13:23-30.

CRAIG, G., and DUCK, S.W. (forthcoming). "Similarity, interpersonal attitudes and attraction: The evaluative-descriptive distinction."

DION, K., BERSCHEID, E., and WALSTER, E. (1972). "What is beautiful is good." Journal of Personality and Social Psychology, 24:285-290.

DUCK, S.W. (1973a). "Personality similarity and friendship formation: Similarity of what, when?" Journal of Personality, 41:543-558.

--- (1973b). Personal relationships and personal constructs: A study of friendship formation. London: Wiley.

--- (forthcoming a). "Enquiry, hypothesis and the quest for validation: Personal construct systems in developing acquaintance."

--- (forthcoming b). "Personality similarity in friendship formation."

DUCK, S.W., and CRAIG, G. (1975). "Effects of type of information upon interpersonal attraction." Social Behaviour and Personality, 3:157-164.

--- (in preparation a). "Attractiveness of judgement similarity as a function of type of information."

--- (in preparation b). "Information type, similarity and attraction."

--- (in preparation c). "Personality similarity and the longitudinal development of friendship: An experimental study."

DUCK, S.W., and SPENCER, C.P. (1972). "Personal constructs and friendship formation." Journal of Personality and Social Psychology, 23:40-45.

HARRE, R. (forthcoming). "Friendship as an accomplishment: An ethogenic approach to social relationships."

HOFFMAN, L.R., and MAIER, N. (1966). "An experimental re-examination of the similarity-attraction hypothesis." Journal of Personality and Social Psychology, 3:145-152.

IZARD, C.E. (1960). "Personality similarity and friendship." Journal of Abnormal and Social Psychology, 61:47-51.

KAPLAN, K.J., FIRESTONE, I.J., DEGNORE, R., and MOORE, M. (1974). "Gradients of attraction as a function of disclosure probe intimacy and setting formality: On distinguishing attitude oscillation from attitude change–Study one." Journal of Personality and Social Psychology, 30:638-646.

KAPLAN, M.F., and ANDERSON, N. (1973). "Information integration theory and reinforcement theory as approaches to interpersonal attraction." Journal of Personality and Social Psychology, 28:301-312.

KELLY, G.A. (1955). The psychology of personal constructs. New York: Norton.

KELVIN, R.P. (forthcoming). "Predictability, power and vulnerability in interpersonal attraction."

KERCKHOFF, A.C. (1974). "The social context of interpersonal attraction." In E.L. Huston (ed.), Foundations of interpersonal attraction. New York: Academic Press.

KERCKHOFF, A.C., and DAVIS, K.E. (1962). "Value consensus and need complementarity in mate selection." American Sociological Review, 27:295-303.

KLECK, R., ONO, H., and HASTORF, A.H. (1966). "The effects of physical deviance upon face-to-face interaction." Human Relations, 19:425-436.

LA GAIPA, J.J. (forthcoming). "Testing a multidimensional approach to friendship."

LEVINGER, G. (1974). "A three-level appraoch to attraction: Toward an understanding of pair relatedness." In E.L. Huston (ed.), Foundations of interpersonal attraction. New York: Academic Press.

LEVINGER, G., SENN, D., and JORGENSEN, B. (1970). "Progress towards permanence in courtship: A test of the Kerckhoff-Davis hypothesis." Sociometry, 33:427-443.

McCARTHY, B., and DUCK, S.W. (forthcoming). "Friendship duration and responses to attitudinal agreement-disagreement."

MITCHELL, H.E., and BYRNE, D. (1973). "The defendant's dilemma: Effects of jurors' attitudes and authoritarianism on judicial decisions." Journal of Personality and Social Psychology, 25:123-129.

MURSTEIN, B.I. (forthcoming). "The stimulus-value-role (SVR) theory of dyadic relationships."

NEWCOMB, T.M. (1961). The acquaintance process. New York: Holt, Rinehart and Winston.

ROBBINS, G.E. (1975). "Dogmatism and information gathering in personality impression formation." Journal of Experimental Research in Personality, 9:74-84.

STROEBE, W. (forthcoming). "Self esteem and interpersonal attraction."

STROEBE, W., EAGLY, A., and STROEBE, M. (forthcoming). "Friendly or just polite? The effects of self esteem on attributions."

WRIGHT, P.H. (1965). "Personality and interpersonal attraction: Basic assumptions." Journal of Individual Psychology, 27:127-136.

Chapter 7

INTERPERSONAL EPISTEMOLOGY AND INTERPERSONAL COMMUNICATION

Charles R. Berger, Royce R. Gardner, Malcolm R. Parks, Linda Schulman, and Gerald R. Miller

THE PROCESS of coming to know other persons is viewed by most members of our society as both important and intriguing. Evidence of people's preoccupation with knowing others abounds in everyday communicative activities. Popular songs tunefully proclaim the joy of "getting to know you"; adages and clichés acknowledge differences in interpersonal epistemology (e.g., "I can read her like a book" as opposed to "She's got a real poker face"); and inscrutable, hard-to-read individuals are the object of frequent curiosity and inquiry (e.g., "You've worked with Fred for a long time; what's he *really* like?"). Moreover, people often acknowledge differences in their levels of social understanding of others by such comparative statements as, "I feel as though I know Mary very well, but I've never been able to get to know her sister."

Our purpose in this paper is to explicate some of the ways that persons come to know others through interpersonal communication. More specifically, we address three major concerns. First, we consider the conditions which give rise to interpersonal knowledge or understanding, with primary interest directed at answering the question, Under what conditions are individuals willing to say that they "know" or "understand" another person and their relationship to him or her? Second, we examine some of the communicative strategies used to gain knowledge about other persons in an interpersonal relationship. Finally, we present data from several studies which demonstrate the knowledge-gaining processes discussed earlier in the paper.

CONDITIONS FOR INTERPERSONAL UNDERSTANDING

Levels of Knowledge

We view the process of achieving interpersonal knowledge or understanding as taking place at several different levels of increasing complexity. When someone asserts that he or she "knows" someone else, an auditor may attach several meanings to the assertion. For instance, if a man is heard to say, "I know that woman is my mother," an observer might conclude that the man is merely capable of identifying the woman who is his mother. By contrast, if a woman says, "I know my mother believes that most persons can't be trusted," the woman's statement conveys a level of "knowledge" about her mother that is more significant and complex; not only can she identify her mother but she also appears to know something about her mother's beliefs. The first statement is descriptive, since it involves only identification. The second statement requires an inference, since it asserts something about the state of affairs within the mother's head.

It is possible to distinguish at least three levels of knowledge about others. First, there are descriptive statements which are relatively easy to verify empirically. Such things as a person's height, weight, and other physical features are subject to relatively easy verification by others. Usually persons have little difficulty agreeing that someone is tall or short, fat or thin, young or old, etc. Observation without actual measurement is generally sufficient to achieve something approaching social consensus. Similarly, it is relatively easy to identify persons who occupy various role positions—e.g., "That person is the teacher."

A second level concerns the person's beliefs on issues. Such knowledge is more difficult to attain, for while the statement "Mary is tall" can be verified relatively easily by observation, the statement "Mary believes that abortion on demand should be extended to all women" is less subject to direct verification. In the first case, others can determine Mary's "tallness" by unobtrusively observing her. Moreover, it is relatively difficult for Mary to hide her height from view. However, even if others hear Mary assert that she endorses abortion on demand for all women, they cannot be certain that she is telling the truth. In other words, they can never know with complete certainty what Mary "really" thinks.

A third level of knowledge concerns others' ability to explain a person's actions and beliefs. This level presupposes that others "know" that a person behaves and/or believes in particular ways; knowing this, they seek answers to the question of *why* the person behaves in certain ways and believes in certain things. This is not to say that people are always concerned with this level of knowledge. When they interact with a shopkeeper who conforms to their expectations by giving them particular goods in exchange for money, people do not normally expend energy to speculate about why the shopkeeper behaved in this way. However, if the shopkeeper deviates from their expectations concerning appropriate behavior—e.g., if the shopkeeper is rude or beseiges them with personal problems—they well may wonder why the shopkeeper behaves so atypically. By contrast, people usually attempt to arrive at explanations for the behaviors and/or beliefs of those with whom they have significant relationships. When asked to explain typical behavior patterns of close friends, they have an easier time generating explanations than when asked to explain the behavior of a relative stranger. Again, this third, explanatory level of knowledge does not occupy people's awarenesses frequently; however, if asked to explain behaviors or beliefs, this level requires the most cognitive effort, since there are usually many plausible explanations for another's behavior.

Obviously, the same three levels of knowledge also operate vis-à-vis oneself. People can know themselves in terms of (1) easily accessible surface attributes, (2) less directly accessible attributes such as beliefs, and (3) reasons for their behaviors and beliefs. As they become capable of generating more and more plausible explanations for their thoughts and actions, they achieve more stable self-identities and possess more self-knowledge. Here again, it should be noted that people are not always preoccupied with questions concerning why they are behaving or believing in particular ways. Moreover, under some conditions, people may be unable to explain their behavior a priori, and only after they have behaved are they capable of generating causal attributions for it (Bem, 1972). In general, however, it can be reasonably assumed that if persons are called upon to explain a certain series of behaviors, some will be capable of providing a considerable number of motive attributions while others will not.

The three levels of knowledge or understanding described above involve *description, prediction,* and *explanation* respectively. The idea that interpersonal communication is largely a prediction-making activity employing psychological level data has been advanced by Miller and Steinberg (1975). Berger and Calabrese (1975), as well as Pope and Siegman (1972), have used the notion of uncertainty as a central explanatory construct for various communication phenomena. Berger and Calabrese, who were concerned mainly with initial interactions between strangers, argue that persons generate predictions and explanations about others' behaviors and beliefs so that they can select advantageous responses from their available repertoires. The present formulation extends the theoretical positions cited above by recognizing the necessity of formulating descriptive attributions and by emphasizing the various levels of complexity.

Up to this point, we have used the terms "knowledge" and "understanding" interchangeably. Hamlyn (1974:5) contends that the two terms are not synonymous. He asserts that "It is possible and legitimate for us to say 'I know him very well, but I don't really understand him; indeed I doubt if I understand him at all.' " Hamlyn goes on to point out, however, that the necessary conditions for knowing and for understanding a person are probably identical. In the present paper, we view description and prediction as prerequisites for both knowledge and understanding. Nevertheless, most people are probably unwilling to assert that they understand a person until they have constructed a rather elaborate set of causal schemata to explain important facets of the person's behaviors and beliefs. Understanding is not achieved until such causal explanations have been elaborated and verified.

Types of Predictions

People can make several kinds of predictions about others. Berger and Calabrese (1975) point out that the types of information generally exchanged during the course of initial interactions often lead to predictions about attitudes and beliefs that have not yet been revealed. For example, when one party to an initial conversation discovers that the other person is a steel worker, he or she may infer that the other person holds politically conservative attitudes. As Miller and Steinberg (1975) emphasize, using such sociological data to make predictions about an individual is dangerous since the probability that such stereotypes are erroneous is relatively high. Nevertheless, it is useful to remember that such predictive attempts are often aimed at moving from the sociological level to the psychological level without directly sampling the latter level.

A second kind of prediction involves dispositional consistency across situations. Jones and Davis (1965) have explicated the conditions under which persons are likely to make *correspondent inferences,* i.e., to infer that acts are accurate indicators of underlying dispositions. If a person has formed a number of correspondent inferences about another, his or her best prediction might be that during subsequent encounters the person will act in ways which continue to yield the same correspondent inferences. In other words, the observer might predict consistency from encounter to encounter. Thus, if the actor's pattern of behavior leads the observer to infer the disposition "friendly," the observer would expect to see friendly actions in the next encounter with the actor. Moreover, if such friendly behaviors were not forthcoming, the observer would be strongly motivated to generate an explanation for this deviation from expected behavior.

A third kind of prediction is roughly equivalent to a statistical interaction. Such interaction predictions are more complex than the first two types because they stipulate that a person will display different patterns of behaviors or beliefs in differing social situations. These predictions require more time to test and to verify since they demand observation in various social contexts. Furthermore, because of their complexity, greater cognitive effort is required to formulate them.

To the extent that these three types of predictions are verified by subsequent observations, people are willing to say that they know another person. Kelley (1967) has suggested a number of relevant criteria in establishing attributions to an entity. Given the entity's distinctiveness, when predictions of various types are confirmed repeatedly over time and across differing situations, and when other observers arrive at the same predictions about the target person, people will be willing to say that they *know* the target person, in the sense that they are more confident that the person possesses a particular attribute. Notice that the process of assessing predictive accuracy can be carried out alone or in concert with other observers. The process of verifying predictions via interaction with third parties is a communicative phenomenon worth study in its own right. People spend considerable time asking others their opinions of particular target persons. Such communicative behavior is an obvious instance of the prediction-testing process described above.

At times, the difference between predictions and descriptions may be difficult to determine by studying everyday discourse. For example, assume that two persons, A and B, are talking about a third person, C. Moreover, assume that A has known C for a long time while B has never met C. Suppose A tells B that C is very friendly. From A's perspective, that statement about C is descriptive. By contrast, from the viewpoint of B, the statement is predictive and must be verified at some future time. Person B only *knows* that A has *said* that person C is friendly, not that C is, in fact, friendly.

Types of Explanations

Just as there are different types of predictions that can be made about others' beliefs and behaviors, numerous kinds of explanations can be employed to account for others' actions. For instance, explanations can be classified as either *internal* or *external* (Heider, 1958). When people's behaviors are explained by such factors as personality dispositions, motivations, or intentions, internal causal attributions are being employed. When behaviors are explained by invoking such causal attributions as luck or task difficulty, external forces are being used. In almost any situation, the behavior of a given individual can be attributed to either internal or external causes, or a combination of the two.

Moreover, it is possible to differentiate between two subtypes of external causality: personal and impersonal. For example, the behavior of a target individual in a work situation might be explained by asserting, "Jones did it because his boss made him do it." In this example, Jones' behavior has been judged to result from the orders given him by his boss; thus, the cause of Jones' behavior is personal and external to him. By contrast, if it were argued that

"Jones did it because it is a warm day," the cause would be external to Jones, but impersonal. One kind of attribution which may be crucial to the development of understanding is the external-personal attribution in which the attributor perceives *himself or herself* to be the agent of external influence over the other; i.e., "Jones did it because *I* behaved in a particular way." Moreover, when an attributor perceives his or her *own* behavior to be at least partially caused by the other person, the perception of an *interpersonal relationship* may begin to emerge; e.g., "Jones did X because I behaved in a particular way, *and* I did Y because Jones behaved in a certain manner." This perception of mutual influence in a limited domain may lead to interpersonal or mutual understanding if extended to numerous other areas.

The same consistencies across time, situations, and other persons play a critical role in the process of verifying explanations of another's behavior. For example, in attempting to determine why a particular child has a generally friendly communicative style, people may observe the behavior of the child's parents across a variety of situations. If they, too, consistently display a friendly communicative style and if other observers agree that they are friendly persons, most people would probably conclude that the parents' friendly interaction style at least partially causes (and hence explains) the friendly interaction style of the child. To the extent that explanations are verified through the various processes described above, people are likely to assert that they know or understand the other person.

Interpersonal Understanding

Thus far, we have considered the necessary conditions for a person to achieve an understanding of another. We have used the terms "observer" and "observation" to refer both to situations where persons may be only observing the target person and to situations where they are in direct communication with the target. To achieve *interpersonal understanding,* the persons must be engaged in a symbolic exchange which both sets the knowledge generation processes in motion and serves to verify a considerable number of mutual descriptions, predictions, and explanations. If one party to the relationship is not expending effort directed toward knowledge generation and verification, interpersonal or mutual understanding cannot be realized. Moreover, if the interacting parties are unable to describe, predict, and explain each other's behaviors and beliefs with some degree of accuracy, they will not achieve interpersonal understanding. When the observer is involved in symbolic exchange with the observational target, he or she has one additional source of verification not available to the passive or unobtrusive observer. Specifically, the interactive observer can attempt to verify predictions and explanations about the target person through direct questioning. This possibility also enables the target to question the observer directly, and once this opportunity is provided through symbolic exchange, mutual understanding can result.

An additional point concerning the nature of understanding should be clarified. Under certain conditions, an outside observer might have a better understanding of a person's behavior than the person himself. Jones and Nisbett (1972) have pointed out that actors tend to overattribute their behavior to the environment, while observers are biased toward attributing behavior to the dispositions of the actors. These biases would lead individuals away from attributing their behaviors to their own internal dispositions. However, an observer who had been sensitized to attribute the actor's behavior to internal factors might be able to communicate these dispositional attributional possibilities to the actor. The actor would not only gain better self-understanding but, if he or she agreed to accept the observer's attributions, might also attribute "interpersonal sensitivity" to the observer. In turn, if the actor were able to help the observer gain self-understanding by assuming the role of observer, the level of mutual understanding in the relationship would increase. Thus, in a therapist-client relationship, the therapist may initially assume the role of observer to help the client more accurately identify the reasons for particular behaviors. But as the relationship progresses, the client may occasionally assume the observer role and provide attributions for certain behaviors of the therapist. To the extent that such reciprocal role-taking occurs, mutual understanding should be enhanced.

As our remarks have probably implied, the opportunity for mutual understanding increases if both parties are primarily concerned with questions about the reasons for the other's beliefs and behaviors, i.e., if they are operating at the third level of knowledge discussed earlier. After all, a dominant, aggressive person may coerce another into espousing certain beliefs or performing certain behaviors, and as a result the aggressor may be able to make fairly accurate predictions about certain of the victim's behaviors. To say that the aggressor "understands" the victim would be generally regarded as inaccurate, except in those relatively infrequent situations where the aggressor accurately perceives the victim as a masochist who enjoys being dominated and coerced. What is more probable is that the oppressed party will deny even a modicum of understanding on the part of the oppressor ("He doesn't even begin to know how I feel!") and may, eventually, take steps to terminate the relationship.

Similarly, mutual understanding is more likely to occur when both parties perceive that the relationship is important to them and when both have invested considerable resources in it. The dramatic cliché regarding unrequited love has considerable validity; although the spurned lover may expend enormous amounts of energy attempting to understand *why* the disinterested party believes and behaves in certain ways, his or her concern for causal knowledge is not likely to be reciprocated. Precisely because the degree of knowing and understanding represented at level three requires so much cognitive effort, it is usually reserved for a person's truly significant, important relationships.

In virtually all interpersonal relationships, complete descriptions, predictions, and explanations of another person's beliefs and behaviors are impossible to achieve. Moreover, when people do generate such knowledge about another, some predictions and explanations are likely to be disconfirmed by further interaction. Even persons who have been engaged in long, intimate relationships occasionally violate each other's predictions. When people say, "I didn't think he could do such a thing!" they are expressing their amazement at the disconfirmation of a confident prediction. Finally, remember that over time one or both parties to the relationship are likely to change their beliefs and behaviors. When such changes occur, interpersonal understanding suffers. Consider what happens when a college freshman who has been away from home a relatively short period of time reports that many relationships with his or her family and friends have become awkward or have even been disrupted. In fact, it may be necessary to update the relationship to achieve previous knowledge levels and to restore the fluidity of the relationship. This updating process itself deserves research attention.

STRATEGIES FOR KNOWLEDGE GENERATION

In this section, we will identify strategies used by persons to gain knowledge about each other. Not all of these strategies necessarily require direct communication between the interacting parties; knowledge about another can sometimes be gained by unobtrusive observation or through third parties. For the most part, however, use of communicative behavior is central to the strategies considered. Knowledge-generating strategies may be thought of as patterns of communication used by an individual to gain information about another person's beliefs, motives, and intentions. In this sense, we view persons employing these strategies as social scientists using their communicative capacity as an independent variable to produce observable effects that will provide insights into the other person.

Strategy 1: Interrogation

One way to get information about another person is to ask for it. Some studies (Berger, 1973; Calabrese, 1975) have demonstrated that when strangers are instructed to "get acquainted with each other," the first minute or two of the interaction is dominated by question asking. The questions usually request background and demographic information. Berger (1975) has shown how similarities and dissimilarities in background information are used to make proactive attributions or predictions about similarities and dissimilarities in attitudes. The same research also revealed how persons use similarities and dissimilarities in background to form retroactive attributions or causal explanations for subsequent attitudinal disagreements.

As an initial interaction progresses, the number of questions declines significantly. Calabrese (1975) found that during the first minute of conversation an average of about four questions was asked by each participant. By the 13th minute, the average number of questions declined to less than one. As time passes, the types of questions also change. Initially, persons ask for what Miller and Steinberg (1975) have called sociological level information which is largely descriptive, e.g., "What is your occupation?" As the conversation progresses, however, persons are more likely to ask each other to *explain* their feelings about an issue. Thus, in all probability, there is a shift from requests for descriptive information to requests for explanatory information. Obviously, explanatory information helps develop causal attributions for beliefs and behaviors.

There are, nevertheless, limits on the extent to which persons can use interrogation as a means for gaining knowledge about each other. Calabrese (1975) reported a strong tendency for the number of questions asked during initial encounters to be reciprocal. This finding supports the notion that a reciprocity norm (Gouldner, 1960) acts to govern initial interactions. Underlying this reciprocity norm is the tacit understanding that if a person asks another person a question in an initial interaction, he or she should be willing to answer the same question. Thus, one must be willing to divulge the same information requested from the other. When persons continue to ask for information but refuse to provide the same information when it is requested of them, the information asker's level of desirability will probably decline in the eyes of the information giver. Data relevant to this generalization have been provided by Sermat and Smyth (1973).

A second limitation of interrogation in initial interaction situations is that one cannot ask for relatively intimate information in the beginning stage of the relationship. Typically, a male who desires a sexual relationship with a female would be rebuked if he asked, "How do you feel about going to bed with men you have just met, like me?" Thus, even if both parties to a relationship wish to know the same thing about each other, norms governing the appropriate level of communicative intimacy may prohibit them from asking questions to elicit the desired information.

A third limitation of interrogation lies in the number of questions persons are permitted to ask each other. If question asking is used extensively to obtain knowledge about another, the interaction takes on the qualities of a formal interview situation. Such a formal tone seems undesirable for informal social interaction. Although we know of no data bearing directly on this issue, it seems worthwhile to determine if there is an upper limit to the number of questions people can ask each other before their levels of attraction for each other will be adversely affected.

A fourth inherent limitation of question asking as a means of gaining information about others has already been mentioned: to accept information obtained via questioning involves the tacit inference that the respondent is being truthful, rather than deceptive. In initial interactions, even commonplace queries may be answered untruthfully; e.g., the respondent may seek to enhance status by saying he or she is a doctor, rather than a restaurant employee. Initial encounters by members of the opposite sex may find one or both parties trying to maximize their credentials through a strategy of exaggeration: a 2.8 grade average may blossom to a 3.5, or a parental income of $15,000 may inflate to $30,000. And even in long-standing, intimate relationships, some questions may be too painful or threatening to answer truthfully. Thus, a certain air of contingency is always associated with the fruits of interrogation, although a high degree of trust may reduce uncertainty to a minimum.

It is worth reemphasizing that persons may also ask others for their opinions about a particular target person. Such indirect interrogation generates attributional stability through the observer consensus process explicated by Kelley (1967). The antecedent conditions associated with this kind of indirect information seeking are worth investigating. Perhaps when people are thinking of establishing a relatively long-term or highly intimate relationship, they seek the opinions of third party observers. Moreover, knowledge of the kinds of persons who are sought out as information sources may produce insights into how persons form friendship networks.

Strategy 2: Self-Disclosure

One of the most effective ways of eliciting information from others is to disclose information about oneself. The rule of reciprocity (Gouldner, 1960) mentioned above implies that if one party to a relationship is willing to reveal information about his or her behaviors and beliefs, the other party is likely to respond in kind. Indeed, if both parties enter into self-disclosure honestly and openly, the relationship will eventually yield a relatively high degree of mutual understanding.

The cautious tone of the last statement is occasioned by a distinction between *genuine* and *apparent* self-disclosure drawn by Miller and Steinberg (1975). According to them, genuine self-disclosure occurs when an individual reveals information that he or she perceives as personally private. Apparent self-disclosure, on the other hand, takes place when an individual reveals information that most members of the society would define as personally private, but which is not, for some reason or another, seen as personally private by the "discloser." In other words, apparent self-disclosure is a manipulative strategy that seeks to gain information or behavioral compliance from another by creating a false sense of frankness or intimacy. In some cases, the information may not even be true; e.g., some sales pitches rely upon "disclosing" to the customer a supposed physical handicap or malady suffered by the salesperson, when in fact, the salesperson may be perfectly healthy.

During initial stages of an interaction, excessive self-disclosure, like overly intimate interrogation, may be viewed negatively, or even suspiciously. Social norms generally prohibit high levels of disclosure to new acquaintances, particularly under circumstances where the interactants are likely to come into repeated contact. The assembly line worker who immediately deluges his new work partner with a detailed account of economic and sexual problems will probably be viewed rather skeptically. The studies reported in the next section of this paper address this possibility.

Self-disclosure is by far the most extensively studied of the strategies discussed here (e.g., Jourard, 1971; Cozby, 1973; Pearce and Sharp, 1973) and is a major topic of several papers in this volume (e.g., see the chapters by Duck and by Gilbert). That it provides a viable strategy for gaining knowledge about the other is unquestionable; that its relative success in generating information depends on a number of individual and relational variables is documented by the research cited above.

Strategy 3: Deception Detection

As we have indicated, one limitation of direct interrogation as a knowledge-generating communicative strategy is simply that the person being interrogated may, for a variety of reasons, misrepresent himself or herself. Even when information is gathered from third party observers, the target person may have successfully misrepresented something to them. Thus, quite early in a relationship, participants often attempt to determine whether their perceptions of each other lack validity because of misrepresentation or deception. Misrepresentation might occur because a person omits certain information, withholds negative information about himself, or overemphasizes favorable self-attributes.

Jones (1964) and Jones and Wortman (1973) have suggested several ingratiation strategies used to curry favor with others: among these are opinion agreement, flattery, self-presentation (i.e., leaking only positive information about oneself to enhance attractiveness), and rendering favors. The strategy of deception detection can be used to unmask attempts at ingratiation. For example, when a person agrees with an opinion and the other suspects that the person is only agreeing for purposes of ingratiation, the other can quickly clarify the opinion so that it now opposes the opinion originally advocated. If the suspected ingratiator follows suit, additional support is provided for an ingratiation interpretation of his or her behavior. If, on the other hand, the person sticks to the original opinion, even though the other has changed, it becomes more likely that the person is expressing a true opinion, rather than engaging in ingratiation. Of course, it is possible that the other person saw through the strategy and is still misrepresenting even while expressing the original opinion.

Compliment giving is a potentially powerful tool of the ingratiator; however, there are communicative strategies that can be used to ascertain the probable sincerity of complimentary behavior. Frequently, when persons are complimented, they deny that they possess the praised attribute. For example, when complimented for good cooking, they might respond that the meal really wasn't *that* good or *that* exotic. The compliment receiver then observes whether the compliment giver is willing to recompliment the same performance or attribute. If the compliment is repeated, most people are more likely to believe that it is sincere. Persons who offer too many compliments or show too much opinion agreement are viewed with greater suspicion than persons who offer an appropriate number of compliments for a particular situation. Data discussed later in this paper bear directly on this issue.

A communicative strategy for dealing with both self-presentation and favor rendering involves avoiding any response to the positive information, in the case of self-presentation, and failing to reciprocate favors, in the case of favor rendering. If a person continues doing favors when they are not reciprocated, greater sincerity is often attributed. Since such moves cannot totally erase doubts about the motives of the target person, the indirect interrogation strategy discussed earlier can also be used: the information seeker asks others whether the target person always presents himself or herself in a favorable light or whether the target person characteristically renders favors. Moreover, indirect interrogation can be useful in gaining knowledge about a person's opinions, in order to test for opinion agreement, and in finding out whether the target person frequently flatters others and, if so, for what reasons.

Of course, direct interrogation may also be used to detect deception. Parents frequently ask their children, with varying success, whether they are telling the truth. However, in an informal social relationship involving persons of equal status, such direct questioning is generally inappropriate.

Strategy 4: Environmental Structuring

Under certain conditions, persons purposely arrange a physical or social environment to gain knowledge about the persons who will inhabit it. An example of such behavior sometimes occurs when people entertain others in their homes. In arranging seating, the host may structure the situation such that certain others are cast into an interaction situation. A common way in which this occurs is by seating suggestions for the dinner table. Aside from considerations of guest comfort, the host may wish to put certain individuals together so that he or she may gain information. This information may be gained either by directly observing their interaction or by later interrogating one of the parties. In work settings, a person may put questionable employees in interaction with a trusted employee so that he or she can "keep an eye on them."

At the other extreme, persons sometimes create high-stress environments to learn if others are capable of coping. Simulated stressful situations are employed by the military and by NASA. Businesses also use stressful interviews to determine if a particular candidate can make decisions under high-stress conditions. Whether a stressful environment simulation analogue exists in informal social interaction situations is an interesting question. Perhaps persons who are contemplating marriage raise personal crises to determine how their potential partner operates under stress. Of course, such naturally occurring events as severe illness or family death can also provide information about a person's ability to cope with stress.

Persons structure environments in numerous other ways to gain knowledge of others. For example, the individual who has a potential romantic partner to dinner may create a situation with candlelight, soft music, and wine to determine the potential partner's feelings about their relationship. Of course, it may be difficult to separate the information-gathering aspects of such environmental structuring from the persuasive attributes of the situation; i.e., the host might intend to induce the guest to view their relationship in a particular way.

Under certain conditions, an individual might structure a *social* environment to determine how another person feels about their relationship. For example, a person who is contemplating marriage but who is unsure about the other's feelings may try to ascertain them by placing the other into interaction with persons who already have the desired relationship. Thus, instead of interacting with other single persons, the inquirer might suggest spending more time with married couples. The partner's reaction to the general idea, as well as his or her specific responses in the actual interaction situation, may give the inquirer insights into the partner's feelings on the marriage issue. Here again, however, it may be difficult to separate the information-gaining aspects of the situation from the persuasive effects of the interactions.

Strategy 5: Deviation Testing

Berger and Calabrese (1975) have noted that initial interactions between strangers are highly ritualized and evidence considerable control by social rules and norms. Strangers know how to communicate with each other without setting up communicative conventions, because they have tacit knowledge about how they should communicate with other members of their culture in particular situations; from the perspective of Miller and Steinberg (1975), they base initial communicative predictions on cultural data. As far as understanding others is concerned, Jones and Davis (1965) have argued that conformity to role requirements does not lead to the development of correspondent inferences and confident dispositional attributions about the other. They point out that when persons conform to social expectations, they are behaving like all other members of a particular social group or culture. Consequently, the observer finds it difficult to view the person as an *individual.* Their reasoning leads to the conclusion that behavior which conforms to widely shared cultural rules is relatively useless as a source of information for gaining an understanding of another. Jones and Davis go on to assert that only when persons deviate from socially desirable expectations can observers generate confident dispositional attributions about them.

We believe that the position of Jones and Davis is too extreme. When persons confrom to rules or norms, others do gain insights, albeit limited ones, into them as individuals. Specifically, the observers at least learn whether or not the person is "normal" in the sense that he or she knows the appropriate behaviors in particular situations. Data presented in the following section directly address the issue of the impact of rule violations on perceptions of the rule violator.

As active participant observers in social interaction, some people may intentionally violate situational rules of conduct to give others information about them *as individuals* and to see the kind of response elicited by the deviation. For instance, assume you have met someone for the first time and have enjoyed talking to him or her. Since the beginning of the conversation you have both addressed each other by title plus last name. You are interested in determining whether the other person is also enjoying the relationship and whether he or she wishes to continue it on a more informal level. Thus, you begin to call the person by his first name. The move from title plus last name to first name signals a move from formality to informality and a step toward solidarity (Brown, 1965).

If your use of first name is reciprocated, you know, with some probability of error, that your partner defines your relationship in terms similar to yours. If your partner continues to address you with title plus last name, you have learned that he or she views your relationship from a different perspective. In some situations, the move from formal to informal address might be perceived as a violation of social convention. Nevertheless, making the move provides you with some knowledge of how the other views your relationship. An even more extreme violation would be to commence your conversation with the stranger by using first name only. The stranger's response to this strategy might be even more informative than in the situation where you move from the formal to the informal level.

In all likelihood, the five general strategies discussed above do not exhaust all the possible communicative strategies used to generate knowledge about others. Nevertheless, they appear to be worthy of further investigation. Even an obvious strategy such as interrogation merits study. To our knowledge, no one has yet investigated changes in the kinds of questions that persons ask one another as their relationship develops. Furthermore, frequency of question asking may be a useful indicator of relational growth, stability, and decline. Certainly, the strategy of deviation testing would also profit from research attention. The studies reported in the following section provide some insight into this strategy as well as the deception detection strategy.

STUDIES OF NORM VIOLATION

The three studies reported in this section were conducted to examine the effects of norm violation in the context of initial interaction between strangers. Studies I and II were concerned with the effects of violating the normal pattern of information sequencing. Study III varied the number of compliments given in a conversation between strangers as a form of the ingratiation strategy. All three studies focused on perceptions of the attractiveness and mental health of the norm violator. Furthermore, the confidence with which subjects could predict and explain the feelings, attitudes, and behaviors of the norm violater was measured. Additional variables will be discussed as they relate to the individual studies.

STUDIES I AND II

Methodology: Study I

Subjects. The subjects for this study were 231 residents of Wilmette, Illinois. A cluster sample of 100 areas was drawn from census tract data; households within each area were then randomly selected. Subjects ranged in age from 17 to 83 years of age (M = 40.39 years). The sample consisted of 66.1% females and 33.9% males, and 69.3% of the total sample were married.

Design. Subjects were randomly assigned to one of 18 conditions in a 3 x 3 x 2 design. Independent variables were (1) conversational sequencing (low deviance, moderate deviance, high deviance), (2) background similarity (similar, dissimilar, no information), and (3) reciprocity (reciprocal, nonreciprocal). The dependent measures included perceptions of the participants' attractiveness and included the subject's ability to predict the attitudes, feelings, and behavior of the participants.

Manipulations and Procedures. Respondents were asked to read a transcript of the first two minutes of a conversation between strangers. The conversations in this study were based on the findings of a previous study conducted in Wilmette (Berger, Gardner, Clatterbuck, and Schulman, 1975). In that research, subjects sorted 150 conversational statements along a time continuum, indicating at which point in a two-hour conversation between strangers a particular statement might first occur. The present study randomly selected statements that were sorted into the initial, middle, and last time slots by the respondents in the earlier study. The *low deviance* transcript was constructed primarily of biographic-demographic statements; the *moderate deviance* conversation dealt with attitudes toward public affairs, religion, and nonintimate family and personal information; and the *high deviance* transcript was composed of statements concerned with intimate personal issues, such as marital problems and sexual matters.

The conversations were either *reciprocal* or *nonreciprocal.* Subjects in the reciprocal conditions read transcripts which had participants revealing information of the same quality and at the same rate. Disclosure patterns were "matched." In the nonreciprocal conversations, only one participant disclosed information while the other participant responded minimally (e.g., "I see," or "uh-huh").

The *background similarity* of the participants was manipulated by inserting a brief biographic-demographic participant profile in the questionnaire. One-third of the subjects received a similarity manipulation in which participants were described as very similar to one another; one-third read a profile which contained information stressing dissimilarities between the participants; and one-third read the conversation without benefit of information about the participants.

Subjects were told that they were reading a transcript of the first two minutes of a conversation between strangers who had met at a party at the home of a mutual friend. To increase the salience of norm violations, subjects were also told that the participants in the conversation would meet and talk again in the near future (Kiesler et al., 1967).

After reading the transcript, subjects were asked to answer a series of questions concerning their perceptions of the communicators. One series of questions focused on the perceived attractiveness of the participants, with questions relating to characteristics such as sincerity and likableness. The subjects' ability to predict confidently the behavior, attitudes, and feelings of the participants was assessed by means of an uncertainty measure.

Methodology: Study II

Subjects. The participants in this study were 94 males and 96 females who were enrolled in an introductory communication course. Subjects ranged from 17 to 31 years of age (M = 19.14). Almost all (96%) were unmarried.

Design. The design was a 2 x 2 x 2 fixed effects analysis of variance: *level of norm violation* (low versus high) by *sex of the subject* by *sex of the other* (the person in the conversation). Subjects were randomly assigned to the eight experimental conditions. The dependent variables were designed to assess the following negative consequences of norm violation: (1) attraction, (2) desire for future interaction, (3) perceived mental stability, (4) perceived similarity, (5) perceived sincerity, and (6) uncertainty.

Manipulation and Procedures. In the low norm violation conditions, the 51 statements comprising the conversation were arranged in the order in which a pretest had indicated that they would normally occur. In the high norm violation condition, the statements were arranged in reverse order from the low violation condition. The 51 statements were drawn from a set of 112 statements generated by students who were asked to list things that they might say in a 60-minute conversation with a stranger at a friend's party. Statements were drawn on the basis of low variance in terms of position in the 60-minute conversation.

The two sex variables (sex of subject, sex of other) were included. A series of studies have indicated sex differences in self-disclosure (Cozby, 1973). Such differences were believed relevant given the differences in timing of self-disclosure in the two violation conditions. Furthermore, it seemed reasonable that persons might approach same- and opposite-sex interactions differently —especially in a party situation.

Subjects were instructed to read through a booklet of 51 statements. They were told to imagine that the statements were being made by a person whom they had just met at an informal party at the home of a friend. Subjects were told that the encounter was to "last" about 60 minutes. When subjects had completed the booklet containing the statements, they were given a brief questionnaire. Global evaluations of liking, desire for future interaction, perceived mental stability, perceived similarity, and perceived sincerity were made on 9-point, Likert-type scales. Two aspects of the uncertainty variable were investigated: how certain the subject was about his or her own judgments concerning the other, and how predictable the other's behavior or internal states were to the subject.

Results: Studies I and II

Subjects in Study I viewed the low deviant conversation as most typical for a first meeting between strangers ($F = 12.8$, $df = 1/193$, $p < .001$), as well as rating the reciprocal conversation as more typical than the nonreciprocal interaction ($F = 5.23$, $df = 1/193$, $p < .025$). In Study II, the low violation condition was seen as more structurally similar to the subjects' own interaction style ($t = 5.43$, $df = 164$, $p < .001$) and to that of most people ($t = 7.16$, $df = 164$, $p < .001$). Thus, manipulations for both studies were judged to be successful.

Main effects for attraction were found in both studies. Subjects were most attracted to persons in the low violation (low deviance) condition (Study I: $F = 40.97$, $df = 2/213$, $p < .05$; Study II: $F = 3.97$, $df = 1/165$, $p < .05$). This was true regardless of the sex of the subject in Study I and the sex of the subject or the sex of the other in Study II. Subjects in Study I also viewed participants in the reciprocal conversations as more attractive than persons in nonreciprocal interactions ($F = 12.9$, $df = 1/213$, $p < .001$). Whereas Study I found that perceived mental health was rated higher for participants in the low deviance condition ($F = 67.1$, $df = 2/197$, $p < .001$) and the reciprocal condition ($F = 5.00$, $df = 1/197$, $p < .025$), Study II found no significant differences for perceived mental stability between the violation conditions.

Subjects in Study I were more confident of their predictive attributions for participants in reciprocal conditions than in nonreciprocal conditions ($F = 21.5$, $df = 1/213$, $p < .001$). No main effects for level of norm violation were found for the uncertainty measure in either study. There were, however, significant interactions in Study II for the uncertainty of the subjects' predictions about the other ($F = 4.19$, $df = 1/165$, $p < .05$), and for the uncertainty of the subjects' own judgments ($F = 5.67$, $df = 1/165$, $p < .025$). In both cases, uncertainty was greater for males in the low violation conditions but greater for females in the high violation conditions. This was true regardless of the sex of the other person in the conversation–i.e., no three-way interactions were found.

Background similarity-dissimilarity appeared to have no effect on the subjects' perceptions of the attractiveness of the participants or the confidence with which the subjects could predict the feelings, attitudes, and behavior of the participants, although the check for background manipulation was successful ($F = 10.09$, $df = 2/17$, $p < .001$). It appears, however, that similarity-dissimilarity mediated the effects of the reciprocity manipulation, for subjects rated participants in the reciprocal condition to be more similar to one another than in the nonreciprocal condition ($F = 104.5$, $df = 1/17$, $p < .001$). In Study II, no differences among the violation conditions for perceived similarity were found.

STUDY III

Methodology

Subjects. The participants in this study were 195 residents of Wilmette, Illinois. Sampling procedures were the same as those of Study I. Respondents ranged in age from 15 to 96 ($M = 40.9$). The sample consisted of 64.2% females and 35.8% males, of whom a majority (78.8%) were married.

Design. Respondents were randomly assigned to one of 12 conditions in the 3 x 2 x 2 design, or to one of 3 control conditions. Independent variables were (1) number of compliments (0 or control, 2, 8), (2) background similarity (similar, dissimilar, no information provided), and (3) reciprocity (reciprocal, nonreciprocal). The dependent measures included perceptions of the attractiveness of the participants in the conversation, and the ability with which subjects felt that they could confidently predict the behavior, attitudes, and feelings of the participants.

Manipulation and Procedures. Subjects were asked to read a transcript of an initial conversation between strangers. The basic transcript remained the same throughout all conditions. In the reciprocal conditions, participants each expressed two or eight compliments; their complimenting behavior was equal. In the nonreciprocal transcripts, one person complimented the other two or eight times, while the other participant in the conversation neither acknowledged the compliments nor complimented the other. Compliment giving in the nonreciprocal transcripts was one-sided. Compliments were randomly selected from among statements that were rated very complimentary or extremely complimentary on a pretest. The choice of two and eight compliments for the primary manipulation was made after a pretest suggested that these conditions were seen as significantly different from each other and from a no compliment condition in terms of compliment level.

Background similarity was manipulated by inserting a brief description of the participants before the transcript of the conversation in which they were supposed to have engaged. One-third of the subjects read an introduction in which participants were described as being very similar to one another; one-third received a dissimilarity manipulation which focused on differences between the participants; and one-third read the transcripts without benefit of background information.

Subjects were told that the participants in the conversation were strangers who had met at a party at the home of a mutual friend. They were also told that the interactants would meet and talk again in the near future. The commitment to future interaction was included to increase the salience of the violation of the norm of reciprocity and to make extreme compliment giving in initial interactions more uncertainty-producing (Kiesler et al., 1967).

After reading the conversation, respondents were asked to answer a series of questions designed to tap their perceptions of the attractiveness of the participants. Another series of questions measured predictive confidence as an indicator of uncertainty.

Results

All the manipulations involved in this study were successful. Respondents viewed the two compliment conditions as most typical for an initial conversation between strangers and the eight compliment conditions as least typical ($F = 53.08$, $df = 1/135$, $p < .001$). Reciprocal conditions were seen as more balanced in terms of conversational give-and-take than were nonreciprocal conditions ($F = 10.01$, $df = 1/135$, $p < .01$). The participants were viewed as trying to be more complimentary in the eight compliment conditions than in the two compliment conditions. Participants in the no compliment control conditions were seen as least complimentary ($F = 16.28$, $df = 1/135$, $p < .001$). Subjects also felt that the participants' backgrounds were most similar in the similar conditions, followed by the no information conditions, and least similar in the dissimilar conditions ($F = 6.45$, $df = 2/11$, $p < .025$).

Two main effects for attraction were found. Subjects viewed the compliment giver as most attractive in the two compliment conditions and least attractive in the eight compliment conditions ($F = 33.92$, $df = 1/145$, $p < .001$). The participants were also seen as more attractive in the reciprocal conditions ($F = 3.92$, $df = 1/145$, $p < .05$). Included within the attractiveness scale was a question dealing with the perceived mental health of the participants. The participants were seen as most healthy in the reciprocal conditions ($F = 7.97$, $df = 1/121$, $p < .01$). The number of compliments given also affected judgments of mental health, such that the participants were seen as least healthy in the eight compliment conditions ($F = 48.97$, $df = 1/121$, $p < .001$). Although both the number of compliments and the reciprocity main effects were found for attraction and mental health, no interactions were observed.

Uncertainty reduction was also facilitated by giving a small number of compliments. Subjects felt that they were able to predict the behaviors, attitudes, and feelings of the participants in the interaction with most confidence in the two compliment conditions ($F = 5.24$, $df = 1/128$, $p < .025$). In addition, female subjects were more confident of their predictive ability than males in all conditions ($F = 3.86$, $df = 1/129$, $p < .05$).

Discussion

The results of all three studies indicate that norm violations or deviations affect the perception of communicator attractiveness and impede the pursuit of interpersonal knowledge. Given the context of an initial conversation between strangers, violating the norms of information sequencing, reciprocity, and appropriate compliment giving leads to negative consequences for the norm violator. Subjects consistently viewed participants in deviant conversations as least attractive. Many theorists contend that a norm violater is perceived as an unpredictable person (Thibaut and Kelley, 1959; Kiesler et al., 1966). By their behaviors, individuals implicitly define what they consider to be appropriate conduct. When someone violates a conversational norm, the other party probably feels that his or her definition of the situation, and perhaps even his or her definition of himself or herself, has been rejected (Goffman, 1959). Thus, uncertainty is introduced into the interaction, which in turn decreases attractiveness (Berger and Calabrese, 1975).

Studies I and III found that norm violators are judged as less mentally healthy. This finding was not replicated in Study II. There is some evidence indicating that a person's behavior is not perceived to be as important or salient when a commitment to future interaction is lacking (Kiesler et al., 1967). Study II did not include a future interaction possibility. Future research might productively explore the ramifications of norm violations in a live setting where future interaction is expected.

The confidence with which persons are able to predict and explain the behavior of communication participants seems to vary with the degree of deviance. In Study I, subjects were more confident of their predictive attributions in the reciprocal condition than in the nonreciprocal condition. This difference may be due to subjects perceiving reciprocity as an indication of similarity. Previous research suggests that similarity reduces uncertainty (Berger and Calabrese, 1975). Varying the number of compliments in a conversation also seems to affect uncertainty. When participants in a conversation expressed too many compliments, the subjects' ability to predict confidently decreased. Compliment giving produces a number of alternative explanations, among which may be sincerity, ingratiation, or manipulative intent. Having to choose from among numerous attributional options increases uncertainty.

The findings relating sex of subject to judgmental confidence were equivocal. There were no sex effects at all in Study I; the interaction effect in Study II indicated that uncertainty was greater for males in low violation conditions but greater for females in high violation conditions; in Study III, however, females were more confident than males across all conditions. The inconclusiveness of these findings suggests that more work needs to be done in this area.

Studies I and III included a degree of background similarity manipulation. Although the manipulation checks were successful, no effects for attractiveness or confidence were observed. Perhaps background characteristics have less predictive and explanatory importance once people are exposed to actual communication behavior. Attitudinal and personal similarity, as revealed in the conversations, appears to be more informative. It may also be that placing subjects in the observer role affected the salience of the background manipulation.

Taken together, these three studies demonstrate that violation of communication norms decreases the subjects' perception of the norm violator's attractiveness and also affects their ability to confidently predict and explain behavior. Further research is needed to determine whether the increase in uncertainty stimulates the search for more information or whether the unattractiveness of the violator leads to an early termination. It should be noted, however, that these studies did not indicate that violators were heavily sanctioned. This would seem to suggest that persons are relatively free to vary their initial interaction behavior quite widely—within some general limits. To the extent that such freedom exists, persons would be able to employ a greater variety of information-seeking strategies. Obviously, further research which more directly addresses these assumptions is essential.

CONCLUSION

Our brief excursion has but touched on the many conceptual and empirical issues related to the role of communication in interpersonal epistemology. As we indicated at the outset, people are persistently concerned with knowing others (or at least, knowing *some* others); and, in quest of this objective, communication is the primary tool for acquiring increased understanding. Hence, the effectiveness of various communicative strategies for gathering information, as well as their perceived appropriateness at various points in the process of developing mutual understanding, should be of concern and interest to students of communication. Moreover, none of the strategies discussed occur in social voids, and the relational consequences of using each of the various strategies should also be of considerable interest.

Perhaps the best way to summarize the results of this paper is to draw an analogy with the three levels of interpersonal knowledge discussed earlier. We feel that the distinctions established and the preliminary typology described in the first two sections of the paper should help us, and other like-minded persons, to "know" more about interpersonal epistemology at the basic, descriptive level–the most rudimentary level of interpersonal knowledge explicated earlier. Moreover, the studies reported in the third section of the paper represent our initial attempt to move to the second, more complex, predictive level. As for the *why* questions–the most complex, third level, explanatory phase–we have hardly scratched the surface. A great deal of conceptual and empirical spadework must be done if a theory of interpersonal epistemology, and the role of communication in that process, is to be developed.

REFERENCES

BEM, D.J. (1972). "Self-perception theory." In L. Berkowitz (ed.), Advances in experimental social psychology (vol. 6). New York: Academic Press.

BERGER, C.R. (1973). "The acquaintance process revisited: Explorations in initial interaction." Paper presented at the annual convention of the Speech Communication Association, New York.

--- (1975). "Proactive and retroactive attribution processes in interpersonal communications." Human Communication Research, 2:33-50.

BERGER, C.R., and CALABRESE, R.J. (1975). "Some explorations in initial interaction and beyond: Toward a developmental theory of interpersonal communication." Human Communication Research, 1:99-112.

BERGER, C.R., GARDNER, R.R., CLATTERBUCK, G.W., and SCHULMAN, L.S. (1975). "Perceptions of information sequencing in relationship development." Paper presented at the annual convention of the Speech Communication Association, Houston.

BROWN, R. (1965). Social psychology. New York: Free Press.

CALABRESE, R.J. (1975). "The effects of privacy and probability of future interaction on initial interaction patterns." Unpublished doctoral dissertation, Northwestern University.

COZBY, P.C. (1973). "Self-disclosure: A literature review." Psychological Bulletin, 79:73-89.

GOFFMAN, E. (1959). The presentation of self in everyday life. New York: Doubleday.

GOULDNER, A.W. (1960). "The norm of reciprocity: A preliminary statement." American Sociological Review, 25:161-178.

HAMLYN, D.W. (1974). "Person perception and our understanding of others." In T. Mischel (ed.), Understanding other persons. Oxford: Basil Blackwell.

HEIDER, F. (1958). The psychology of interpersonal relations. New York: John Wiley.

JONES, E.E. (1964). Ingratiation. New York: Appleton-Century-Crofts.

JONES, E.E., and DAVIS, K.E. (1965). "From acts to dispositions: The attribution process in person perception." In L. Berkowitz (ed.), Advances in experimental social psychology (vol. 2). New York: Academic Press.

JONES, E.E., and NISBETT, R.E. (1972). "The actor and the observer: Divergent perceptions of the causes of behavior." In E.E. Jones, D.E. Kanouse, H.H. Kelley, R.E. Nisbett, S. Valins, and B. Weiner (eds.), Attribution: Perceiving the causes of behavior. Morristown, N.J.: General Learning Corp.

JONES, E.E., and WORTMAN, C. (1973). Ingratiation: An attributional approach. Morristown, N.J.: General Learning Corp.

JOURARD, S.M. (1971). Self-disclosure: An experimental analysis of the transparent self. New York: John Wiley.

KELLEY, H.H. (1967). "Attribution theory in social psychology." In D. Levine (ed.), Nebraska symposium on motivation. Lincoln: University of Nebraska Press.

KIESLER, C.A., KIESLER, S.B., and PALLACK, M.S. (1967). "The effects of commitment to future interaction on reactions to norm violation." Journal of Personality, 35:585-599.

KIESLER, C.A., ZANNA, M., and DE SALVO, J. (1966). "Deviation and conformity: Opinion change as a function of commitment, attraction, and presence of a deviate." Journal of Personality and Social Psychology, 3:458-467.

MILLER, G.R., and STEINBERG, M. (1975). Between people: A new analysis of interpersonal communication. Palo Alto, Calif.: Science Research Associates.

PEARCE, W.B., and SHARP, S.M. (1973). "Self-disclosing communication." Journal of Communication, 23:409-425.

POPE, B., and SIEGMAN, A.W. (1972). "Relationship and verbal behavior in the initial interview." In A.W. Siegman and B. Pope (eds.), Studies in dyadic communication. New York: Pergamon.

SERMAT, V., and SMYTH, M. (1973). "Content analysis of verbal communication in the development of a relationship: Conditions influencing self-disclosure." Journal of Personality and Social Psychology, 26:332-346.

THIBAUT, J.W., and KELLEY, H.H. (1959). The social psychology of groups. New York: John Wiley.

Chapter 8

COMMUNICATION STRATEGIES, RELATIONSHIPS, AND RELATIONAL CHANGE

Michael E. Roloff

DESPITE A LONG-STANDING INTEREST in human relationships, social psychologists and students of communication have been unable to capture the variable that would allow them to distinguish between types of relationships. Recently, however, four theoretical perspectives have emerged that provide insight into the various types of relationships and their development. Furthermore, these perspectives focus on communication as an important element in distinguishing between relational types. Altman and Taylor (1973) argue that interpersonal relationships develop as a process in which people's interactions progress from nonintimate communication to deep self-disclosures. Writing about relationship formation and development, Duck (1973) points out that people choose which relationships they wish to escalate to the friendship level on the basis of how they perceive others. Berger and Calabrese (1975) theorize that relationships move through phases during which different kinds of information about self-concepts are shared. Finally, Miller and Steinberg (1975) categorize relationships into types according to the kinds of communication predictions that relational partners make about each other.

These four perspectives have three common assumptions:

(1) As people communicate, they share information about each other.

(2) As people share more information about each other, the nature of their predictions changes; i.e., they move from making stereotypic or generalizing predictions to making discriminating predictions about each other.

(3) As people make predictions based on discriminating information, their relationships escalate; as people rely on stereotypic or generalizing information, their relationships deescalate.

The four theoretical perspectives also share several important strengths. First, they identify changes in the attitudes and behaviors of relational partners that indicate change in the relationship. All four perspectives point to the ability to make certain kinds of predictions as a key indicator of relational change. Furthermore, they suggest methodologies that might be used to measure these indicators of relational change.

Second, each perspective examines the totality of the relationship, not just the individuals who are involved. For example, Miller and Steinberg (1975) stress the importance of this transactional point of view when they argue that interpersonal relationships are rarely formed or maintained by unilateral effort or commitment; both parties must consider themselves to be part of the relationship or it will not escalate.

Finally, each perspective assumes that relationships change; relationships will be modified as the relational partners gain information about each other. This movement can vary from some degree of generality or superficiality to some degree of uniqueness or depth. An important point made by both Altman and Taylor (1973) and Duck (1973) is that relationships may deescalate as well as escalate.

Obviously, the four perspectives represent a giant step forward; however, each stops short of a very important area. This paper contends that we should begin to examine the communication strategies involved in relational development. The four perspectives mentioned here and examined in detail later in the paper only partially discuss the role of communication strategies in relational development. Indeed, they limit their discussion to the role of self-disclosure in relationships, which largely ignores the communicative goals motivating disclosure. This limitation is apparent in the research on self-disclosure; researchers frequently ask people how often they self-disclose with friends, or researchers put people together who are strangers and measure their disclosing behavior. Both methods ignore the goals of self-disclosure in communication. Since people communicate to affect their environments, self-disclosure should also be viewed in that framework.

For instance, a great deal has been written about communication and conflict within relationships. Simmel (1950) argued that conflict often serves the function of identifying problem areas in the relationship and providing information about relational partners. Within this context of conflict, researchers may find different self-disclosure patterns when comparing interactions between strangers or friends. Furthermore, the importance of the object of the conflict to the individuals and to the relationship may affect the degree of self-disclosure in the modes of conflict resolution used.

By focusing on self-disclosure apart from the communicative goals which motivate it, the utility of a paradigm is limited. As indicated above, self-disclosure is often examined in some pure state, i.e., unshaded by the communicative context in which it takes place. People dealing with communication problems (therapists, for example) are less likely to observe self-disclosure in such an uncontaminated manner. Rather, they are likely to observe self-disclosure within a large variety of communication strategies and situations. They must be concerned with the degree of self-disclosure within the communication strategies and with how self-disclosure affects the outcome of these strategies. Furthermore, therapists could then relate the amount of self-disclosure in a given communication strategy to relational problems such as divorce. I will expound on this idea later in this paper.

Many discussions of self-disclosure, while conceptually rich, are not particularly useful to social scientists due to measurement difficulties. For example, Miller and Steinberg (1975) distinguish between genuine and apparent self-disclosure. Genuine self-disclosure occurs when someone provides information about the self which he or she considers personally private, with the disclosure of such information involving considerable risk. Apparent self-disclosure occurs when someone releases information which others might believe to be personally private. Obviously, apparent self-disclosure involves less risk than genuine self-disclosure. This conceptualization is particularly useful when applied to relational escalation. For example, a person might seek to escalate a relationship by releasing information that appears to be intimate. If the relational partner responds in a similar manner, the person could obtain important information which might improve predictive accuracy while actually releasing very little information and encountering very little risk.

However, using this conceptualization to study self-disclosure may precipitate problems. If genuine self-disclosure involves significant risks, researchers are not likely to observe it in a research setting; people in this setting may not be willing to release such information. If researchers focus on the release of such information as part of a communication strategy, they could increase their ability to measure it. People might be willing to indicate when they would include such information in a communication strategy, whereas they might hesitate to release such information directly.

This paper attempts to describe communication strategies within the context of communicative goals. In addition, these strategies are applied to communication relationships and relational change. The first section of the paper describes communication strategies, relationships, and relational change —focusing on definitions, types, and functions. The second section develops propositions which integrate the three variables.

COMMUNICATION STRATEGIES

Definition

Communication strategies refer to certain kinds of attempts by people to obtain relational rewards. The focus of this definition on the functional aspects of communication carries several important implications.

First, the definition implies a broad view of communication. Communication has often been restricted to a symbolic process between people. Such an approach excludes behavior that is not involved in verbal or written messages. By taking a broader view, researchers may be able to enrich their approaches to communication by including processes not normally examined. For example, people often use withdrawal techniques to affect their environment. Watzlawick et al. (1967) observe that some people communicate their attitudes or feelings by attempting not to communicate. Furthermore, some people often use physical aggression to affect others. Although a great deal of research has investigated the acquisition of violent behavior from the mass media, researchers have not thoroughly examined how physical aggression might be used as an alternative strategy to affect a person's environment.

Second, the definition does, however, limit communication to intentional behavior. The word "strategy" seems to imply that a person systematically develops some plan to obtain rewards. Indeed, the conceptualizations and research discussed here focus on the strategies that people intentionally use to affect others.

Third, the definition does not preclude undesirable or unsuccessful attempts to achieve relational rewards. An important area of communication research involves attention to those techniques which may be harmful to relationships, rather than dealing only with beneficial strategies.

Types

Several communication theorists have dealt with various types of communication strategies. This section will examine three of these typologies.

Patterns of Communicative Control. Miller and Steinberg (1975:92) discuss five patterns of communicative control:

> Each individual has a personal repertory of control messages, a personal way of transmitting these messages, and a personal way of reacting to the responses he or she gets from other communicators. We call the combination of these things the individual's pattern of communicative control (PCC).

The first PCC is the *dangling carrot* or reward technique. The goal is to change the rate and/or the direction of a person's behavior, and the primary procedure is to have the person associate a behavior with rewards or satisfaction. By associating certain behaviors with rewards, the communicator can establish a pattern which permits control of the person's behavior. Obviously, this control increases the communicator's chances of obtaining relational rewards from the person.

The second PCC is the *hanging sword* or punishing strategy. Miller and Steinberg assume that people use hanging sword techniques in three ways: presenting another with aversive stimuli, withdrawing a reward, or facilitating profit loss. Research indicates that the presentation of aversive stimuli produces sharper, more rapid effects than the other two techniques (D'Amato, 1969). The important point is that by creating or by threatening to create some undesirable state, the communicator can induce the other person to behave in a manner congruent with the communicator's intentions.

The third strategy is the *catalyst* technique, of which there are several types: the communicator may prompt the listener, implying that he knows the listener is going to act in a certain way and that now is the appropriate time; the communicator may supply the receiver with information which suggests that the compliant response is more desirable; or the communicator may appeal to a person's rationality or common sense. When using the catalyst strategy, the source does not directly ask the receiver to conform; instead, the source suggests that if the receiver behaves in a certain way, it will be in his or her best interest.

The fourth PCC is the *Siamese twin* strategy. For this strategy to work, two people must be involved in a relationship that entails a great deal of mutual dependence, and both persons must have relatively equal power. If these conditions exist, the participants can attain rewards due to the nature of the relationship. On a destructive level, one person may take advantage of the other due to the realization that relational dependence is high.

The final PCC is the *fairyland* strategy, which relies on self-induced feelings of control. Fairyland strategists tend to ignore undesirable responses, distort undesirable responses by giving them a positive interpretation, or overrate or deny responsibility for eliciting responses. In short, the fairyland strategy produces an illusion of control, rather than actual control.

Compliance-Gaining Techniques. A second typology of communication strategies results from an analysis of compliance-gaining techniques by Marwell and Schmitt (1967). Marwell and Schmitt were interested in developing clusters of persuasive techniques which people see themselves as using (p. 351):

> A strategy is here defined as a group of techniques towards which potential actors tend to respond similarly. Persons who see themselves as likely to perform one of the techniques from a cluster will tend to see themselves as likely to perform the others. Conversely, tendencies to use techniques within one cluster will not predict well responses to techniques in other clusters.

Marwell and Schmitt reviewed several theoretical perspectives to derive 16 compliance-gaining techniques. Table 1 presents the descriptions of these techniques. Marwell and Schmitt sought to develop a typology of compliance-gaining strategies from the 16 techniques. University students were asked how likely they would be to use each of the 16 techniques in four different situations. Their responses were summed across the situations for each of the techniques and then factor-analyzed. The analysis yielded five factors.

The first factor, labeled *rewarding activity,* consisted of pregiving, liking, and promise. The second factor represented a negative manipulation of the target's environment (e.g., threat and aversive stimulation); it was labeled *punishing activity.* The third factor, called *expertise,* consisted of positive and negative expertise. The fourth factor contained seven techniques: positive and negative self-feeling, positive and negative altercasting, positive and negative esteem, and moral appeal. Marwell and Schmitt argued that all seven represent a form of strategy that relies on activation of commitments. Due to the absence of personal commitment techniques (debt and altruism), they labeled this factor

TABLE 1
MARWELL AND SCHMITT'S COMPLIANCE-GAINING TECHNIQUES

Promise	"If you comply, I will reward you."
Threat	"If you do not comply, I will punish you."
Expertise (positive)	"If you comply, you will be rewarded because of 'the nature of things.' "
Expertise (negative)	"If you do not comply, you will be punished because of 'the nature of things.' "
Liking	The actor is friendly and helpful in order to get the target in a "good frame of mind" so that he will comply with the request.
Pregiving	The actor rewards the target before requesting compliance.
Aversive stimulation	The actor continuously punishes the target, making cessation contingent on compliance.
Debt	"You owe me compliance because of past favors."
Moral appeal	"You are immoral if you do not comply."
Self-feeling (positive)	"You will feel better about yourself if you comply."
Self-feeling (negative)	"You will feel worse about yourself if you do not comply."
Altercasting (positive)	"A person with 'good' qualities would comply."
Altercasting (negative)	"Only a person with 'bad' qualities would not comply."
Altruism	"I need your compliance very badly, so do it for me."
Esteem (positive)	"People you value will think better of you if you comply."
Esteem (negative)	"People you value will think worse of you if you do not comply."

activation of impersonal commitments. The final factor, *activation of personal commitments,* consisted of four items: altruism, negative esteem, debt, and negative altercasting.

When Marwell and Schmitt correlated these oblique factors, they found two second-order factors. The first consisted of rewarding activity, expertise, and activation of impersonal commitments; the second consisted of punishing activity and activation of personal commitments. They argue that the second-order factors occurred largely on the basis of their social acceptability: the first second-order factor was labeled *socially acceptable techniques* and the second *socially unacceptable techniques.*

Modes of Conflict Resolution. The final typology of communication strategies to be examined (Roloff, 1975) resulted from a study of how people attempt to resolve conflict. *Modes of conflict resolution* were defined as the attempt by one or more people in a relationship to achieve some solution to their perceptions of contradictory attitudes or behavior. A scale was developed consisting of 44 possible ways to resolve a conflict. Roloff asked high school students how likely they would be to use each of the 44 means of conflict resolution if something important were taken from them. The students were asked how likely their favorite television character would be to use each of the 44 strategies in a similar situation. The responses were cluster-analyzed, with five clusters or modes of conflict resolution obtained for the television characters and four for the students. Two of the TV character clusters were combined into one cluster for the students, and the rest of the clusters remained the same. The five clusters were *revenge, regression, verbal aggression, prosocial,* and *physical aggression.* Table 2 presents the items that made up each of the clusters.

The revenge cluster consisted of items involving deception; there was no honest confrontation between individuals in conflict. Regression contained items similar to the behavior of children. Verbal aggression consisted of attacks upon the self-concept of the other person. The prosocial mode of conflict resolution represented the ways in which people can resolve conflict through open and rational discussion; it included forgiveness, honesty, and understanding. Finally, physical aggression represented violent behavior directed at the other person.

Roloff then categorized these modes of conflict resolution on the basis of their effect on social relationships. Mead (1934) distinguished between social and antisocial behavior. Social behaviors are the building blocks of relationships, and eventually, society; whereas antisocial behavior is destructive to the formation of relationships and societies.

Roloff drew a similar distinction between pro- and antisocial modes of conflict resolution. Prosocial modes of conflict resolution are likely to facilitate relational growth and development. Only one mode of conflict resolution, the prosocial mode, would allow two people to discuss their problems and positions without seeking to intimidate each other in any way. Instead of damaging the

TABLE 2
ROLOFF'S MODES OF CONFLICT RESOLUTION AND THEIR ITEMS

Revenge	
Hate the person	
Destroy something that the person has	
Cheat the person	
Get drunk	
Take a pill	
Take something from the person	
Turn others against the person	
Chase the person away	
Lie to the person	
Give the person something for returning the object	
Ignore the missing object	
Joke about it	
Regression	*Physical Aggression*
Ask someone what to do	Shoot the person
Cry	Hit the person
Plead with the person	Stab the person
Pray for return of the object	Kick the person
Worry	Punish the person
Pout	Shove the person
Feel guilty that someone took something from you	
Not know what to do	
Run away	
Verbal Aggression	*Prosocial*
Argue with the person	Help the person reform
Trick the person	Feel sorry for the person
Shout at the person	Forgive the person
Insult the person	Talk to the person
Take the object back	Be honest with the person
Threaten the person	Think about what to do
Tell someone about it	Try to persuade the person
Make the person feel guilty	Let the person alone
Ask others' help	

relationship, such a discussion should help the people to understand each other and allow the relationship to grow.

Antisocial modes of conflict resolution are likely to impede relational growth or development. The least antisocial of the modes of conflict resolution is regression, which seems to be a withdrawal tactic; it does not rely on intimidation but represents an attempt to resolve the conflict through internalization or consolation from others. The shortcoming of such a technique is that it results in little contact between the people in the relationship; their communications are largely unrevealing.

The revenge mode is also antisocial. It is designed to get even through deceit, and deception is likely to be detrimental to relational growth. Verbal aggression is antisocial because the person's self-concept is attacked. The physical aggression mode seeks to force the person to give in, rather than elicit information about the other person or release information about the self. Certainly, some relationships are formed through violent initiation ceremonies, but, within conflict situations, physical aggression takes on an antisocial characteristic.

Pro- and Antisocial Communication Strategies. The distinction between pro- and antisocial communication strategies is an important one which appears to run through other typologies of communication strategies as well. Miller and Steinberg (1975) state that some forms of PCCs can be used for the construction of relationships while others can be employed for relational destruction. Marwell and Schmitt (1967) indicate that their compliance-gaining dimensions can be viewed as socially acceptable or socially unacceptable.

The distinction between pro- and antisocial communication strategies might be generalized even further. Prosocial communication strategies reflect people's attempts to obtain relational rewards by techniques that facilitate understanding of their attitudes and needs. As with the distinction made about modes of conflict resolution, these strategies would be expected to facilitate relational growth and development.

On the other hand, antisocial communication strategies represent people's attempts to obtain relational rewards by imposing their position on another through force or deception. Communicators who use antisocial strategies are concerned with obtaining relational rewards, but they are not concerned with providing any information about themselves. Such use of force or deception might be expected to impede relational growth or development.

Function

The function of communication strategies is to obtain relational rewards. This paper argues that communication strategies are designed to realize specific kinds of rewards, i.e., those obtained in a relationship; people design their communication strategies for someone they know in a relationship. Within this paper, mass media communication strategies will not be discussed, since mass media communication is not often aimed at a particular person.

Relational rewards are of two types: short-term and long-term. *Short-term* rewards are those that are relatively minor in their effect on the relationship. These kinds of rewards are sought each day; they represent the vast majority of rewards sought in relationships. A person may seek free time at work or at home. Loss of these rewards can be troublesome, but rarely catastrophic. *Long-term* rewards are those that are essential for people to continue their relationships. If these rewards are not available, the relationship will likely fail.

For example, love or companionship may be thought of as long-term rewards. They may take considerable time to develop, and they benefit both partners in the relationship. In addition, it can also be argued that some minimal level of short-term rewards must be obtained in order to continue the relationship. For example, a person may be able to withstand the loss of a short-term reward on a given day, but if the person never gets the reward, the relationship may not continue.

RELATIONSHIPS

Second of the three variables to be discussed is relationships. The focus will be on communication as a distinguishing factor in defining and typing relationships.

Definition

A *relationship,* regardless of type, represents mutual agreement, implicit or explicit, between people to interact in order to maximize rewards. This definition suggests several important implications.

First, a relationship involves some degree of mutual agreement. This implication relates to the transactional notion that Miller and Steinberg (1975) discuss. Relationships go beyond the involved individuals to represent a combination of both persons; thus, the rules governing the relationship are, to some degree, mutually agreed upon.

Second, a relationship is functional. Relationships are formed to serve some function–in this case, to realize rewards from the environment. The approach taken in this paper does not argue that all relationships provide rewards, but it does contend that people form their relationships in order to *attempt* to gain some reward from their environment. For example, some people may have relationships that are not totally rewarding even though the original formation of the relationship was prompted by the need to obtain rewards.

Third, relationships involve either implicit or explicit agreement or knowledge that the relationship exists. This simply means that people know with whom they have relationships even though they may not have formally acknowledged relational formation. This fact suggests that relationships can be categorized in terms of their formality. Even though people are aware of a relationship, they need not necessarily agree on the nature of the relationship. Indeed, in some relationships implicitly agreed upon, the nature may never be specified, causing misperceptions and conflict.

Finally, this definition leaves open the types of relationships that are possible. Since relationships involve communication between people, a typology can be developed from the communication patterns that are manifested. Indeed, it can be argued that the types of communication patterns in the relationships will affect the ability of persons to attain rewards.

Types

Miller and Steinberg (1975) argue that relationships can be categorized according to the type of information which the relational partners use to predict the outcomes of their communication to each other. These authors posit three types of information. Cultural information consists of data about a person derived from the culture to which he or she belongs. Obviously, these data are the most general and superficial. Sociological information is data derived from the groups to which a person belongs. While not as general as cultural data, sociological information is still very broad and superficial. Both cultural and sociological information are categorized as *noninterpersonal information.* By contrast, the third type of information is psychological data, which represents data about a person that allows another to discriminate the person's uniqueness: psychological information is *interpersonal.*

These information types combine to form three kinds of relationships: noninterpersonal, interpersonal, and mixed level. Noninterpersonal relationships are those in which two people base most of their communicative predictions on cultural or sociological information. Miller and Steinberg argue that noninterpersonal relationships occur most frequently in everyday life. While most noninterpersonal relationships are typified as stranger or business acquaintances, some marriages may be noninterpersonal relationships, if the spouses base their predictions about each other on noninterpersonal data. Furthermore, Miller and Steinberg hold that noninterpersonal relationships require less energy to maintain than interpersonal relationships, since little effort is required in gaining information about the other person. Thus, noninterpersonal relationships are common, rely on generalizations, and are useful.

Interpersonal relationships are those in which people base most of their communicative predictions on psychological data. These relationships are usually emotionally intense and highly valued. They are likely to have been developed over a long period of time and are rather rare.

Mixed-level relationships are those in which one partner makes most communicative predictions at the psychological level while the other partner makes most communicative predictions at the sociological or cultural level. Such relationships are highly conducive to conflict. Usually, the person who is able to discriminate the other's needs will be better able to meet those needs (or to thwart their fulfillment, for that matter). The person who relies on generalizing data may be unable to reciprocate the same degree of rewards. Furthermore, the person who relies on psychological data is in a position to exert considerable over the other since he or she can more accurately predict the person's ıor. The person who relies on sociological or cultural information may not ıle to counter such manipulation.

Iiller and Steinberg's typology fits well into the present definition of relationship. It focuses on the interaction of two people and relates the different types of relationships to success in obtaining relational rewards.

Function

The function of human relationships is to maximize rewards through environmental control. Exchange theorists have long argued that relationships are designed to gain rewards from the environment. Thibaut and Kelley (1959) contend that the evaluation of a relationship hinges upon the degree of success that it provides in gaining rewards. They hold that three variables affect the evaluation: outcomes, comparison level, and comparison level for alternatives. *Outcomes* represent the rewards attained within the relationship; the *comparison level* represents the standard for evaluating the relationship; and the *comparison level for alternatives* represents the potential rewards to be gained from entering into a new relationship. The combination of these three variables predicts the stability and satisfaction of the relationship.

RELATIONAL CHANGE

As current marriage and divorce rates testify, people are frequently changing formal relationships in extreme ways; however, relationships also change less drastically. This section describes the theoretical perspectives dealing with the third variable of relational change.

Definition

Relational change suggests the ability of one or more persons involved in a relationship to make predictions about another person on the basis of discriminating (intimate) or generalizing (superficial) information changes. This definition has several implications.

First, relationships change because of the need to increase or decrease the likelihood of attaining a reward. It is assumed that some decision or condition occurs that affects the decision to change the relationship. For example, Miller and Steinberg (1975) suggest that relationships are likely to escalate when a person has few interpersonal relationships or when increased relational rewards are likely to be attained through escalation.

Second, this definition of relational change assumes that a decision or condition to change can be made by one or both persons in the relationship. In other words, one or both partners in the relationship can attempt to change the nature of the relationship through communication.

Third, changes in the relationship are caused by changes in the content of communications between relational partners. People can escalate their relationship by providing information about themselves or seeking more information about the other. This increased information allows one person to make predictions that recognize the uniqueness of the other person and thereby change the nature of the relationship.

Finally, the definition assumes that change can move in any direction: relationships can escalate (i.e., move from generalization to discrimination); they can deescalate; or they can be terminated.

Types

Altman and Taylor (1973:6-7) argue that relational change is a process involving social penetration, the gathering of personal or intimate information. Social penetration involves four hypotheses:

> Specifically, it is hypothesized that interpersonal exchange gradually progresses from superficial, nonintimate areas to more intimate, deeper layers of the selves of the social actors. That is, people are generally believed to let others know them gradually, first revealing less intimate information and only later making more personal aspects of their lives accessible. Our second hypothesis is that people assess interpersonal rewards and costs, satisfaction and dissatisfaction, gained from interaction with others, and that the advancement of the relationship is heavily dependent on the amount and nature of the rewards and costs. According to the theory, people assess the reward/cost balance of an ongoing or immediately preceding interaction and also forecast or predict implications of future interactions at the same and at deeper levels of exchange. . . .
>
> The theoretical framework also considers how the social penetration process is affected by the personal characteristics of people; for example, those with predispositions to reveal themselves would show a different history of social penetration than those more reluctant to enter into relationships with others. . . .
>
> Another facet of the theory concerns the deterioration of interpersonal relationships. Our position is that development (or penetration) and dissolution (or depenetration) follow the same principles with regard to orderliness of progress and the movement from superficial to intimate areas of discourse. A relationship undergoing a process of deterioration should move from more to less intimate and from greater to lesser amounts of interaction—contrary to the forward penetration process.

Obviously, communication plays an important role in the social penetration process. People communicate information about themselves so that relationships progress or deteriorate, depending on the kind of information communicated.

Berger and Calabrese (1975:100) theorize along similar lines, arguing that human relationships develop in three phases—the entry phase, the personal phase, and the exit phase:

> Findings . . . indicate that during the entry phase, communication content is somewhat structured. For example, message content tends to be focused on demographic kinds of information. The amount of information asked for and given by the interactants tends to be symmetric. During the latter phases of the entry stage, persons begin to explore each other's attitudes and opinions. The kinds of attitude issues explored are of rather low consequence or low involvement. By the end of entry phase, the interactants have a fairly confident estimate of whether or not they will develop their relationship toward a more intimate level.
>
> The second phase of the communication transaction we have labeled the personal phase. This phase begins when the interactants engage in communication about central attitudinal issues, personal problems and basic values. . . . During this phase, persons may talk about socially undesirable aspects of their personalities and social relations. In the entry phase, such information is not usually sought or given.
>
> The final phase of the transaction we have called the exit phase. During this phase decisions are made concerning the desirability of future interaction. Frequently, these decisions are discussed and plans for future interaction made.

In their perspective, Berger and Calabrese assume that a change in the relationship is commensurate with a change in communication content; specifically, the information described becomes less formal and more intimate. Moreover, they assume that some stage is reached at which the relationship is evaluated. While they do not specifically consider an end to the relationship, it is possible that it could terminate as a result of evaluation.

As described earlier, Miller and Steinberg (1975) discuss three relationships: noninterpersonal, interpersonal, and mixed level. They indicate that one important function of noninterpersonal relationships is to serve as a springboard to interpersonal relationships. While they do not discuss stages, Miller and Steinberg do argue that certain conditions affect escalation: the social context of the time, the decision to make the change, and the probability of increasing profits. Communication plays a central role in the process (p. 225):

> The premise we want to advance is this: an important basis of interpersonal relationships is not that people share similar internal states, but that they can communicate with each other—people tend to develop relationships with people with whom they can communicate.

After reviewing several experiments and their effect on relational development, Duck (1973:141) concludes:

> However, it is clear from the experiments and the hypothesis which has come from them that the observed progression up the hierarchy (in whatever form it is conceptualized) during the construal of others involves the broad process of progression from viewing them in terms of "stereotypes" to a greater individuation and differentiation of them.

Function

Relational change functions to facilitate or to impede the ability to obtain relational rewards. All four perspectives discussed above endorse this functional view. If people perceive that a relationship will be rewarding, they will try to escalate it; if the relationship is likely to be unrewarding or is unrewarding, they will allow it to deescalate (assuming an available alternative).

The next section of this paper interrelates the three variables of communication strategies, relationships, and relational change. Six propositions develop the link between the three variables. The propositions deal with the following six areas: type of communication, type of relationship, variety of communication strategies, speed of relational change, power, and satisfaction.

PROPOSITIONS

Proposition 1

> *TYPE OF COMMUNICATION. Prosocial communication strategies are more common in interpersonal relationships than antisocial communication strategies; antisocial communication strategies are more common in noninterpersonal relationships than prosocial communication strategies.*

This proposition is derived from the notion that prosocial communication strategies involve release of information about the self within the context of some goal. Because this information is released, one might expect that it would be used to maintain interpersonal relationships, using Miller and Steinberg's terminology. Antisocial communication strategies involve deception and force (physical or verbal); these strategies are likely to be counterproductive for maintaining or developing interpersonal relationships. Antisocial strategies can be effective in noninterpersonal relationships; for in these relationships, it is not usually a primary concern that participants understand each other's psyches in order to maintain the relationship. Indeed, prosocial communication strategies require greater energy and risk since the persons must provide psychological or intimate information about themselves. Consequently, because they demand less effort, antisocial communication strategies are more likely to be used in noninterpersonal relationships than prosocial communication strategies.

There is some empirical support for this proposition. When investigating modes of conflict resolution, Roloff (1975) asked adolescents how likely they would be to use certain modes of conflict resolution with a stranger (noninterpersonal relationship) and with a friend (interpersonal relationship). For strangers, the most likely modes of conflict resolution to be used were antisocial. Indeed, verbal aggression was significantly ($p < .001$) more likely to be used than all other modes of conflict resolution. However, the prosocial mode of conflict resolution was the second most likely mode to be used. It was significantly ($p < .001$) more likely to be used than the remaining antisocial modes of conflict resolution (order of frequency of use: regression, revenge, and physical aggression).

In conflicts with friends, the prosocial mode was significantly ($p < .001$) more likely to be used than all the antisocial modes of conflict resolution. Verbal aggression was the second most likely mode of conflict resolution to be used.

Thus, some support was found for Proposition 1. Prosocial communication strategies are more likely to be used with a friend than antisocial communication strategies. Furthermore, at least one of the antisocial modes of conflict resolution was more likely to be used with a stranger than the prosocial mode. It is important to note that the prosocial mode was very likely to be used in both types of relationships.

Miller et al. (forthcoming) investigated the use of the compliance-gaining strategies discussed by Marwell and Schmitt (1967) in both interpersonal and noninterpersonal relationships. Two forms of interpersonal and noninterpersonal situations were used: those with short-term relational consequences and those with long-term relational consequences. Subjects were asked to indicate how likely they would be to use each of the 16 strategies to gain compliance in the four relationships.

Reward-oriented strategies and activation of commitment strategies with positive connotations were very likely to be used in both interpersonal situations; the high use of threat in long-term interpersonal relationships was the only exception. In interpersonal situations, punishing activities such as aversive stimulation were unlikely to be used, along with activation of commitments strategies which have a negative connotation. Thus, the findings of Miller et al. lend additional support for Proposition 1.

Proposition 2

> *TYPE OF RELATIONSHIP. Prosocial communication strategies are more common in interpersonal relationships than in noninterpersonal relationships; antisocial communication strategies are more common in noninterpersonal relationships than in interpersonal relationships.*

This proposition is derived from the notion that people are more likely to expend energy and to take the risks involved in self-disclosure through prosocial communication strategies when dealing with interpersonal relationships than when dealing with noninterpersonal relationships. Antisocial communication strategies are more likely to be used in noninterpersonal relationships, since they restrict information about the self and hence require less energy expenditure and risk. Even though such behaviors may threaten a relationship, the persons may employ antisocial strategies because the relationship is not unique. Thus, antisocial forms of communication represent an efficient and safe way to obtain rewards in noninterpersonal relationships.

Roloff's (1975) investigation of the use of modes of conflict resolution provides some empirical support for this proposition. Four of the five modes of conflict resolution strategies showed significant ($p < .0001$) differences of use for conflicts with strangers as opposed to friends. Verbal aggression, physical aggression, and revenge (all antisocial strategies) were significantly more likely to be used to resolve a conflict with a stranger than with a friend, while the prosocial mode was significantly more likely to be used to resolve a conflict with a friend than with a stranger. Regression showed no significant difference between conflicts.

Proposition 3

> *VARIETY OF COMMUNICATION STRATEGIES. As a relationship escalates from noninterpersonal (generalization) to interpersonal (discrimination), the variety of communication strategies will decrease; as a relationship deescalates from interpersonal (discrimination) to noninterpersonal (generalization), the variety of communication strategies will increase.*

The four perspectives discussed earlier concur that, initially, relational partners have little intimate or psychological data on which to base predictions. If, as hypothesized here, people rely on antisocial communication strategies in noninterpersonal relationships, it is understandable that little information about the self will be discerned. Consequently, the communication strategies formed by the predictions are more likely to be inaccurate. Various strategies will probably be employed until successful ones can be discovered. Furthermore, a person may experiment with certain communication strategies to gather information about the other person to reach a decision about whether to continue the relationship (see Chapter 7 in this volume by Berger et al.). Therefore, at the early stages of a relationship, a wide variety of strategies will probably be used. As successful ones are discovered, or if the relationship appears to be a rewarding one, the variety of strategies will decrease.

As indicated earlier, relationships are also likely to deescalate; people lose track of their partner's progress as a person or simply lose interest in the relationship. Assuming that one of the participants wants to rejuvenate a relationship, he or she would probably attempt to reattain the interpersonal level. This attempt would require an increase in the variety of communication strategies in order to find the right pattern to escalate the continuation of the relationship.

Some empirical support is available for this proposition. Miller et al. (forthcoming) found that, when compared with interpersonal relationships, noninterpersonal relationships may be characterized as containing more strategies that have a higher likelihood of use:

> It is plausible to conclude that in the noninterpersonal situations persons are somewhat more uncertain as to what type of strategy to employ and, hence, tend to rate more strategies as highly likely to be used. This interpretation follows closely from Miller and Steinberg's argument that interpersonal relationships, which are based upon psychological data, facilitate one's ability to predict the other's behavior. This ability to predict, in turn, produces the ability to control by choosing an appropriate persuasion strategy to produce the desired behavioral effect. But in noninterpersonal situations such data on others are lacking, and prediction and, hence, control becomes a somewhat more tenuous process. In response to their uncertainty, persons may grab at any strategic straw which promises to produce some measure of control over an uncertain environment.

Proposition 4

SPEED OF RELATIONAL DEVELOPMENT.

A. *Prosocial communication strategies promote rapid relational escalation from noninterpersonal (generalizing) to interpersonal (discriminating) relationships; antisocial communication strategies impede relational escalation from noninterpersonal (generalizing) to interpersonal (discriminating) relationships.*

B. *Antisocial communication strategies promote rapid relational deescalation from interpersonal (discriminating) to noninterpersonal (generalizing) relationships; prosocial communication strategies impede relational deescalation from interpersonal (discriminating) to noninterpersonal (generalizing) relationships.*

These propositions argue that people can use communication strategies to influence the rate of relational change. By increasing the use of prosocial communication strategies, the rate of relational escalation can be accelerated through an increase in the amount of self-disclosure. Operating from a reciprocity principle, it can be argued that prosocial strategies from one person are likely to produce prosocial strategies from another. In other words, two people engaged in conflict may both seek to resolve the conflict with a prosocial strategy. When using prosocial communication strategies, they release information about each other; this leads to a rapid increase in the ability of the relational partners to make discriminating or psychological predictions. Since disclosing information through prosocial communication strategies will probably stimulate reciprocal behavior, the two people should move rapidly toward the interpersonal level.

Similarly, the use of prosocial communication strategies is likely to impede deescalation. People who are attentive to such strategies are likely to be successful in keeping relationships at the interpersonal level. By providing a constant flow of information about the changes that one is experiencing, the chances are reduced that he or she will be stereotyped by past behavior. Relationships can remain at the interpersonal level by partners recognizing the changes that each is going through.

Antisocial communication strategies will probably retard the process of escalation. Since these strategies release little psychological data, the ability to reach the interpersonal level is impeded. Indeed, people may use antisocial strategies to retard relationships which they feel are progressing too rapidly.

Furthermore, antisocial communication strategies are quite likely to be employed to produce rapid relational deescalation. By employing force, deception, or withdrawal techniques, the relationship can begin to deteriorate. Again, these techniques restrict the availability of psychological information or even information about one's reasons for behaving in a given manner. Such a restriction of information is likely to dampen a person's desire to continue the relationship.

It should be noted that no data are available to support these propositions. Certainly this suggests an area for future research.

Proposition 5

POWER. Powerful communicators maximize short-term rewards through appropriate styles in relationships; powerful communicators maximize long-term rewards by controlling the rate of relational escalation.

Power means that one person in a relationship may attempt to maximize rewards regardless of the effect on the other person. Such manipulation paradigms have been discussed by Berne (1964) and Shostrom (1967). From this power-oriented point of view, the individual-oriented communicator can maximize short-term rewards through either prosocial or antisocial strategies. This paper takes the position that either can be effective, but that antisocial strategies are likely to be more effective.

For example, a person can attempt to discuss some conflict or issue openly (prosocial), but he or she may lose. When discussing an issue openly, people take the risk of presenting a weak argument or displaying some other weakness, and during the discussion it may be recognized that they are wrong and they may lose. However, if they use antisocial communication strategies, they can force the issue or deceive the other person. In this case little information about oneself or one's position is released. Thus, the focus on the validity of the position is obscured, and skill as a manipulator becomes the determinant of the success or failure. Furthermore, if the longevity of the relationship is of no concern, antisocial methods are particularly useful.

In order for individual-oriented communicators to maximize long-term rewards, they must utilize communication strategies selectively to control the rate of relational escalation. For example, they might self-disclose some information in a compliance-gaining or conflict situation to give the appearance of wanting to escalate the relationship. While this communication might actually self-disclose the communicator's position, it may be more likely to describe what he or she perceives that the receiver wants to hear.

Recall the Miller and Steinberg (1975) distinction between genuine and apparent self-disclosure. Apparent self-disclosure is prosocial because it provides information about the self, but it is also slightly deceptive because it gives the appearance that it is intimate or psychological information. Communicators could use apparent self-disclosure to produce a rapid escalation in a relationship. If the relationship develops too rapidly, they could slow it down by using an antisocial strategy to exert control over their partners.

Proposition 6

> *SATISFACTION. From a transactional point of view, relational satisfaction is maximized when mutual short-term rewards are maximized through prosocial communication strategies; mutual long-term rewards are maximized through mutual control over the rate of relational change.*

This proposition argues that relationships will be mutually satisfying when both partners use prosocial communication strategies. By relying on prosocial strategies, they can achieve short-term rewards while not threatening the relationship. People can openly display their needs for rewards and negotiate for them. Obviously, this does not mean that prosocial strategies will always achieve short-term rewards. The achievement of the reward will depend on the person's arguments and the negotiation with the other person, rather than on force or deception.

Furthermore, people will be able mutually to control the rate of relational change by employing prosocial strategies. Both relational partners can become aware of each other's position and reach mutual decisions about their desire to change the relationship. Instead of unilateral decisions that are likely to be deceiving, the two people share in decision making about the relationship. Their awareness and understanding of each other's position makes their decision about relational change more open and accurate. While they may decide to deescalate the relationship, the decision is bilateral. Thus, it is likely to be less destructive to both persons than a unilateral decision to continue the relationship or a decision by one person to end the relationship.

Several cautions are necessary. Such behavior could lead to manipulated, one-sided relationships. A relational partner could withhold information to reduce the other partner's predictive power, resulting in a mixed level relationship, in Miller and Steinberg's terminology.

The use of prosocial strategies does not ensure a successful relationship. It is entirely possible that two people may learn enough about each other to realize that they are totally incompatible. Prosocial communication strategies cannot guarantee that people will like each other; all they can ensure is that people will have reliable information about what relationships they want to maintain. Prosocial communication strategies can identify the causes of conflict, but they cannot ensure that people will want to expend the energy to resolve the conflict. It may be easier to let the relationship end.

CONCLUSIONS

This paper has attempted to formulate a perspective that relates specific communication strategies to relationships and relational change. Several of the implications of this formulation are important.

If the effect of communication strategies on relationships and relational change can be predicted, the potential usefulness of this perspective to therapists, for example, is great. Relational problems can be observed not only in terms of their causes, such as money, but also in terms of the difficulties arising from how people attempt to resolve these problems. Eventually, it may be possible to predict which of the various compliance-gaining strategies or modes of conflict resolution are most likely to resolve specific problems and not endanger the relationship or its development.

For communication scientists, the questions raised by the paradigm are exciting. Researchers can begin to examine the role of communication strategies in various stages of relational change. It can be predicted that certain strategies are more likely to be used in early or noninterpersonal stages of a relationship. Furthermore, it is possible to observe the strategies at work in relational dissolution, such as divorce. The impact of some of these strategies on the children of divorced parents could be great; for example, modeling such strategies could create serious harm for children and their relationships.

Furthermore, subcultural differences may affect strategy selection. Certain low-income groups, or perhaps particular ethnic groups, may deviate significantly from the predictions generated herein. The generalization of these predictions represents an important future research area.

The use of communication strategies may also vary with personality types. For example, Christie and Geis (1970) suggest that persons high in Machiavellianism may rely on antisocial strategies; this would affect their ability to form and maintain relationships.

Finally, the model might later be expanded to deal with the variable of attraction. At this point, the model assumes that the relationship has begun. Perhaps observation of certain communication strategies, or certain physical characteristics, may prompt a decision to create a relationship. As the communication strategies continue to release information about a person, a decision can be made to continue or discontinue the relationship.

REFERENCES

ALTMAN, I., and TAYLOR, D.A. (1973). Social penetration: The development of interpersonal relationships. New York: Holt, Rinehart and Winston.

BERGER, C.R., and CALABRESE, R.J. (1975). "Some explorations in initial interaction and beyond: Toward a developmental theory of interpersonal communication." Human Communication Research, 1:99-112.

BERNE, E. (1964). Games people play. New York: Grove Press.

CHRISTIE, R., and GEIS, F.L. (1970). Studies in Machiavellianism. New York: Academic Press.

D'AMATO, M.R. (1969). "Instrumental conditioning." In M. Marx (ed.), Learning: Processes. London: Macmillan.

DUCK, S.W. (1973). Personal Relationships and personal constructs: A study of friendship formation. New York: John Wiley.

MARWELL, G., and SCHMITT, D.R. (1967). "Dimensions of compliance-gaining behavior: An empirical analysis." Sociometry, 30:350-364.

MEAD, G.H. (1934). Mind, self and society. Chicago: University of Chicago Press.

MILLER, G.R., BOSTER, F., ROLOFF, M.E., and SEIBOLD, D. (forthcoming). "Compliance-gaining message strategies: A typology and some findings concerning effects of situational differences."

MILLER, G.R., and STEINBERG, M. (1975). Between people: A new analysis of interpersonal communication. Palo Alto, Calif.: Science Research Associates.

ROLOFF, M.E. (1975). "Mediated and unmediated social influences on modes of conflict resolution." Unpublished Ph.D. dissertation, Michigan State University.

SHOSTROM, E.L. (1967). Man the manipulator: The inner journey from manipulation to actualization. Nashville: Abingdon.

SIMMEL, G. (1950). The sociology of Georg Simmel (K.H. Wolff, trans.). New York: Free Press.

THIBAUT, J.W., and KELLEY, H.H. (1959). The social psychology of groups. New York: John Wiley.

WATZLAWICK, P., BEAVIN, J., and JACKSON, D. (1967). Pragmatics of human communication. New York: Norton.

Chapter 9

EMPIRICAL AND THEORETICAL EXTENSIONS OF SELF-DISCLOSURE

Shirley J. Gilbert

I am convinced that the crucial factor in what happens both inside people and between people is the picture of individual worth that each person carries around with him.

V. Satir (1972:21)

In every sort of interpersonal relationship, from business partnerships to love affairs, the exchange of self disclosure plays an important role.

Z. Rubin (1973:168)

WITHIN THE AREA of interpersonal communication, research interests have come to focus on individual and situational variables which influence the exchange of information and impressions between people. The impression that an individual forms from observing the appearance and behavior of another is influenced and affected by numerous variables. Among these determinants are the attributes that characterize the other person as a stimulus object, the relationship between perceived and perceiver, and the nature of the communication content, as well as the cognitions, motives, beliefs, personality, and other psychological states of the perceiver and the perceived, including self-conception. Self-conception refers to "the person's subjective cognitions and evaluations of himself" (Gordon and Gergen, 1968:3). The evaluative way in which one perceives oneself is believed to be related to the manner in which one presents oneself (Rogers, 1961). The verbal aspects of self-presentation refer to the process of self-disclosure. Self-disclosure, a special instance of communication, is a primary concern of interpersonal systems and is a tool in helping to determine the direction of interpersonal relationships.

SELF-DISCLOSURE: WHAT IT IS AND IS NOT

Self-disclosure, for too long, has been used to designate nearly anything that anyone says about oneself to anybody. Culbert's distinction between self-disclosure and self-description is useful in this regard (1967:2):

> Self disclosure refers to an individual's explicitly communicating to one or more persons information that he believes these others would be unlikely to acquire unless he himself discloses it. . . . Self description designates self-data that an individual is likely to feel comfortable in revealing to most others.

Similarly, Miller and Steinberg (1975) have conceptualized disclosure as being either "genuine" or "apparent." Genuine disclosure is construed as a personally private act as evidenced by one's reluctance or embarrassment to share it with most other persons, and it is revealed when it "creates or strengthens a bond of trust between the transactants" (p. 324). Unlike apparent disclosure, it is usually communicated as a means of personal or relational growth, not as a message strategy to be utilized for exploitative purposes. Apparent disclosure is the process of sharing information which is not really perceived as private; in the process, most undesirable consequences are nonexistent. Unlike genuine disclosure, it is not characterized by much risk, nor is it likely to be perceived as a social reward within the framework of interpersonal trust or attraction for the recipient.

While self-disclosure may arise out of varying motivational frameworks, "relational escalation"–the process of establishing interpersonal relationships, some of which may be characterized as "intimate"–is the primary function of genuine self-disclosure and is the concern of this chapter.

Sidney Jourard (1959), a pioneer in the arena of self-disclosure, has advanced the thesis that self-disclosure is an important and often overlooked aspect of interpersonal communication. He conceives of it as a healthy act which, when enacted discriminately, can produce and increase attraction between persons, thus forming the foundation for establishing close, interpersonal relationships.

A recurrent theme in self-disclosure is the importance of interpersonal attraction. That is, disclosers do not randomly reveal themselves indiscriminately (not if they are playing with a full deck, that is). Rather, if relational escalation is desired, one's choice of recipients is likely to be based on attraction of one form or another. Reported research on self-disclosure indicates that it is an act which often follows an attitude of trust, affection, and attraction. It is a gift. "The self's disclosure in language means that it is a giving–and perhaps the fundamental gift and giving as a human activity is words" (Tiryakian, 1968:81). The person who communicates genuine disclosure is likely indicating that he or she likes and trusts the disclosure recipient, thereby implying that he or she might value the establishment of a relationship with the recipient.

Disclosure may serve not only to communicate information and to establish trust but to create commitment in a relationship; that is, intimacy, a special instance of self-disclosure, is one possible outcome.

> Humans are relational beings and speech communication enables relating. . . . Emotional intimacy is the potential bonding force that occurs between human beings. . . . The communication of and experience of intimacy is one of the primary/potential outcomes of human communication that links people with people. [Sutton, 1975:2-3]

DISCLOSURE: REWARDS AND RISKS

> When we reveal to another person something of our true self, we must be prepared for the possibility that he will examine what we have revealed and find it wanting. [Rubin, 1973:160]

The thesis has been advanced that accurate portrayal of the self to others is a condition for achieving self and relational understanding and that, in fact, the two are intertwined: "no man can come to know himself except as an outcome of disclosing himself to another person" (Jourard, 1971b:6).

> Openness to relatedness with other persons and the search for self-identity are not two problems but one dialectical process; as one finds more relatedness with other persons one discovers more of oneself; as the sense of one's own identity becomes clearer and more firmly rooted, one can more completely go out to others. It is not a loss of oneself, an "impoverishment," but a way of finding more of oneself when one means most to others whom one has chosen. [Lynd, 1968:226]

In addition to the rewards of self and relational understanding, Jourard has asserted that self-disclosure is a symptom of healthy personality, as is having a positive self-conception. He further contends that one's mental health is dependent upon the directness and intimacy of one's communications:

> Every maladjusted person is a person who has not made himself known to another human being and in consequence does not know himself. Nor can he be himself. More than that, he struggles to avoid becoming known by another human being. . . . One's self grows from the consequence of being. . . . Alienation from one's real self not only arrests personal growth, *it tends to make a farce of one's relationships with people.* [Jourard, 1971b:32-33; emphasis added]

Risk is inherent in Jourard's argument for advancing the rewards of self-disclosure which may make disclosure choices more difficult, particularly for those of low self-opinion. "I believe that other people come to be stressors to an individual in direct proportion to his degree of self-alienation" (Jourard,

1968:426). That is, if one accepts the premise that self and relational understanding are greatly influenced by one's disclosure, mental health notwithstanding, a dilemma is imminent for those with considerable reluctance to being "known." Seemingly, it requires the *courage to be:* "There is probably no experience more horrifying and terrifying than that of self disclosure to 'significant others' whose probable reactions are assumed, but not known" (Jourard, 1968:425).

> The reason two people are reluctant to . . . [disclose] . . . is because in doing so they make themselves vulnerable and give enormous power over themselves to the other. How awful, how deadly, how catastrophically they can hurt each other, wreck and ruin each other forever! How often, indeed, they end by inflicting pain and torment upon each other. Better to maintain shallow, superficial affairs; that way the scars are not too deep. . . . Getting to know someone, entering that new world, is an ultimate, irretrievable leap into the unknown. The prospect is terrifying. The stakes are high. The emotions are overwhelming. [Cleaver, 1968:139]

And so, "if I tell you who I am, you may not like who I am and it is all that I have" (Powell, 1969:20).

SOME FINDINGS IN THE STUDY OF SELF-DISCLOSURE

Self-disclosure is generally regarded as a process in which relationships proceed from nonintimate to intimate areas of exchange with regard to content (Taylor and Altman, 1966) and which may be largely determined by reward-cost factors of present, past, and projected interchange (Thibaut and Kelley, 1959) and/or by the need for the reduction of uncertainty (Berger and Calabrese, 1975).

Whether or not people actually disclose themselves to another person has been found to depend on the nature of the target person (Jourard and Lasakow, 1958; Vondracek and Marshall, 1971), the relationship between the discloser and the target person (Shapiro et al., 1969) and the category of information to be disclosed (Taylor and Altman, 1966; Gilbert and Whiteneck, forthcoming a). In addition, it appears that in the development of interpersonal relations, disclosures tend to be reciprocal ("dyadic effect") and to become more intimate as relationships proceed over time (Jourard and Richman, 1963).

In general, it is reported: women are characteristically higher disclosers than men (Jourard, 1971b); women are likely to disclose more on the basis of liking, whereas men disclose more on the basis of trust (Jourard and Landsman, 1960); perceived appropriateness exerts strong influences on recipients of self-disclosure (Kiesler et al., 1967); self-esteem may affect both the output and reception of self-disclosure (Shapiro, 1968; Gilbert, forthcoming a); mothers are the favorite chosen recipient of self-disclosure by children (Rivenbark, 1971); more disclosure occurs to parents from children who perceive them as nurturant and supportive (Doster and Strickland, 1969); the most consistent intimate disclosure occurs in the marital relationship (Jourard and Lasakow, 1958); valence of disclosure affects relational development (Blau, 1964; Levinger and Senn, 1967; Bienevenu, 1970; Dies and Cohen, 1973; Gilbert and Horenstein, 1975); and privacy needs affect disclosure choices and outcomes (Karlsson, 1963; Simmel, 1964). (For an extended review of the literature on self-disclosure, see Cozby, 1973.)

Researchers have seemingly devoted considerable attention to the *why* and less to the *how* of the disclosure process. This focus needs to change. Also, disclosure needs to be studied *qualitatively* as it affects the development of interpersonal relationships as well as relational intimacy. Undoubtedly, this will not be an easy task. Contextual influences, dispositional characteristics of the discloser and the recipient, norms of perceived appropriateness, content as delineated by degree of personalness as well as valence, interactive effects of self-conception and self-disclosure, as well as the perceptual influences on the entire process of information exchange will need to be examined. The disclosure process, as it exists at any given time, is a function of so many complex variables, known and unknown, as to nearly defy explanation.

DISCLOSURE, SELF-ESTEEM, AND INTERPERSONAL ATTRACTION

Clearly, self-esteem and self-disclosure are threads which run throughout the disclosure literature. Yet, in an era when alienation is the rule more than the exception and when loneliness is a common theme among persons, there is surprisingly little research which seeks to illuminate the interactive effects of self-esteem and self-disclosure on relational development.

Jourard (1971a) conducted a study to determine the effects of self-conception on disclosure behavior. Fifty-two unmarried female undergraduates, whose mean age was 18 years, served in the study. The data revealed that the attitudes of these young women toward themselves were positively related to their disclosure to their parents. A study by Shapiro (1968) also revealed that subjects high in self-esteem could be expected to be comparatively high in self-disclosing behavior. Mullaney (1963), in a study of the relationships among self-disclosure, personality, and family interaction, concluded that disclosure appears to depend both on personality factors and on the degree to which the self is perceived to be socially desirable.

Gilbert (forthcoming a) conducted a study which revealed that subjects with intermediate levels of self-esteem were the *most* receptive to a disclosing other, followed by subjects of low and finally high self-esteem. This same finding was demonstrated in an earlier study by Gilbert (1969) in which subjects were shown motion pictures of an actor behaving positively in two situations and negatively in two situations. Utilizing the same measure of self-esteem as in the later study (*Tennessee Self Concept Scale*), subjects of moderate levels of self-esteem perceived the actor as being more similar to themselves and liked him better than either high or low self-esteem subjects. Thus, it *may* be that persons of moderate self-esteem have a wider latitude of acceptance for others in providing for both positive as well as negatively valenced disclosures.

The relationship between self-esteem and self-disclosure, at present, appears to be ill-defined, hazily conceptualized, and poorly understood. Researchers would do well to formulate clearer conceptualizations of "self" and refine their research efforts as a prerequisite to understanding how these constructs interact to influence interpersonal relationships. Because of the complexity of the theory and research which focuses on "self," (Gordon and Gergen, 1968), an often confounding variable, this will not be an easy task; yet, it is nonetheless essential.

DISCLOSURE, ATTRACTION, PERSONALNESS, AND VALENCE

Although there is some research which would suggest that self-disclosure may result in attraction, previous studies do not suggest the existence of an unequivocal relationship between them. A positive relationship between disclosure and attractiveness of the discloser to another has been found in conditions of reciprocal disclosure and in situations where disclosure was perceived as a social reward (Fitzgerald, 1963; Worthy et al., 1969). However, negligible or nonsignificant relationships (Jourard and Landsman, 1960; Ehrlich and Graeven, 1971) and significant negative relationships (Culbert, 1968; Weigel et al,. 1972; Chaikin and Derlega, 1974) between attractiveness to others and self-disclosure also have been found. Culbert (1968) reported a preference for the low-disclosing person among subjects who were strangers to each other. In a setting which emphasized self-disclosure (a sensitivity training group), he found that subjects were less inclined to enter into a relationship with a high-disclosing than with a low-disclosing trainer. Similarly, Weigel et al. (1972:47), in a study of members of five sensitivity groups, two psychotherapy groups, and two marathon groups, found that "group members perceive therapists' self-disclosure as a negative indicator of mental health." These studies suggest the existence of norms governing self-disclosure which exert powerful influences to regulate times when it is socially acceptable and rewarding to divulge personal information about oneself to another. That is, while previous research on self-disclosure suggests that it must be perceived as a social reward in order to produce a positive effect, it must also be perceived as appropriate behavior.

Intimate disclosure, inappropriately timed, could be perceived as maladjustment or inappropriate socialization, which would likely result in lack of attraction for another since it violates social norms (Kiesler et al., 1967). The relationship between disclosure and appropriateness was the subject of a study undertaken by Chaikin and Derlega (1974). They found that "intimate disclosure to a stranger or an acquaintance was seen by observers as less appropriate and more maladjusted than non-disclosure" (p. 588). Thus, the appropriateness of disclosure, as it is perceived by the *recipient,* is an important determinant of the effect that it is likely to have on the relationship.

Blau (1964:21) suggests that another's attraction to oneself "depends on the anticipation that the association with him will be rewarding." Thus, in the early stages of acquaintance, a person attempts to appear impressive and to present qualities which make him an attractive person, such that the expectation of associating with him will be rewarding. That is, the reason that a person is an attractive associate is that he has impressed others as someone with whom it would be rewarding to associate. Thus, according to Blau, one must present oneself in a positive way, particularly in the initial acquaintance stage, in order for attraction to occur. He further explains that in an initial encounter, to disclose aspects of oneself which are negative does not meet the social conditions within which attraction usually occurs (p. 49):

> A display of his deficiencies does not make one attractive. . . . Hence, unless the weaknesses to which a person calls attention are less significant than the attractive qualities he has exhibited, he will not have succeeded in demonstrating to others that he is approachable as a peer as well as attractive but only in convincing them that he is fundamentally not an attractive associate at all.

Thus, social exchange theory would suggest that positive disclosure in an initial interaction would be more likely than negative disclosure to produce the anticipation that a relationship with a discloser would be rewarding.

Within this framework, Gilbert and Horenstein (1975) conducted a study which sought to separate two distinct aspects of self-disclosure: namely, the degree of personalness (nonintimate to intimate) and the valence (postiveness or negativeness) of self-disclosure and their relationship to interpersonal attraction. The major hypothesis of their study was that subjects would report greater interpersonal attraction for the discloser in the positive valence condition, regardless of the degree of intimacy of self-disclosure.

To test this hypothesis, a factorial design was employed. Degree of intimacy and valence of self-disclosure to another were experimentally manipulated. The dependent variable was interpersonal attraction for the discloser.

To vary disclosure, a male confederate communicated a set of either intimate (high disclosure) or nonintimate (low disclosure) statements about himself to a subject. In addition, valence was also manipulated so that the confederate

TABLE 1
MEAN SCORES OF INTERPERSONAL ATTRACTION AS A FUNCTION OF SEX, DEGREE OF INTIMACY, AND VALENCE OF SELF-DISCLOSURE

Valence of Content	*Self-Disclosure*					
	High			*Low*		
	Male	*Female*	*Total*	*Male*	*Female*	*Total*
Positive	.75	.83	.79	.85	.88	.86
Negative	.55	.60	.57	.46	.60	.53

communicated a set of either positive or negative statements about himself to the subject.

The results of the study demonstrated that the valence of the content was of far greater significance in determining the effects on the recipient than the degree of personalness of disclosure, though the latter is the focus of most disclosure studies. Subjects clearly expressed greater attraction for the confederate when he offered positive disclosing statements rather than negative disclosing statements (Tables 1 and 2).

The data in Gilbert and Horenstein's study reflected the importance of more clearly differentiating the current construct of self-disclosure as it is typically operationalized; that is, disclosure should not be categorized into camps of those who do and those who don't. There are specific aspects of disclosure which need to be differentiated–i.e., degree of personalness, valence, and disclosure recipient. Because of the suggested importance of valence and degree of personalness in affecting disclosure outcomes, an obvious question became evident–namely, the nature of their *interactive* effects. Thus, a follow-up study was conducted by Gilbert and Whiteneck (forthcoming) in an effort to

TABLE 2
ANALYSIS OF VARIANCE OF INTERPERSONAL ATTRACTION AS A FUNCTION OF SEX, DEGREE OF INTIMACY, AND VALENCE OF DISCLOSURE

Source	*SS*	*df*	*MS*	*F*	*p*
Sex	.111	1	.111	2.85	
Degree of intimacy (high or low)	.002	1	.002	.0645	
Valence (positive or negative)	1.515	1	1.515	38.65	<.001
Sex x Level	.001	1	.001	.0198	
Sex x Valence	.001	1	.001	.1989	
Level x Valence	.064	1	.064	1.6431	
Sex x Level x Valence	.019	1	.019	.4982	
Error	2.822	72	.039		

determine the influence which these variables exert on disclosure behaviors independently and/or interdependently with varying disclosure recipients.

DISCLOSURE, PERSONALNESS, VALENCE, AND TARGET

A four-way factorial design was employed. Personalness and valence were manipulated, along with blocking for gender. In addition, the variable of disclosure recipient (target) was manipulated by asking subjects to separately indicate whether or not they would disclose a particular statement to five targets: stranger, acquaintance, parent, friend, and spouse. The goal was to determine the combined influence of these four independent variables on the likelihood of disclosure occurring.

Thirty-eight subjects (19 males and 19 females) were asked to indicate with which of the five target recipients they would likely talk about each of the 27 disclosure statements (Table 3). For each subject, 45 likelihood-of-disclosure scores were computed—one for each combination of the five targets and the nine cells in the personalness-valence matrix. Each score was expressed as a percentage of the statements in that personalness-valence cell which the subjects indicated that they would likely disclose to a particular target. Thus, the dependent variable was the percentage probability or likelihood of disclosure. A four-way repeated-measures analysis of variance was performed on the data: three levels of personalness by three levels of valence by two levels of gender by five levels of target. Table 4 summarizes the results of that analysis.

The results demonstrated three highly significant main effects due to personalness, valence, and target. As hypothesized, the less personal the statements, the greater the likelihood that they would be disclosed: the likelihood of disclosure was 79% for the nonintimate statements, 59% for the moderately intimate statements, and 52% for the intimate ones. The more positive the statements, the greater the likelihood that they would be disclosed: 69% for positive statements, 62% for neutral statements, and 60% for negative statements. Differences in the target recipients resulted in the greatest differences in disclosure rates: the likelihood of disclosing was 31% for strangers, 42% for acquaintances, 64% for parents, 89% for friends, and 91% for spouses (which, interestingly, leaves a 9% "privacy" margin). There was no significant main effect for the gender of the discloser.

While there were significant main effects due to the individual influences of personalness, valence, and target, there were also significant interaction effects due to *all the possible combinations of these variables.* The likelihood of disclosure probabilities for the cells of these interactions is summarized in Table 5.

The standard type in part A of Table 5 indicates the likelihood of disclosure

TABLE 3
A LISTING OF PROTOTYPICAL DISCLOSURE STATEMENTS BY PERSONALNESS AND VALENCE

Valence	Degree of Personalness: Nonintimate	Moderately Intimate	Intimate
Positive	. Kinds of group activity I enjoy . How much I like traveling with others . My strong admiration for professionals	. The kind of people I find it easy to talk to . My expectations for others . My ability to support others	. My good reputation with others . My sexual prowess and fulfillment . My capacity to be open with others
Neutral	. Whether or not I laugh at dirty jokes . Whether or not I enjoy the excitement of a crowd . The amount I drink at parties	. Which I value more: friendship or money . Whether or not I like being the center of attention . My feelings about people who are different from me	. Things I don't like to talk about with others . My problems in interpersonal relationships . My tendency to keep distance between myself and others
Negative	. My aversion to crowds . My strong aversion to another's snoring . My problems with liquor	. Things that bug me about others . Lies that I have told my friends . My tendencies to get even with people I dislike	. Things that would cause me to break up a friendship . How I feel when someone doesn't accept my friendship . Times when others have made me feel uncomfortable

TABLE 4

ANALYSIS OF VARIANCE SUMMARY TABLE FOR STUDY TWO

Source of Variation	*SS*	*df*	*MS*	*Error Term*	*F*	*p*
Personalness	22.527	2	11.263	PS(G)	119.369	.01
Valence	2.343	2	1.171	VS(G)	21.453	.01
Target	101.276	4	25.319	TS(G)	124.459	.01
Gender	.318	1	.318	S(G)	.460	ns
Subjects (Gender)	24.894	36	.692			
Personalness x Valence	4.603	4	1.151	PVS(G)	18.932	.01
Personalness x Target	14.821	8	1.853	PTS(G)	35.868	.01
Personalness x Gender	.048	2	.024	PS(G)	.253	ns
Personalness x Subjects (Gender)	6.793	72	.094			
Valence x Target	.926	8	.116	VTS(G)	2.716	.01
Valence x Gender	.412	2	.206	VS(G)	3.774	.05
Valence x Subjects (Gender)	3.931	72	.055			
Target x Gender	1.714	4	.429	TS(G)	2.106	ns
Target x Subjects (Gender)	29.294	144	.203			
Personalness x Valence x Target	2.091	16	.131	PVTS(G)	3.940	.01
Personalness x Valence x Gender	.253	4	.063	PVS(G)	1.042	ns
Personalness x Valence x Subjects (Gender)	8.754	144	.061			
Personalness x Target x Gender	.616	8	.077	PTS(G)	1.490	ns
Personalness x Target x Subjects (Gender)	14.875	288	.052			
Valence x Target x Gender	.754	8	.094	VTS(G)	2.212	.05
Valence x Target x Subjects (Gender)	12.276	288	.043			
Personalness x Valence x Target x Gender	.481	16	.030	PVTS(G)	.906	ns
Personalness x Valence x Target x Subjects (Gender)	19.103	576	.033			

TABLE 5
CELL MEANS FOR PERSONALNESS, VALENCE, AND TARGET

PART A	Degrees of Personalness			PART B
Valence	Nonintimate	Moderately Intimate	Intimate	All Valences
Positive	88%-All Targets *76%-Stranger* *87%-Acquaintance* *88%-Parent* *97%-Friend* *92%-Spouse*	67%-All Targets *22%-Stranger* *43%-Acquaintance* *79%-Parent* *95%-Friend* *96%-Spouse*	51%-All Targets *11%-Stranger* *25%-Acquaintance* *48%-Parent* *78%-Friend* *92%-Spouse*	79%-All Targets *61%-Stranger* *73%-Acquaintance* *75%-Parent* *97%-Friend* *91%-Spouse*
Neutral	79%-All Targets *58%-Stranger* *76%-Acquaintance* *70%-Parent* *98%-Friend* *90%-Spouse*	60%-All Targets *19%-Stranger* *32%-Acquaintance* *71%-Parent* *88%-Friend* *88%-Spouse*	47%-All Targets *11%-Stranger* *8%-Acquaintance* *43%-Parent* *85%-Friend* *90%-Spouse*	59%-All Targets *17%-Stranger* *32%-Acquaintance* *68%-Parent* *89%-Friend* *90%-Spouse*
Negative	71%-All Targets *48%-Stranger* *56%-Acquaintance* *66%-Parent* *95%-Friend* *90%-Spouse*	50%-All Targets *11%-Stranger* *21%-Acquaintance* *53%-Parent* *77%-Friend* *87%-Spouse*	59%-All Targets *19%-Stranger* *32%-Acquaintance* *59%-Parent* *89%-Friend* *95%-Spouse*	52%-All Targets *13%-Stranger* *22%-Acquaintance* *50%-Parent* *84%-Friend* *92%-Spouse*
PART C All Degrees of Personalness	69%-All Targets *36%-Stranger* *51%-Acquaintance* *72%-Parent* *90%-Friend* *93%-Spouse*	62%-All Targets *29%-Stranger* *39%-Acquaintance* *61%-Parent* *90%-Friend* *89%-Spouse*	60%-All Targets *26%-Stranger* *37%-Acquaintance* *59%-Parent* *87%-Friend* *91%-Spouse*	

for each cell in the personalness x valence interaction (averaged across all targets). It can be seen that the previously described main effect due to valence (positive statements having the greatest likelihood of disclosure, then neutral, with negative statements having the least likelihood) held *only* for the nonintimate and moderately intimate levels of personalness. For intimate disclosure, negative statements had the *greatest* likelihood of disclosure, followed by positive, then neutral statements. This same ordering of valence for intimate disclosures was replicated in another study by Gilbert and Whiteneck (forthcoming). This research suggests that a multidimensional approach to the study of the content of self-disclosure may be required.

Currently, there is a dearth of research which conceptualizes disclosure within the framework of valence and its impact on relationship development; yet, from the results of current research, it would appear that this line of study might prove fruitful. A particularly interesting line of research would involve a multidimensional study of disclosure which includes not only the interactive effects of personalness, valence, and target in relational development, but also the interactive effects of these variables in relation to the self-esteem of both the discloser and the recipient. From this line of thinking, the question begins to emerge, "What, then, is the nature of relational intimacy?"

RELATIONAL INTIMACY: CURVILINEAR VERSUS LINEAR [1]

Several investigators speak to the issue of indiscriminant disclosures and speculate as to their implications for continuing relationships (Karlsson, 1963; Simmel, 1964; Cutler and Dyer, 1965; Rutledge, 1966). Gilbert (forthcoming b) has reported, from a descriptive research review of disclosure studies, support for a curvilinear relationship between self-disclosure and satisfaction in the maintenance of interpersonal relationships. That is to say, a moderate degree of disclosure appeared to be the most conducive to maintaining relationships over time. Yet, Jourard (1971b:46) apparently takes the position that moderate disclosure and maintenance of relationships are not the ideal.

> The optimum . . . in any relationship between persons, is a relationship between I and Thou, where each partner discloses himself without reserve.

Figure 1 contrasts the linear and curvilinear views of the relationship between self-disclosure and relational satisfaction.

These two perspectives on disclosure illustrate a conceptual differentiation among individuals concerned with the relationship between disclosure and relational intimacy. The curvilinear perspective suggests a point of diminishing return; i.e., high levels of disclosure in a relationship may be associated with lowered levels of interpersonal satisfaction and may interfere with the maintenance of interpersonal relationships. The linear view argues for an unchanging positive relationship between disclosure and satisfaction across all levels of disclosure. Whenever two apparently inconsistent points of view exist, especially if these points of view are readily translatable into theoretical propositions, our strategy should be to explore the merits of each, rather than to accept one and dismiss the other.

One way to bring about a resolution of the two points of view is to attend specifically to the underlying claims of each. The first claims that, in those relationships actually studied, disclosure functions so as to deepen the relationship, move it to more intimate levels, and establish interpersonal bonds from which relational satisfaction may be derived. However, as disclosures accumulate through the history of a relationship and as the nature of the

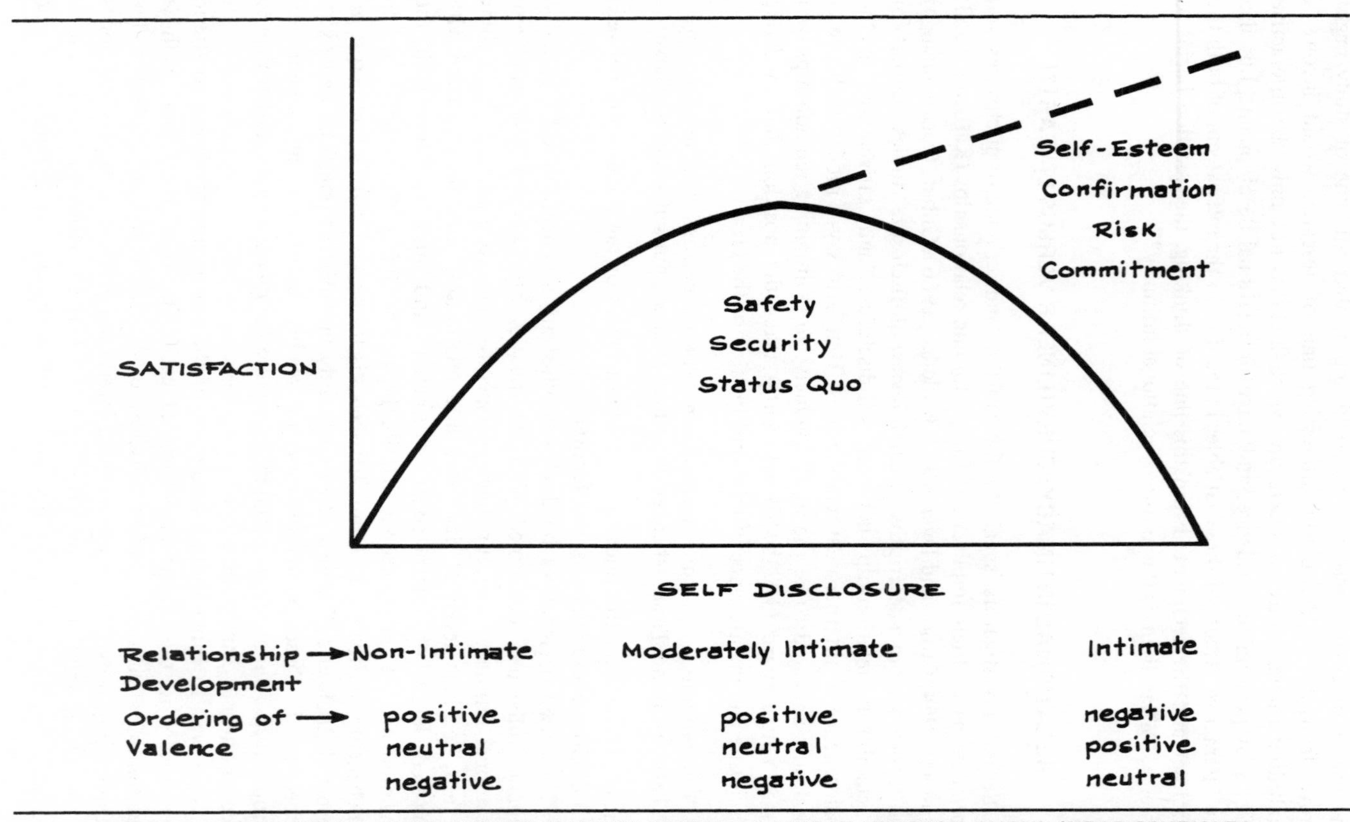

Figure 1: DISCLOSURE PROCESSES IN RELATIONSHIP DEVELOPMENT: A LINEAR VERSUS A CURVILINEAR SCHEMATA

relationship itself changes, then the connection between disclosure and relational satisfaction reverses from a positive to a negative association. The underlying claim in the first point of view is that this is the way disclosure functions for most relationships.

The underlying claim in the second point of view is that disclosure may, and indeed should, remain a positive source of relational satisfaction throughout the history of the relationship. What is implied is that this is the way that things should be and could be for more relationships than is presently the case. The second point of view clearly describes an optimum state of affairs. The optimum in a relationship of which Jourard speaks is, undoubtedly, the exception rather than the rule. In other words, optimum is an ideal and seldom the way relationships *are.*

What becomes necessary, therefore, is for proponents of the linear point of view to specify the conditions under which the optimum is realistically attainable. Since I believe in the general validity of the curvilinear point of view and am committed to the promise of the linear perspective, let me suggest a set of conditions which must be present in order for the optimum to be achieved.

If in intimate relationships negative disclosures are, indeed, most likely to occur first, as suggested by the reported research, then it may be that disclosures of a negative valence function positively, to further the relationship, *only* after there has occurred a verbalized or understood acceptance of the other person. Stated differently, the degree of confirmation or the certainty of acceptance by the other will likely influence the effects that negative disclosures exert on relationship development. One certainly has a great deal more to lose and much more to protect in intimate relationships. And it may be argued that the impact of disclosure in intimate relationships may be understood not by simply focusing on the effects of the disclosure on the other, as has most frequently been the case in the past, but by focusing on the effects that the *response of the other* has on the person engaging in the disclosure. Thus, the first condition which may allow the pursuit of optimum levels of disclosure is a healthy "self," capable of accommodating to and ameliorating the consequences of one's disclosures for the other. Healthy self-love may be the catalyst to establishing and maintaining intimate relationships. Jourard (1968:427-428) makes a strong statement to this effect.

> If we are to learn more about man's self, then we must learn more about self-disclosure—its conditions, dimensions and consequences. Beginning evidence . . . shows that actively accepting, empathic, loving, non-punitive responses—in short, love—provides the optimum conditions under which man will disclose. . . . It follows that if we would be helpful (or should I say *human*) we must grow to loving stature and learn, in Buber's terms, to confirm our fellow man in his very being. Probably, this presumes that we must *first* confirm our *own* being.

The curvilinear and linear conceptualizations of self-disclosure described in Figure 1 indicate that the issue in disclosure for optimal relationships may be in learning how to deal with information, disappointments, and conflicts at the far end of the disclosure continuum. Indeed, conflict management has been suggested as the most accurate index of the stability of a relationship. Thus, this parameter can be, though the literature reports it is more often not, linear in nature. Most likely, explorations at the far end of the disclosure continuum may force issues and resolutions that go beyond just the maintenance of the relationship, particularly long-term relationships. What is being suggested is a need to rethink what is happening at the far end of the disclosure continuum. For example, "satisfaction" for most long-term relationships might inevitably decline as the history of the relationship mounts. Declining satisfaction might result in heightened disclosure of a more intense and potentially negatively valenced character. The results of the previously cited descriptive research are as readily explainable by assuming that declining satisfaction is driving the disclosure variable as by assuming, as is often implicitly the case in the descriptive research, that disclosure is driving satisfaction. If this is the case, then a second condition should be imposed on the point of view which promises optimum levels of disclosure in a relationship. This second condition is simply *willingness to risk.* A commitment to the relationship—and a desire not only to maintain it at its present level but to push its potentials into areas of greater intimacy and satisfaction—may require a high degree of willingness to risk. To achieve the optimum of which Jourard speaks, one must certainly be willing to risk alienation from the other, or even termination of the relationship. For most of us, such risks are of great consequence. And an unwillingness to take such a risk might help to explain why things are as they are, rather than as they should and could be.

The interaction of the first two conditions, self and risk, suggests a third condition. Relational satisfaction, as a curvilinear dimension of disclosure, appears to be strongly related to maintenance and needs for security and safety in a relationship. Consequently, the far end of the disclosure continuum may be characterized more by a reciprocity of disclosures which goes beyond satisfaction with the relationship, as it is typically operationalized, to include *an affective response of acceptance and commitment, in its deepest form, of not only the disclosures but of the person making them.* The existential meaning of the term "confirmation" may find its most genuine application at the far end of the disclosure continuum. In the absence of genuinely reciprocal confirmation the presence of the first two conditions may, in the long run, be irrelevant!

From the explicit descriptions of the researchers and the more implicit prescriptions of the theoretically oriented humanists, a still hazy picture begins to emerge. There are interpersonal price tags attached to intimate relationships. Intimacy, as a dimension of affect, may not be a unidimensional construct. It seems to be comprised of not only feelings (satisfaction) but also commitment (willingness to risk). Intimacy refers not only to the depth of exchange, both verbally and nonverbally, but also to the depth of acceptance or confirmation which characterizes a relationship. Thus, "intimate disclosure" and "intimate relationships" need to be clearly conceptualized and differentiated in future disclosure studies. While disclosure has been established as an index of communicative depth in human relationships, it does not guarantee an intimate relationship.

Implicit in the descriptive researcher's curvilinear cautions is a word of advice to the humanistically oriented theorist: in order to attain a future ideal, there are aspects of human relations about the way in which intimate relationships are presently constituted which need to be far better understood. And in the reassurances of the humanist, there is a word of advice to the researcher: there may be dimensions of relationships at least as deserving of empirical attention as satisfaction ratings. And if students of self-disclosure take into account some of these other dimensions, perhaps even their conclusions about satisfaction might change.

NOTE

1. The thoughtful assistance of Dr. Carl Larson in helping to clarify and organize the ideas in this section is gratefully acknowledged.

REFERENCES

BERGER, C.R., and CALABRESE, R.J. (1975). "Some explorations in initial interaction and beyond: Toward a developmental theory of interpersonal communication." Human Communication Research, 1:99-112.

BIENEVENU, M.J., Sr. (1970). "Measurement of marital communication." Family Coordinator, 19:26-31.

BLAU, P.M. (1964). Exchange and power in social life. New York: Wiley.

CHAIKIN, A.L., and DERLEGA, V.J. (1974). "Variables affecting the appropriateness of self disclosure." Journal of Consulting and Clinical Psychology, 42:588-593.

CLEAVER, E. (1968). Soul on Ice. New York: Dell.

COZBY, P.W. (1973). "Self disclosure: A literature review." Psychological Bulletin, 79:73-91.

CULBERT, S.A. (1967). Interpersonal process of self disclosure: It takes two to see one. Washington, D.C.: N.T.L. Institute for Applied Behavioral Science.

--- (1968). "Trainer self-disclosure and member growth in T-groups." Journal of Applied Behavioral Science, 4:47-73.

CUTLER, B.R., and DYER, W.G. (1965). "Initial adjustment process in young married couples." Social Forces, 44:195-201.

DIES, D.R., and COHEN, L. (1973). "Content consideration in group therapist self-disclosure." Paper presented at the convention of the American Psychological Association, Montreal.

DOSTER, J.A., and STRICKLAND, B.R. (1969). "Perceived child-rearing practices and self disclosure patterns." Journal of Counseling and Clinical Psychology, 33:382.

EHRLICH, H., and GRAEVEN, D. (1971). "Reciprocal self disclosure in a dyad." Journal of Experimental Social Psychology, 7:389-400.

FITZGERALD, M.P. (1963). "Self disclosure and expressed self esteem, social distance and areas of self revealed." Journal of Social Psychology, 56:405-412.

GILBERT, S.J. (1969). "An investigation of self esteem and cognitive complexity in the impression formation process." Unpublished M.A. thesis, University of Kansas.

--- (forthcoming a). "Differential effects of unanticipated self disclosure on subjects of varying levels of self esteem."

--- (forthcoming b). "Self disclosure, intimacy, and communication in families."

GILBERT, S.J., and HORENSTEIN, D. (1975). "The dyadic effects of self disclosure: Level versus valence." Human Communication Research, 1(summer):316-322.

GILBERT, S.J., and WHITENECK, G.G. (forthcoming). "Toward a multi-dimensonal approach to the study of self disclosure."

GORDON, C., and GERGEN, K. (1968). The self in social interaction. New York: Wiley.

JOURARD, S. (1959). "Healthy personality and self-disclosure." Mental Hygiene, 43:499-507.

--- (1968). "Healthy personality and self disclosure." Pp. 123-134 in C. Gordon and K. Gergen (eds.), The self in social interaction. New York: Wiley.

--- (1971a). Self disclosure: An experimental analysis of the transparent self. New York: Wiley-Interscience.

--- (1971b). The transparent self. New York: Van Nostrand.

JOURARD, S., and LANDSMAN, M. (1960). "Cognition, cathexes and the 'dyadic effect' in men's self-disclosing behavior." Merrill-Palmer Quarterly, 6:178-186.

JOURARD, S., and LASAKOW, P. (1958). "Some factors in self disclosure." Journal of Abnormal and Social Psychology, 56:91-98.

JOURARD, S., and RICHMAN, P. (1963). "Factors in the self disclosure inputs of college students." Merrill-Palmer Quarterly, 9:141-148.

KARLSSON, G. (1963). Adaptability and communication in marriage. Totowa, N.J.: Bedminster.

KIESLER, C., KIESLER, S., and PALLAK, M. (1967). "The effects of commitment to future interaction on reactions to norm violations." Journal of Personality, 35:385-399.

LEVINGER, G., and SENN, D.J. (1967). "Disclosure of feelings in marriage." Merrill-Palmer Quarterly, 13:237-249.

LYND, H.M. (1968). "Shame, guilt, and identity: Beyond roles." In C. Gordon and K. Gergen (eds.), The self in social interaction. New York: Wiley.

MILLER, G.R., and STEINBERG, M. (1975). Between people. Palo Alto, Calif.: Science Research Associates.

MULLANEY, A.J. (1963). "Relationships among self-disclosure behavior, personality and family interaction." Psychological Abstracts, 64:2420.

POWELL, J. (1969). Why am I afraid to tell you who I am?" Niles, Ill.: Argus Communications.

RIVENBARK, W.H. (1971). "Self-disclosure patterns among adolescents." Psychological Reports, 38:35-42.

ROGERS, C. (1961). On becoming a person. Boston: Houghton-Mifflin.

RUBIN, Z. (1973). Liking and loving. New York: Holt, Rinehart and Winston.

RUTLEDGE, A.L. (1966). Premarital counselling. Cambridge: Schenkman.

SATIR, V. (1972). Peoplemaking. Palo Alto, Calif.: Science and Behavior Books.

SHAPIRO, A. (1968). "The relationship between self concept and self disclosure." Dissertation Abstracts, 39(3-b):1180-1181.

SHAPIRO, J.G., KRAUSE, H.H., and TRUAX, C.B. (1969). "Therapeutic conditions and disclosure beyond the therapeutic encounter." Journal of Counseling Psychology, 16:290-294.

SIMMEL, G. (1964). The sociology of Georg Simmel (K.H. Wolff, trans.). New York: Free Press.

SUTTON, M. (1975). "A theory of the valence dimension of self-disclosure." Unpublished manuscript, University of Denver.

TAYLOR, D., and ALTMAN, I. (1966). Intimacy scaled stimuli for use in studies of interpersonal relationships. Bethesda, Md.: Naval Medical Research Institute.

THIBAUT, J.W., and KELLEY, H.H. (1959). The social psychology of groups. New York: Wiley.

TIRYAKIAN, E.A. (1968). "The existential self and the person." Pp. 75-86 in C. Gordon and K. Gergen (eds.), The self in social interaction. New York: Wiley.

VONDRACEK, F.W., and MARSHALL, M.J. (1971). "Self-disclosure and interpersonal trust: An exploratory study." Psychological Reports, 18:235-240.

WEIGEL, R.G., DINGES, N., DYER, R., and STRAUMFJORD, A.A. (1972). "Perceived self-disclosure, mental health, and who is liked in group treatment." Journal of Counseling Psychology, 19:47-52.

WORTHY, M.A., GARY, I., and KAHN, G.M. (1969). "Self-disclosure as an exchange process." Journal of Personality and Social Psychology, 13:59-63.

Chapter 10

THE FACE IN FACE-TO-FACE INTERACTION

Randall P. Harrison

THE FACE is perhaps our most powerful nonverbal communicator. It is pervasive in mass media communication, in newspapers and newsmagazines, in ads, in the "talking head" shots of television, in the reaction shots and close-ups of cinema. In Western art, the head and face have classically been used to represent the person, in marble bust or oil portrait. But perhaps nowhere is the head as important as in that communication which is often called, appropriately, face-to-face interaction.

Increasingly, research suggests that facial communication has deep evolutionary roots, that it fundamentally frames the interaction of higher primates, including man (Andrew and Huber, 1972; Chevalier-Skolnikoff, 1973; Redican, 1975). Similarly, emerging evidence suggests that facial interaction sets the stage for communication development in the early life of each human infant (Charlesworth and Kreutzer, 1973; Vine, 1973; Sroufe and Waters, 1975; Waters et al., 1975). Finally, recent investigation points to the potential power of facial cues in adult human interaction (Argyle and Cook, 1975; Ekman and Friesen, 1975) and the availability of specific facial cues for systematic future research (Ekman and Friesen, forthcoming).

This chapter examines some of the recent research on the face, frames possible implications for interpersonal communication, and explores directions for future research.

The face, of course, may provide many different types of information. Argyle (1975), for example, notes that primates use facial expression to communicate identity, status, emotions, and interpersonal attitudes. Facial expressions have been found for each of the "main interpersonal relationships–dominant, submissive, threatening, sexual, parental, playful, etc." (p. 212). In man, he argues, facial expressions are additionally important in communicating personality characteristics and interaction signals.

Meanwhile, in a forthcoming work, Ekman articulates some 20 types of information which can be gleaned from the face, ranging from disease and kinship to beauty and sexual attractiveness. Obviously, not all types of information are equally important for social interaction. But the emerging array of categories underscores what a rich and versatile source of stimulation the face can be during the process of human communication.

Recently, a growing number of books on the face have appeared (e.g., Hjortsjo, 1970; Izard, 1971; Ekman and Friesen, 1975). Similarly, a steadily expanding literature is appearing on the broader topic of nonverbal communication (e.g., Scherer, 1970; Harrison et al., 1972; Harrison, 1974; Weitz, 1974; Key, 1975; Argyle, 1975).

The ethological tradition, only recently discovered by most social scientists, has proven enormously fruitful for the study of nonverbal communication (Altmann, 1967; Sebeok, 1968; Hinde, 1972). We see in primates, and perhaps in other animals, many evolutionary foundations for human patterns of interaction and communication.

The ethological data has been particularly relevant to facial research. Van Hooff (1972), for example, has traced the evolution of human laughing and smiling from its apparent primate origins. And Eibl-Eibesfeldt (1972) has traced the "eyebrow flash" used in greeting and flirting. Other examples of the human ethological approach can be found in Eibl-Eibesfeldt (1970, 1971, 1973), Grant (1968, 1969), and Blurton-Jones (1972).

While there is some convergence on terminology, sharp differences still emerge on basic definitions. Sebeok (1976) concludes, for example, that the term "nonverbal communication" has been applied in so many ways that it is "well-nigh devoid of meaning or, at best, susceptible to so many interpretations as to be nearly useless."

Harrison (1973, 1974) argues that "nonverbal communication" should be reserved for those situations in which "signs" are involved. Thus, not all nonverbal stimuli or behavior would be nonverbal communication. But explorations might still consider relatively idiosyncratic encodings and decodings if information was exchanged. Meanwhile, Cranach and Vine (1973) suggest a *common code* as a requirement for communication. This implies an organized set of signs, and an encoder and a decoder, and perhaps members of a broader community, who understand the code.

Unfortunately, the term "code" has itself been used in a variety of ways in the literature on nonverbal communication. Ekman and Friesen (1969) used "coding" as one of the criteria for categorizing nonverbal behavior, and they distinguished between "arbitrary," "iconic," and "intrinsic" codes. In the latter case, the nonverbal behavior refers to itself.

Wiener et al. (1972), however, argue that this is no longer a "code." In their attempt to distinguish between *nonverbal communication* and *nonverbal behavior* they employ the concept of a code, but their methodology for detecting one ties them closely to verbal language and seems most likely to uncover what Ekman and Friesen have called "illustrators" and "regulators." They also appear to reject the possibility of iconic codes.

Ekman and Friesen (1969) argue that nonverbal behavior might be informative, interactive, or communicative. For the latter category, they require *intent.* While admitting the methodological problems raised by a criterion of intent, they found it a useful way to discriminate *emblems* (p. 54), the category of gesture, such as the A-OK sign, which are typically performed with awareness and an acknowledged hope of communicating a specifiable message.

Other behaviors, such as *regulators* (e.g., head nods and eye movements which regulate the flow of communication) may fall into Ekman and Friesen's interactive category. These behaviors distinctly influence the interaction pattern, but participants typically perform them with low awareness, and intent can only be inferred.

Finally, behaviors such as *adaptors* may be good examples of the informative category. These are the nonverbal manipulations and adjustments which may be part of an individual's habit repertoire, but typically are done without awareness of any intent to communicate or influence the interaction. To a knowledgeable observer, they may be "informative" about the sender's internal state, but they were not "encoded" by the sender for that purpose.

Cranach and Vine (1973) also distinguish among informative, interactive, and communicative movements, but each is defined slightly differently from Ekman and Friesen's categories. A major difference emerges on communicative behavior, where Cranach and Vine see no reason to assume intent if a common code is taken as the defining criterion.

Typically, the construct *code* involves (a) perceptible, variable, controllable stimuli, i.e., code elements, (b) "semantic rules" which link the elements or configurations of elements to referents, i.e., a "meaning" dimension, and (c) "syntactic rules" for organizing elements or configurations of elements into larger patterns (Harrison, 1974:61). Vocal language is, of course, the human code which has been studied most carefully and investigators such as Hockett and Altmann (1968) have used the "design features" of human language to compare other codes, including those in the animal kingdom.

A FACIAL "CODE"?

A facial "code," if one is to be found, may be easiest to see in simple pictographic representations of facial expressions. Resorting to such pictographic stimuli presents both methodological advantages and problems, however.

By drastic leveling, the pictographs can eliminate "structural" facial features and focus attention on mobile facial expressions.[1] In experiments, this may be one way of dealing with a common problem encountered in early research on the face, i.e., poor sampling of stimulus individuals (Bruner and Tagiuri, 1954:637). In most studies, only one actor was used, and responses to the individual's expressions may have been confounded by reactions to unique facial features.

At the same time, if the pictographic expressions are used as test stimuli, it becomes unclear whether the experimenter is researching interpretations of human facial expressions or the artistic conventions used by artists and cartoonists. The latter "pictorial code" may be of interest in its own right. And evidence from this source may be indicative since artistic conventions are likely to be iconic at some level with underlying regularities in the world being portrayed. But such evidence could not be considered conclusive for human interaction.[2]

Pictographic expressions, of course, can be used in at least three ways: (a) strictly for demonstration, i.e., as a visual model for explication purposes, (b) as test stimuli, or (c) as a notation system, to provide a drawn record of events which were originally live or recorded on film or videotape.

In the present context, pictographic representations will be used primarily for demonstration. But data will be reported from research in which these pictographs were used as test stimuli.[3] The responses elicited may be indicative of interpretations made in ongoing interpersonal communication. But that remains an open research question.

Figure 1a shows a basic neutral expression constructed from the fewest possible pictorial elements—a circle, two dots, and straight lines to represent the mouth and eyebrows. Extensive pretesting indicated that this particular placement of features was seen as most normal, given the highly simplified pictorial elements. A configuration with eyes higher and mouth lower tended to

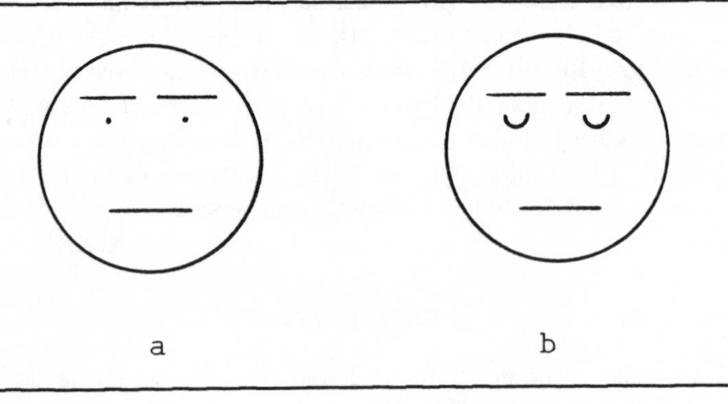

Figure 1.

be seen as unintelligent and sad. If eyes and brows are lowered, the figure is perceived as youthful and perhaps feminine. If features are all raised, the face is described as pugnacious.

Each pictographic expression was presented with 70 adjectives on a 5-point scale, and respondents were asked to indicate, for each label, whether it strongly did or did not apply to the facial expression. The adjectives were selected to highlight judgments which might be important in interpersonal communication.

Four demographic labels were included–young, old, male, female–for control purposes and since it was thought some of the expressions might elicit interactions among judgments. For instance, angry expressions might be assigned to male faces, tired expressions to old faces, etc. The basic neutral expression in Figure 1a was not completely successful in avoiding demographic attributes since it was seen as more male than female.

Six adjectives tapped the individual's *capacity to interact*–i.e., judgments such as robust, frail, intelligent, unintelligent, energetic, lazy, harassed, and unhurried. Another 18 adjectives explored mood, particularly the pleasant-unpleasant and aroused-unaroused dimensions. Labels included happy, unhappy, satisfied, dissatisfied, excited, and relaxed. Predictive implications were explored with terms such as hopeful and fearful.

The final 40 adjectives dealt with two aspects of interpersonal assessment. Half related to implications that the facial expression might have for the relationship itself–e.g., judgments of domineering, submissive, open, withdrawn, helpful, and supportive.[4] The other adjectives related to "comments" that might be made by the face about information being processed–e.g., judgments of believing, disbelieving, confused, comprehending, agreeing, disagreeing, interested, and disinterested.

The neutral face shown in Figure 1a was judged to be intelligent, unhurried, satisfied, relaxed, alert, controlled, helpful, likable, dependable, sincere, honest, understanding, comprehending, and interested.[5] Thus, the face, while showing zero affect, was far from meaningless in terms of judgments which may be important for interaction.

A similar face, with the same brow and mouth, but with eyes closed (Figure 1b), elicited only one of these judgments, unhurried. It would appear that the mere act of attending, even with a relative expressionless face, is an important sign in human interaction.[6]

Figure 2 shows expressions where one feature has been moved while the rest of the face remains unchanged. In Figures 2a and 2b, the mouth has been moved, with, respectively, corners up and corners down. In Figures 2c and 2d, the brow has been shifted, medially upward or medially downward.

Figure 2a elicits many of the same judgments as the neutral expression–e.g., unhurried, intelligent, controlled, comprehending, alert, and satisfied. In addition, it elicits happy, agreeing, and energetic. Figure 2b shows only one

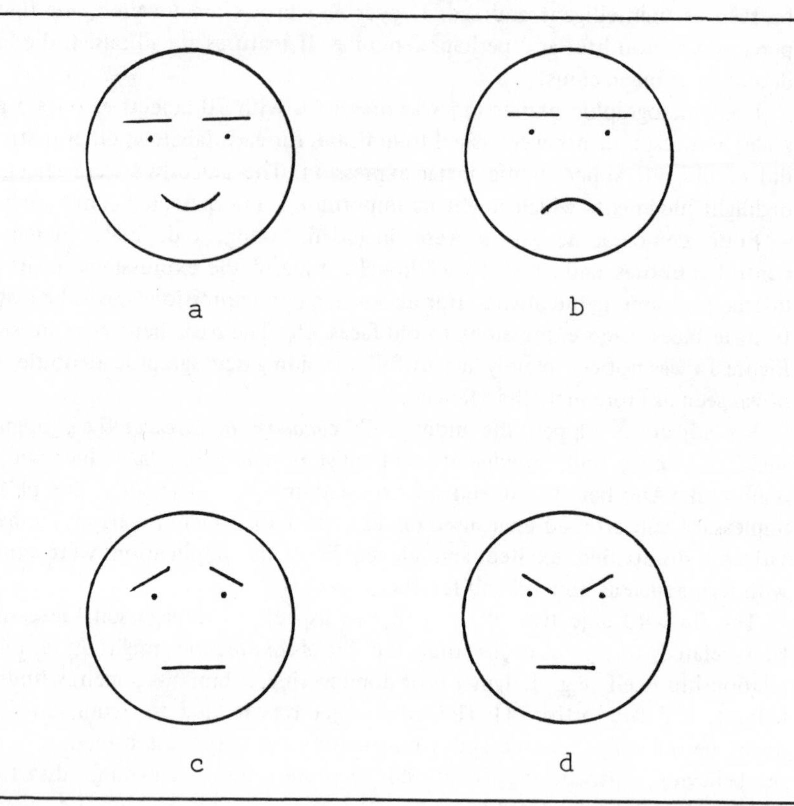

Figure 2.

judgment, sincere, in common with the neutral expression. Instead, the downturned mouth elicits adjectives such as unhappy, dissatisfied, worried, harassed, confused, perplexed, and young.

Figure 2c, with medially upturned brows, is similar in meaning to expression 2b but in addition elicits fearful and skeptical. Meanwhile, Figure 2d elicits a new set of judgments: angry, menacing, overbearing, domineering, unattractive, unlikable, uncontrolled, disagreeing, and disapproving. It, too, is seen as dissatisfied and skeptical.

Synchronic and Sequential Cues

Syntax in the verbal code depends largely on sequential ordering and, to some extent, proximity of elements. In the gestural-visual band, however, cues can occur simultaneously as well as sequentially.[7] These synchronically occurring cues can be (a) redundant, eliciting essentially the same meanings, (b) independent, eliciting separate sets of meanings which are neither redundant nor conflicting, or (c) conflicting, in which case the separately elicited meanings appear to be contradictory or in competition.

Figure 3a is an example of redundant, synchronically occurring cues. It combines the medially upturned brow of Figure 2c and the downturned mouth of Figure 2b. The combination expression, like both components, is seen as unhappy, harassed, perplexed, confused, dissatisfied, and worried. And, like the medially upturned brow, the combination expression is seen as fearful. The only new adjective to emerge is unattractive.

While relatively little new meaning is added, the combination face is seen as more intensely unhappy, etc. This points to another dimension of coding which may be going on in the face. One facial cue (e.g., the upturned brow as opposed to the downturned brow) may elicit a package of meaning as distinct as any word might. But the face also codes analogically or iconically. In general, the greater the excursion of the feature, and the more features involved, the greater the perceived intensity.[8]

Figure 3b may be an example of relatively independent cues. The expression is seen as unhappy, dissatisfied, perplexed, bored, remote, and withdrawn. The first three adjectives are carried over from the downturned mouth (Figure 2b). The last three adjectives are also elicited by just the half-closed eyes when the mouth and brows are neutral.

Figure 3c provides an example of conflicting cues merged into one face. The brows and the mouth, when presented separately, elicit two sets of adjectives in which there is no overlap. In fact, many of the attributes are in direct conflict—e.g., happy for the mouth and unhappy for the brows. The combination expression elicits neither happy nor unhappy. Most of the adjectives attributed to one or the other alone drop out when the cues are combined. But several new adjectives emerge: helpful, approving, open, trusting, likable, believing, hopeful, interested, and young.

This phenomenon appears not unlike the concept of montage in cinema, where the juxtaposition of two visual symbols gives rise to a new meaning not

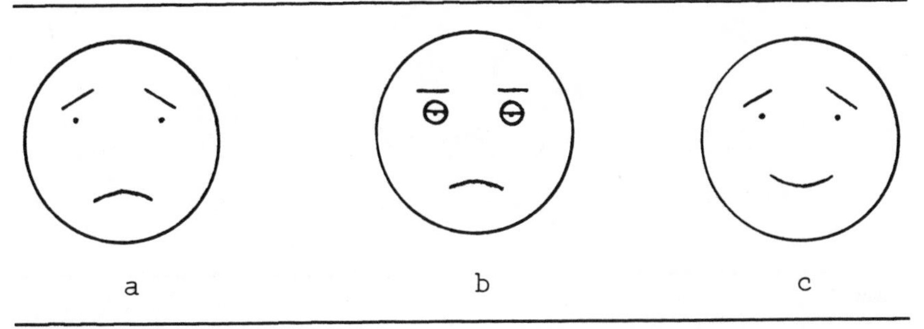

Figure 3.

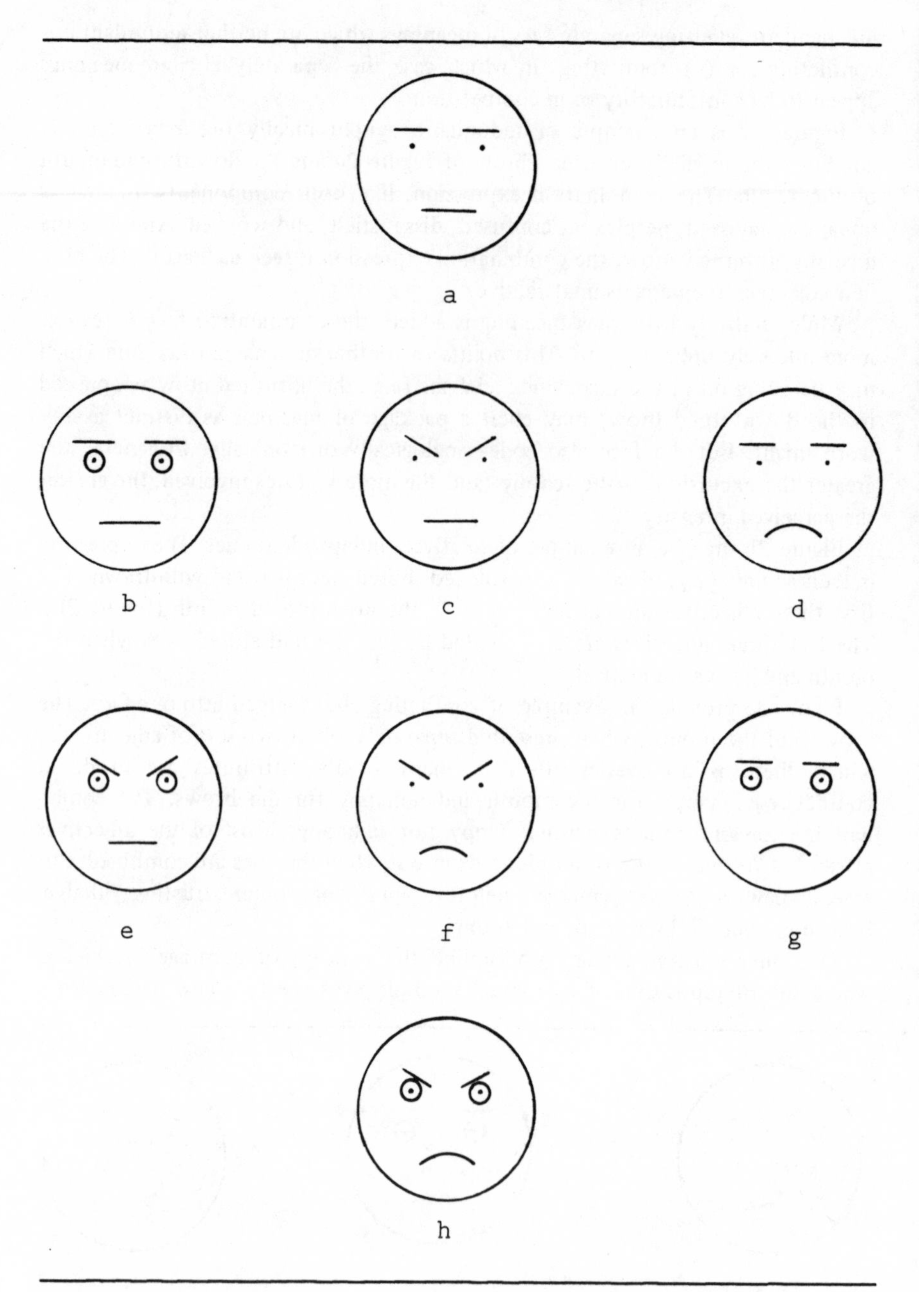

Figure 4.

enjoyed by either symbol alone. In the verbal code, of course, there are also compound words, combinations of morphemes, which range in the degree to which they form a new "gestalt," eliciting meanings quite different from the separate elements.

Figure 4 demonstrates differences which may emerge with the sequential display of cues. Figure 4a is the neutral face of Figure 1a. Figure 4h is the face which was judged to be most angry; brow, eyes, and mouth are activated.[9] In Figures 4b, 4c, and 4d, one facial area has been activated, the eyes, brow, and mouth, respectively. In Figures 4e, 4f, and 4g, two areas have been activated, respectively, brow and eyes, brow and mouth, and eyes and mouth.

Moving from Figure 4a to 4h, there are six different pathways–six ways to get mad, assuming that once a facial area has fired it will remain engaged.[10] From present research, it is not possible to say whether there are typical ways for the face to fire. For instance, in surprise, do brows, eyes, and mouth fire all at once? Do eyes and brow go first, followed by the mouth? Are different types of surprise or anger different in the way in which the face fires? And when someone simulates an expression, or tries to deceive, does the expression move onto the face in a detectably different way?

These are questions which are likely to be explored in the near future. Meanwhile, it does seem clear that there are a number of facial cues which elicit clear interpretations, judgments which may be important in social interaction. These cues, in turn, can be combined, synchronically and sequentially, into larger meaning units. None of the eight faces in Figure 4 have precisely the same meaning. These cues, and combinations of cues, appear to be available to communicators in interaction. Whether and how this potential facial code is used in interpersonal communication remains an open research question. The area which seems most likely to produce immediate evidence on this issue is the well researched field of facial affect.

FACIAL AFFECT

There appears to be little agreement about the underlying structure of emotion (Davitz, 1964; Arnold, 1970; Alloway et al., 1972; Dittmann, 1972; Strongman, 1973). But in the area of facial expressions, there now appear to be enough regularities, in presentation and recognition, so that comparisons might be made with other human codes.

In the display of emotion, there appears to be a basic vocabulary of facial signs, configurations which are reliably linked to internal affective states. Tomkins (1970:107), for example, posited the following primary affects, together with their characteristic facial manifestation:

The positive affects are (a) interest or excitement, with eyebrows down, stare fixed or tracking an object; (b) enjoyment or joy, the smiling response; and (c) surprise or startle, with eyebrows raised and eye blink. The negative affects are (a) distress or anguish, the crying response; (b) fear or terror, with eyes frozen open in fixed stare or moving away from the dreaded object to the side and with skin pale, cold, and sweating and with trembling and hair erect; (c) shame or humiliation, with eyes and head lowered; (d) contempt with the upper lip raised in a sneer; (e) disgust or a deep nausea response and (f) anger or rage, with a frown, clenched jaw, and red face.

Ekman and Friesen (1971; Ekman, 1972) report cross-cultural support for six of these face-affect relationships: anger, fear, sadness, disgust, happiness, and surprise. In a recent work, Ekman and Friesen (1975) present photographically the facial configurations which have been associated with each emotion.

For every emotion, except happiness, there is a *full face* configuration, involving unique brow, eye, and mouth positions. (For happiness, only the eyes and mouth present unique displays; the brow remains neutral.) For anger, two configurations are possible: an open-mouthed anger and a closed-mouthed, tight-lipped anger. Similarly, for sadness, open-eyed or closed-eyed configurations are possible.

Although the full face display, presented in a still photo, reliably elicits the correct emotion label, most of the full face configurations apparently involve considerable redundancy. Surprise, for example, can be elicited by showing only the raised eyebrows, or the wide opened eyes, or the dropped open mouth (Boucher and Ekman, 1975).

One linguistic analogy might be *abbreviation;* i.e., just as "TV" can be used as a shorthand form of "television," it may be that emotional expressions such as surprise are so familiar that only an abbreviated display is necessary to elicit the "surprise" label. Ekman and Friesen (1975:43-44) suggest, however, that surprise has different connotations when expressed in different areas of the face; e.g., the questioning surprise with raised brows and opened eyes versus the astonished surprise of open eyes and open mouth.

An alternate linguistic analogy might argue that the individual facial features are like phonemes, meaningless by themselves, but morphemic, or wordlike, in the proper combination. The Boucher-Ekman (1975:27) data on anger seem to suggest such a parallel. The full face anger is identified as rage by over 70% of the decoders. But seeing just the anger brows, eyes, or mouth, respondents drop below 40% accuracy. At least in that experiment, the individual features work like the letters M-A-D, relatively meaningless as individual elements, but a meaningful symbol in combination.

Drawing any language parallel, of course, raises the question of how the facial expressions come to be encoded. Are they symbols, which can be produced at will to communicate intended or shared meaning? Or, particularly with affect displays, are they more like what Sebeok (1975:239) has called "symptoms?" In other words, are facial expressions of emotion wired in biologically so that wide-open eyes and mouth relate to the internal state of surprise just as red spots on the face might relate to an internal state of measles? In that case, the surprise expression would be informative, perhaps even interactive, but it would not be communicative, except perhaps for a cartoonist or photographer who represents the expression in another medium.

Wiener et al. (1972) argue that facial expressions of emotion are poor candidates for a code if the evidence of universality is accurate. To them, this means that the expressions are invariant and therefore not a code, in their terms. This, however, overlooks the actual complexities involved in producing expressions.

Present evidence suggests that facial expressions, including those related to the emotions, may function as several different types of signs–symbols, signals, symptoms, or indexes (to use the distinctions made by Sebeok, 1975). According to Tomkins's theory (1962, 1963), the unique facial configuration for each affect is fired off by a subcortical program (and the feedback from this event results in the experience of the emotion). At the same time, facial musculature can be controlled cortically so that expressions can be produced at will, and the "natural" or "automatic" reactions can be overridden.

Ekman and Friesen (1975:138) suggest that we have *cultural display rules* which govern the show of emotion. In our culture, for example, females are likely to downplay expressions of intense anger, while males find it inappropriate to show extreme grief (e.g., sobbing in public). In some cultures, it is the males who do the ceremonial weeping, intensifying the display of grief in a way that would be unseemly for an American.

Display rules may include (a) *intensification,* in which the facial display amplifies the felt emotion (e.g., looking very happy upon receiving a mildly pleasing gift), (b) *deintensification,* in which the felt emotion is dampened in its facial display (e.g., looking mildly pleased upon winning a very rewarding competition), (c) *neutralization,* the ultimate stage in deintensification, where the felt emotion is given zero expression (e.g., maintaining a "poker face" while looking at a very good, or very bad, poker hand), and (d) *masking,* where one felt emotion is covered by the display of another affect (e.g., showing anger in the presence of a bully rather than evincing fear). A final rule, of course, may be to not apply any of the above rules, but to just "let it all hang out."

The Ekman-Friesen model suggests that if an individual is alone, experiencing an intense primary affect, he will show the characteristic facial configuration associated with that emotion. If the individual is in a social setting, being observed by even one other human, the culturally learned display rules are likely to come into play (Friesen, 1972).

As far as can be determined now, intact humans will display the characteristic affect expression when experiencing an emotion, although overlearned display rules could presumably lead to the systematic short-circuiting of certain emotions (e.g., anger), even when the individual is alone. Similarly, well-socialized individuals in any culture are likely to use the appropriate display rules, intensifying, deintensifying, and masking, in various social situations.

For facial expression to operate as a common code, of course, it must also be the case that interpreters decode expressions in similar ways. Early research (e.g., Ekman et al. 1972) seemed to indicate very erratic decoding ability. Ekman and Friesen (1975), however, point to several possible reasons for this inconsistency.

A common problem in early research was that the stimulus expressions themselves were what Ekman and Friesen have called "blends," i.e., combinations of an expression in one part of the face and a second affect elsewhere. Surprise, fear, or sad brows, for example, might be combined with anger, disgust, or even happy mouths. With ambiguous or complex stimuli, the interpretations were correspondingly unreliable.

In addition, facial expressions may be difficult to decode if they are "partials," i.e., appearing in only part of the face, or "micromomentary," i.e., involving fleeting expressions which are difficult to detect with the naked eye at normal speeds.

On the decoding side, Ekman and Friesen (1975) note several reasons why decoding accuracy may seem low in interacting situations. For example, they note the barrage of stimuli available in typical interpersonal communication. Affect expressions may be simply missed in the flow of other signals. Similarly, Ekman and Friesen suggest that we are taught not to look at the face continually during interaction. And this, too, means that we may miss some of the expressions which would be available for decoding.

In developing norms on the recognition of pure, full affect displays, Ekman and his associates find a high level of reliable decoding, even when the expressions are presented on a tachistoscope for fractions of a second (Ekman and Friesen, 1975; Boucher and Ekman, 1975). Happy tends to enjoy the best recognition score, in this society and cross-culturally. But all the other major affect displays—surprise, fear, anger, disgust, and sadness—are decoded with an accuracy comparable to the meaning specification for common verbal symbols.

Affects in Interactions

In Ekman and Friesen's own terminology, affect displays are used most clearly as communication when they are employed as emblems. For example, an individual might say, "I was really sad then [sad expression], but I'm much better now [happy expression]." The first expression clearly does not reflect how the person is feeling now. Rather, it is an affect display used as an emblem.

Even the happy face is likely to be emblematic, an exaggerated display done for communication effectiveness.

A more difficult communication discrimination comes in the case in which an individual puts on a facial affect display in the hope of deceiving a receiver. Such a display may be done with intent. An encoder and decoder might apply the same meaning to the display, although in this case the decoder would be in error about the encoder's actual state. (For Ekman and Friesen, accurate decoding, or even a common code, is not required for communicative behavior.)

There may, of course, be typical expressions or variations of expressions which are used in common deception situations. And certain decoders, such as police interrogators or bank loan officers, may know the code better than the average observer.

Affect displays, of course, can also be used as illustrators, punctuating and elaborating verbal statements. If an individual says, "I gave him a smile," and performs the smile expression, the display has served as a *kinetograph,* illustrating a previously produced bodily movement.

Finally, affect displays may be important regulators, guiding the flow of interaction. Just as we have traffic signals to indicate "go," "stop," and "caution" or "slow," facial expressions may perform similar functions. A smile or a look of interest may be a green light, signaling the speaker to continue. A look of surprise or sad confusion may act as a yellow light, signaling caution. And a look of extreme surprise or intense anger or disgust may act as a red light, signaling the speaker to stop, retreat, or repeat.

While a good deal of research has been done on the regulatory functions of eye behavior and head nods, relatively little is known as yet about the regulation provided by affect displays. Similarly, the implications of facial displays are only beginning to be researched in the wider realm of interpersonal communication.

INTERPERSONAL IMPLICATIONS

Ekman and Friesen have been concerned primarily with display rules at a cultural level, to account for the seeming differences found in emotional displays cross-culturally, and more recently with personal display rules (1975:139). But there would appear to be display rules at all levels of social interactions: mass, social, organizational, personal, and interpersonal. So far, no one has articulated a complete profile of rules for any of the levels.

We might expect to find, for example, in a traditional organization, a general rule or norm for deintensifying affect displays: "Get the job done, and don't let your emotions get in the way." A more people-oriented organization might permit a fuller display of affect but still discourage the exhibition of intense, personal emotions. Similarly, in a hierarchical organization, it may be necessary to neutralize or mask feelings of anger toward a superior. It may be more possible to reveal anger in interaction with a peer. And it may be appropriate to display or even intensify expressions of anger in dealing with a subordinate.

At a social level, certain roles require the regulation of affect displays. Doctors and nurses, for example, should not show disgust, no matter how unpalatable the patient's condition. Salesmen are taught to smile even if they, and their business, are depressed. Interrogating officers may try to maintain a "poker face" so the suspect cannot discern which answers are eliciting surprise or satisfaction. Likewise, at a personal level, some individuals make it a point to "keep their cool" no matter what happens, while others adopt a life style which is open and emotional.

Emotions at an Interpersonal Level

Dealing with emotions may be particularly important at an interpersonal level. For one thing, emotions are somewhat contagious, and it is difficult to be happy if someone else in a close interpersonal relationship is miserable or intensely angry. Second, an interpersonal relationship may imply dealing with the "whole" person, as an individual. This means dealing with the other person's feelings: being aware of them, acknowledging them, perhaps taking responsibility for them, perhaps sharing positive affects, or taking steps to alleviate negative affects.

It may be part of an organizational or professional ethic to disregard feelings: "The show must go on" or "Get the task done." But if the same approach is continually applied to a friend or a marriage partner, the other person is likely to feel used. It may stop being an interpersonal relationship.

While we would expect interpersonal systems to be more open in their affect display rules than organizations, individual interpersonal relationships may range from those which maintain a tight rein on emotional displays to those which "let it all hang out." This in itself may reflect the degree of task-orientation of the dyad. For example, some married couples are very task-oriented, dedicated to upward social mobility or "getting the kids raised." For others, the main goal may be the exploration and elaboration of the relationship itself.

A couple may also evolve display rules for different situations or contexts. There may, for example, be rules for "getting through a social evening" or for behaving "when the in-laws are here." For some couples, a public setting requires intensification of displays of satisfaction with each other and a masking of anger. At home after the bridge party, the rules may reverse. For a young couple, there may be deintensification of positive affect in public or in front of parents, but in private the interpersonal display rules permit full vent to the emotions or even require intensification for one or both of the partners.

When two individuals initiate an interpersonal relationship, they are likely to bring to the dyad their personally derived display rules, plus those from their culture and those from their social circumstance, e.g., those appropriate for middle-class dating behavior. If there are sharp differences, these will have to be negotiated or, at least in some cases, the relationship may terminate.

For couples, the emotions and their display may be particularly troublesome where there are differences in the cultural rules. For example, if females are encouraged to be more expressive than males, she may say, "Why don't you let me know how you feel?" Then he may charge, "You're always flying off the handle." Similarly, personalities differ in their handling of emotions. One individual may do a "slow burn" for a long time before exploding in anger. Another individual may have a "short fuse" and a fast recovery time (e.g., Ekman and Friesen, 1975:78). The couple may not be able to change these deeply ingrained patterns of cultural or personal display, but may evolve interpersonal rules to accommodate them. (For example, "When I see you're going to explode, I'll just leave until it blows over.")

Some interpersonal display rules apply to the couple jointly; e.g., "When in public, we will look happy; at home, we'll look any way we want." Others apply differentially to individuals within the relationship; e.g., "When I look angry, you look fearful; when you look angry, I'll look disgusted."

Affects in the Development of Rules

While interpersonal rules may develop the governing of the display of emotions, the face and the show of specific affects may, in turn, play an important role in the evolution of other interpersonal rules. Sometimes, explicit verbal statements are made about the rules governing a relationship–e.g., "to love, honor, and obey" or "I think we ought to . . . " But perhaps typically, the rules evolve nonverbally, with little awareness of the ongoing process of negotiation and adoption, and perhaps even with little ability to verbalize a rule which has obviously been governing the relationship.

This process may begin with the communication of an expectation. Perhaps the most economical way to do that is through simple looking behavior. She looks at him. He thinks, "You expect me to do something" (although he probably typically responds without ever verbalizing, for himself, his interpretation of that message). He searches his repertoire of available options and does or says something.

If she responds with a look of surprise: "Nope, that wasn't it." Again, he may not take time to verbalize his interpretations to himself. He is more likely to respond with a reassuring smile and move on to his second option.

If his behavior is met with a look of joy–"That's it!"–he may find the smile very reinforcing, and the next time the situation comes up he will respond with greater speed and assurance. Soon he will not need the look of expectation; he will recognize the situation coming and anticipate the appropriate behavior. As the pattern becomes embedded in the interaction, a lapse or violation will indeed seem like "breaking a rule."

Just as a smile can be reinforcing, a look of anger, disgust, or contempt may extinguish responses. A look of fear may be similarly inhibiting, a signal that one is about to do something one should not.

In general, expressions of joy are a strong bonding force in a relationship. Expressions of sadness and fear may provide another kind of bonding, particularly if one partner can comfort and reassure the one who is feeling sad and fearful. Anger and disgust, if directed toward a partner, can be very disruptive in a relationship. But on the other hand, such negative expressions may help modify the relationship so that it is more likely to survive. Retribution may be made; expectations may be realigned; rules may be renegotiated.

In sum, emotions have a long evolutionary history, and they continue to function for each new dyad. Similarly, facial expressions, including those not related to the emotions, have a long history for the species, for each individual, and for partners in ongoing interaction. Their role in interpersonal communication is likely to become increasingly clear in current and future research.

NOTES

1. Secord (1958) distinguished between *structural* and *expressive* cues in the face. Harrison (1964) used those terms and added *structural-expressive* for those wrinkles, marks, and changes which endured. Harrison (1974), dealing with nonverbal cues generally, moved to the terms "enduring," "temporary," and "momentary." Temporary cues were those which might remain the same for one interaction (e.g., hair style) but could be changed over time. Cranach and Vine (1973) distinguish between appearance and movement. They place slow changes such as blanching and blushing into appearance. Recently, Ekman and Friesen (1975:70) have used the terms "static," "slow," and "rapid" to describe facial cues.

2. For example, Ekman (1973:198) argues that Cuceloglu's (1970) evidence for cross-cultural universals can only be taken as tentative, since (a) the pictographic representations may not accurately portray known facial movements, and (b) using all possible combinations of elements creates expressions which are rare and perhaps even anatomically impossible.

3. The stimuli were designed and tested by Harrison (1964). Cuceloglu (1967, 1972) used a revised set in international research. Subsequently, Thayer and Schiff (1969) independently developed a set with similar features. The use of drawn faces, of course, goes back to the work of Piderit (1867). And Cline (1956) used drawings to examine facial expressions in interaction.

4. Argyle (1975) summarizes recent research by noting that two major interpersonal dimensions typically emerge: dominant-submissive and hostile-friendly. Mehrabian (1972) explored three major dimensions: immediacy (liking-disliking); power (dominance-submission); and responsiveness.

5. A t test was run for each face-adjective combination. Reported adjectives were significantly related at the .01 level of significance.

6. It is not uncommon for silence or nonmovement to be meaningful in context. See, for example, Sebeok's (1975:233) discussion of "zero signs."

7. Osgood and Sebeok (1954:88) pointed to the possibility of synchronic events within or between bands and suggested that these might involve synchronic complementation or synchronic conflict.

8. Ruesch and Kees (1956:64) suggested that facial expressions provide metacommunication, modifying verbal output, until they reach a certain intensity at which point they become content themselves.

9. On the basis of recent research (Ekman and Friesen, 1975; forthcoming) it should be possible to draw a pictographic face which more clearly matches the known brow, eye, and mouth configurations for anger. Within the set of pictographs used, however, Figure 4h was clearly perceived as the most angry.

10. For further comment and elaboration of this idea, see Osgood (1966) and Stringer (1973).

REFERENCES

ALLOWAY, T., KRAMES, L., and PLINER, P. (eds., 1972). Communication and affect. New York: Academic Press.

ALTMANN, S.A. (ed., 1967). Social communication among primates. Chicago: University of Chicago Press.

ANDREW, R.J., and HUBER, E. (1972). Evolution of facial expression. New York: Arno, 1972.

ARGYLE, M. (1975). Bodily communication. London: Methuen.

ARGYLE, M., and COOK, M. (1975). Gaze and mutual gaze. Cambridge: Cambridge University Press.

ARNOLD, M. (ed., 1970). Feelings and emotions. New York: Academic Press.

BLURTON-JONES, N.G. (ed., 1972). Ethological studies of infant behaviour. Cambridge: Cambridge University Press.

BOUCHER, J.D., and EKMAN, P. (1975). "Facial areas and emotional information." Journal of Communication, 25:21-29.

BRUNER, J.S., and TAGIURI, R. (1954). "The perception of people." In G. Lindzey (ed.), Handbook of social psychology (vol. 2). Reading, Mass.: Addison-Wesley.

CHARLESWORTH, W.R., and KREUTZER, M.A. (1973). "Facial expressions of infants and children." In P. Ekman (ed.), Darwin and facial expression: A century of research in review. New York: Academic Press.

CHEVALIER-SKOLNIKOFF, S. (1973). "Facial expression of emotion in nonhuman primates." In P. Ekman (ed.), Darwin and facial expression: A century of research in review. New York: Academic Press.

CLINE, M. (1956). "The influence of social context on the perception of faces." Journal of Personality, 25:142-158.

CRANACH, M. von, and VINE, I. (eds., 1973). Social communication and movement. New York: Academic Press.

CUCELOGLU, D.M. (1967). A cross-cultural study of communication via facial expressions. Unpublished Ph.D. dissertation, University of Illinois. (University Microfilms No. 68-8046.)

——— (1970). "Perception of facial expressions in three cultures." Ergonomics, 13:93-100.

——— (1972). "Facial code in affective communication." In D.C. Speer (ed.), Nonverbal communication. Beverly Hills, Calif.: Sage.

DAVITZ, J.R. (1964). The communication of emotional meaning. New York: McGraw-Hill.

DITTMANN, A.T. (1972). Interpersonal messages of emotion. New York: Springer.

EIBL-EIBESFELDT, I. (1970). Ethology, the biology of behavior. New York: Holt, Rinehart and Winston.

--- (1971). Love and hate. New York: Holt, Rinehart and Winston.

--- (1972). "Similarities and differences between cultures in expressive movements." In R. Hinde (ed.), Non-verbal communication. Cambridge: Cambridge University Press.

--- (1973). "The expressive behaviour of the deaf-and-blind-born." In M. von Cranach and I. Vine (eds.), Social communication and movement. New York: Academic Press.

EKMAN, P. (1972). "Universals and cultural differences in facial expressions of emotion." In J.K. Cole (ed.), Nebraska Symposium on Motivation, 1971. Lincoln: University of Nebraska Press.

--- (ed., 1973). Darwin and facial expression: A century of research in review. New York: Academic Press.

--- (forthcoming). "Facial signs: Semiotic perspectives."

EKMAN, P., and FRIESEN, W.V. (1969). "The repertoire of nonverbal behavior: Categories, origins, usage, and coding." Semiotica, 1:49-98.

--- (1971). "Constants across cultures in the face and emotion." Journal of Personality and Social Psychology, 17:124-129.

--- (1975). Unmasking the face. Englewood Cliffs, N.J.: Prentice-Hall.

--- (forthcoming). "Measuring facial movement."

EKMAN, P., FRIESEN, W.V., and ELLSWORTH, P. (1972). Emotion in the human face: Guidelines for research and an integration of findings. New York: Pergamon.

FRIESEN, W.V. (1972). "Cultural differences in facial expressions in a social situation: An experimental test of the concept of display rules." Unpublished doctoral dissertation, University of California, San Francisco. (University Microfilms No. 73-3651.)

GRANT, E.C. (1968). "An ethological description of non-verbal behaviour during interviews." British Journal of Medical Psychology, 41:177-184.

--- (1969). "Human facial expression." Man, 4:525-536.

HARRISON, R.P. (1964). "Pictic analysis: Toward a vocabulary and syntax for the pictorial code; with research on facial expression." Unpublished doctoral dissertation, Michigan State University. (University Microfilms No. 65-6079.)

--- (1973). "Nonverbal communication." In I. de Sola Pool and W. Schramm (eds.), Handbook of communication. Chicago: Rand McNally.

--- (1974). Beyond words: An introduction to nonverbal communication. Englewood Cliffs, N.J.: Prentice-Hall.

HARRISON, R.P., COHEN, A.A., CROUCH, W., GENOVA, B.K.L., and STEINBERG, M. (1972). "The nonverbal communication literature." Journal of Communication, 22:339-352.

HINDE, R.A. (ed., 1972). Non-verbal communication. Cambridge: Cambridge University Press.

HJORTSJO, C.H. (1970). Man's face and mimic language. Lund, Swed.: Student-literature.

HOCKETT, C.F., and ALTMANN, S.A. (1968). "A note on design features." In T.A. Sebeok (ed.), Animal communication. Bloomington, Indiana University Press.

IZARD, C.E. (1971). The face of emotion. New York: Appleton-Century-Crofts.

KEY, M.R. (1975). Paralanguage and kinesics (nonverbal communication). Metuchen, N.J.: Scarecrow Press.

LA BARRE, W. (1947). "The cultural basis of emotion and gestures." Journal of Personality, 16:49-68.

--- (1964). "Paralinguistics, kinesics, and cultural anthropology." In T.A. Sebeok, A.S. Hayes, and M.C. Bateson (eds.), Approaches to semiotics. The Hague: Mouton.

MEHRABIAN, A. (1972). Nonverbal communication. Chicago: Aldine-Atherton.

OSGOOD, C.E. (1966). "Dimensionality of the semantic space for communication via facial expression." Scandinavian Journal of Psychology, 7:1-30.

OSGOOD, C.E., and SEBEOK, T.A. (eds., 1954). Psycholinguistics: A survey of theory and research problems. Baltimore: Waverly.

PIDERIT, T. (1867). Wissenschaftliches System, die Mimik und Physiognomik. Detmold, Ger.: Meyers.

REDICAN, W.K. (1975). "Facial expressions in nonhuman primates." In L.A. Rosenblum (ed.), Primate behavior: Developments in field and laboratory research (vol. 4). New York: Academic Press.

RUESCH, J., and KEES, W. (1956). Nonverbal communication. Berkeley: University of California Press.

SCHERER, K.R. (1970). Non-verbale Kommunikation. Hamburg: Helmut Buske.

SEBEOK, T.A. (ed., 1968). Animal communication. Bloomington: Indiana University Press.

——— (1975). "Six species of signs: Some propositions and strictures." Semiotica, 13:233-260.

——— (1976). "The semiotic web: A chronicle of prejudices." Unpublished manuscript, Indiana University.

SECORD, P.F. (1958). "Facial features and inference processes in interpersonal perception." In R. Tagiuri and L. Petrullo (eds.), Person perception and interpersonal behavior. Stanford, Calif.: Stanford University Press.

SROUFE, L.A., and WATERS, E. (1975). "The ontogenesis of smiling and laughter: A perspective on the organization of development in infancy." Unpublished manuscript, Institute of Child Development, University of Minnesota.

STRINGER, P.H. (1973). "Do dimensions have face validity?" In M. von Cranach and I. Vine (eds.), Social communication and movement. New York: Academic Press.

STRONGMAN, K.T. (1973). The psychology of emotion. New York: John Wiley.

THAYER, S., and SCHIFF, W. (1969). "Stimulus factors in observer judgment of social interaction." American Journal of Psychology, 82:72-85.

TOMKINS, S.S. (1962, 1963). Affect, imagery, consciousness (vols. 1 and 2). New York: Springer.

——— (1970). "Affect as the primary motivational system." In M. Arnold (ed.), Feelings and emotions. New York: Academic Press.

Van HOOFF, J.A.R.A.M. (1972). "A comparative approach to the phylogeny of laughter and smiling." In R.A. Hinde (ed.), Non-verbal communication. Cambridge: Cambridge University Press.

VINE, I. (1973). "The role of facial-visual signalling in early social development." In M. von Cranach and I. Vine (eds.), Social communication and movement. New York: Academic Press.

WATERS, E., MATAS, L., and SROUFE, L.A. (1975). "Infants' reactions to an approaching stranger: Description, validation, and functional significance of wariness." Child Development, 46:348-356.

WEITZ, S. (ed., 1974). Nonverbal communication: Readings with commentary. New York: Oxford University Press.

WIENER, M., De VOE, S., RUBINOW, S., and GELLER, J. (1972). "Nonverbal behavior and nonverbal communication." Psychological Review, 79:185-214.

Chapter 11

GROUP DECISIONING: TESTING A FINITE STOCHASTIC MODEL

Leonard C. Hawes and Joseph M. Foley

IT TAKES TALK AND TIME to make decisions. When people in groups make decisions, they get together and talk. This talk is a resource which, when used appropriately, makes decisions in much the same way lumber, hammers, and nails, when used appropriately, make houses. The catch phrase is, "when used appropriately." Talk, as a resource for making social interaction, has different functions. People using talk appropriate for making decisions use talk which functions in certain ways.

It also takes time to make decisions, in large part because it takes time to make an utterance. The passing of time in decisioning groups is punctuated with talk which functions in specified ways. In short, using talk appropriate for making decisions means using talk which functions differently at different points in time. This paper is an empirical description of that activity. It presents an empirically fine-grained description of how people use talk over time to make decisions.

Communication researchers typically use the term "process" when referring to talk embedded in time. Merriam-Webster's *Collegiate Dictionary* defines

AUTHORS' NOTE: This paper is based on research performed pursuant to grant No. OEG-0-4520 from the Office of Education, U.S. Department of Health, Education, and Welfare–a grant awarded the senior author. Points of view or opinions stated do not necessarily represent official Office of Education position or policy. The study was conducted at the Behavioral Science Laboratory at The Ohio State University. The authors wish to thank Gerald R. Miller, Dean E. Hewes, and B. Aubrey Fisher for their critical reviews of an earlier draft of this paper and for their suggestions for strengthening it.

"process" as "a series of actions or operations conducing to an end." Hertel (1972) argues that such a definition of process must take into account (a) a molecular description or specification of the actions or operations being studied, (b) a molar description of the sequential relationship among these units, and (c) the designation of the goal(s) or end point(s) toward which it moves.

FINITE STOCHASTIC MODELS

Given the above conceptualizations of *time, talk,* and *process,* a model was required that would facilitate a detailed and precise description of decisioning activity. The family of finite stochastic models seemed an appropriate place to look. Hertel's (1972) first stipulation for a definition of *process* is a molecular description of the actions being studied. Discussing the capabilities of finite stochastic models, Hewes (1975:271) says, "The term 'finite' implies that at least the dependent variable in these models must be composed of a finite number of discrete, mutually exclusive and exhaustive categories." Constructing a finite number of discrete, mutually exclusive, and exhaustive categories for coding talk during a group decisioning session satisfies Hertel's (1972) definitional stipulation for process and is specifically called for when using a finite stochastic model.

A second attractive feature of finite stochastic models is their theoretical compatability with the above conceptualizations of time, talk, and process. Recall that Hertel's (1972) second stipulation for a definition of process is a description of the sequential relationship among units. Parzen (1962:v) defines stochastic processes as follows:

> The theory of stochastic process is generally defined as the "dynamic" part of probability theory, in which one studies a collection of random variables (called a *stochastic process*) from the point of view of their interdependence and limiting behavior. One is observing a stochastic process whenever one examines a process developing in time in a manner controlled by probabilistic laws.

The collection of random variables is the set of discrete, mutually exclusive, and exhaustive categories. Their sequential relationship can be studied in terms of the interdependence and limiting behavior of these categories on each other over time.

The third stipulation of Hertel's (1972) definition of process is that goals or end points of the process be specified. A specific type of finite stochastic model fits this third stipulation. Hewes (1975:274) says, "the Markov chain becomes an immensely powerful tool for predicting the distribution of attitudes, or other variables, at any point in the future. It is this property which makes such stochastic models highly useful in examining processes." If the goal of decisioning processes is to formulate decisions, use of a model which enables us to predict these goal states, as well as intermediate patterns of states leading to that goal, has exciting theoretic potential.

Before theory can be developed and tested based on our descriptive data, however, it is necessary to determine the goodness of fit between the model selected and the decisioning activity observed and coded. The remainder of this paper discusses the finite stochastic model we used to represent the decisioning process, identifies the assumptions of that model, and reports the results obtained when the model was tested against group decisioning activity. Given the test results, the appropriateness of using the model for subsequent decisioning research is explicated.

DECISIONING AS A DISCRETE MARKOV CHAIN

A discrete Markov chain was selected to model group decisioning activity; its conceptual isomorphism with decisioning, as we defined it, as well as its potential predictive power made it the appropriate model to test. The set of discrete, mutually exclusive, and exhaustive categories into which utterances of talk were coded is the collection of random variables. The ensuing analyses focus not upon the individual or paired codes of talk but upon transitions between coded utterances. More specifically, the procedures focus on the relative frequencies of transitions between utterances rather than on the relative frequencies of the utterances themselves.

Describing decisioning processes by inspecting transition probabilities between codes in a long string, however, was an awkward and inefficient way to proceed. To streamline analysis, transition probabilities between codes were displayed in matrix form. The matrix functioned as a summary of transition probabilities between codes found in the original string. Displaying transition probabilities in matrix form had the heuristic advantage of providing information not only about what could be found, on the average, within a string of coded utterances but also what could be found within all possible strings of coded talk having the same transition probabilities. Once in matrix form, we compared the decisioning processes that the matrices modeled.

A transition matrix ignores all properties of the string of coded utterances except frequencies of transition probabilities in the string. If one is willing to describe a string of coded utterances completely by a matrix, the string of codes can then be examined for Markovian properties. As we pointed out earlier, the advantage of knowing that a process closely resembles a discrete Markov chain is the resulting ability to predict the distribution of coded utterances at any point in the future.

Assumptions to be Tested

In hypothesis testing, the theory is usually identified with the alternative hypothesis to be tested against a null. In model testing, and especially Markov chain model testing, the model is identified with the null hypothesis, and a violation of the assumptions of the model is tested by seeking rejection of the null hypothesis.

To conclude that group decisioning processes can be modeled as discrete Markov chains, we had to test three assumptions: stationarity, order, and homogeneity. First, data being mapped onto a discrete Markov chain must be stationary; transition probabilities are assumed to be stationary across time. Bartos (1967:29) defines a stationary Markov chain as a "process the transition probabilities of which do not depend on t."

Perhaps the most direct test of stationarity is to consider a string of coded utterances linked by transition probabilities to be a probability vector, V, of a given length. Probability vector V can be subdivided into shorter probability vectors, ${}^{t+1}V$, ${}^{t+2}V$, . . . ${}^{t+n}V$, of variable lengths, each considered to have been generated by the same process responsible for generating V. Probability vector V is then transformed into a composite transition matrix, M, and each shorter probability vector, ${}^{t+n}V$, is transformed into an individual transition matrix, ${}^{t+n}M$. Each ${}^{t+n}M$ is then compared to M to determine statistical dependence or independence. The null hypothesis identified with the model is that there are no statistically significant differences between each ${}^{t+n}M$ when compared to M. If the null hypothesis is not rejected, it is concluded that each ${}^{t+n}V$ was generated by the same process and that the process remained stationary for the time duration being studied.

The second assumption to be tested is that data mapped onto a discrete Markov chain are of first order. The alternative hypothesis is that the string of coded utterances is second or higher order. Consider a string of codes representing sequential utterances made during a decisioning session. That string is a first order Markov chain if any given code in the string can be maximally predicted knowing only the immediately preceding code in the string. If we must know the preceding two codes to maximally predict the next code, the string is second order. A third order string means we must know the preceding three codes to maximally predict the next, and so forth.

The third assumption to be tested is that data mapped onto a discrete Markov chain are homogeneous; there are no radically different subgroups being modeled. Stated another way, the initial probability vector, V, and the transition matrix, M, are assumed to represent all subgroups in the sample. Procedures used to test the homogeneity assumption are similar to those used to test the stationarity assumption. The null hypothesis identified with the model is that there are no statistically significant differences between each submatrix, ${}^{t+n}M$, when compared to their composite matrix, M.

GENERAL PROCEDURES

Seven meetings of three established academic committees were videotaped, audiotaped, and transcribed. Each of these seven meetings lasted approximately two hours. All three were established committees (i.e., groups with histories prior to the study). Two were university committees; the third was a departmental committee. The first university committee (A) consisted of eight faculty and four student members. The second university committee (B) consisted of nine faculty and five student members. The departmental committee (C) consisted of one faculty and 10 student members. Faculty members were the appointed chairpersons of all three committees. Two meetings of committees A and B and three meetings of committee C were recorded.

Coding Categories

Fisher (1970) constructed a four-dimensional coding system for the talk of the groups he studied. We used a modified version of one of those dimensions. Fisher's (1970) *mode* dimension is comprised of two categories–*assert* and *request*. These two modes indicate when talk functions to assert information and when it functions to request information pertinent to the topic being talked about. We added *propose* to the mode dimension because we were interested in when utterances functioned to propose a specific formulation of a decision.

We were interested also in the role of the person doing the asserting, requesting, and proposing. Group members were classified as chairperson, faculty, and student. As mentioned earlier, the three chairpersons were faculty. Utterances of chairpersons were counted only once; they were not coded as faculty utterances.

The result was a set of nine source-mode categories: (1) chairperson assert, (2) chairperson request, (3) chairperson propose, (4) faculty assert, (5) faculty request, (6) faculty propose, (7) student assert, (8) student request, and (9) student propose.

Coding Reliability

Obtained values of unitizing reliability were determined by expressing the difference between two coders as a percentage of the sum of the numbers of coded utterances obtained by each coder. A unit was an uninterrupted utterance or an utterance-part with a single function. In other words, if one utterance was long and uninterrupted but its function changed from, say, an assertion to a request, two units were coded. Using these obtained values of unitizing reliability, we used Guetzkow's (1950) formula to obtain estimates of coder unitizing reliability. Obtained values of unitized reliability ranged from .05 to

.12 when two coders unitized three segments of transcripts, each segment consisting of approximately 100 units of talk. The most conservative obtained value, .12, can be expected only one time in 100 when the coefficient of variation for two coders is .03. This estimate of unitizing reliability was considered quite satisfactory.

The obtained values of categorizing reliability for two coders were computed by summing the units that they classified identically and those units that they classified differently and then dividing by the total number of units coded. These obtained proportions of agreement (P′) were then used as single estimators in Guetzkow's (1950) formula for determining the theoretical proportion of agreement (P). Seven obtained values of categorizing reliability—ranging from .89 to .97—were used as estimators. The most conservative P′ produced expected limits of the theoretical proportion of categorizing reliability between two coders of .88 ± .05, or .83 to .93, which was considered quite satisfactory.

TESTING STATIONARITY

The meetings of each committee were modeled as separate decisioning processes. Committees A and B each generated two probability vectors, V. Committee C generated three probability vectors, V. The probability vectors that each committee generated were transformed in two ways. First, the vectors that each system produced were combined and transformed into one composite transition matrix, M; the seven probability vectors, V, became three transition matrices, M.

Each of the seven probability vectors, V, was also subdivided into four shorter probability vectors, ${}^{t+n}V$, of equal length (in terms of number of coded utterances and corresponding transition probabilities). Each ${}^{t+n}V$ was then transformed into a transition matrix, ${}^{t+n}M$, which was compared to the composite transition matrix, M. For committees A and B, eight ${}^{t+n}M$'s (two meetings, each subdivided into fourths) were compared to their respective M's. For committee C, 12 ${}^{t+n}M$'s (three meetings, each subdivided into fourths) were compared to their M. If each decisioning process was stationary, the transition matrices, ${}^{t+n}M$'s, should not differ significantly when compared to each other and to the composite matrix, M. In short, the transition matrices should not differ significantly from quarter to quarter during the meetings. Therefore, the first null hypothesis posits no statistically significantly differences among the transition matrices, ${}^{t+n}M$'s, when compared to their composite matrix, M, for the two meetings of committee A.

$$H_1: {}^{t+1}M_{A1} = {}^{t+2}M_{A1} = {}^{t+3}M_{A1} = {}^{t+4}M_{A1} = {}^{t+1}M_{A2} = {}^{t+2}M_{A2} = {}^{t+3}M_{A2} = {}^{t+4}M_{A2} = M_A$$

The first null hypothesis reads as follows. There are no statistically significant differences between the transition probabilities from all nine source-mode states in the four transition matrices of meeting No. 1, the four transition matrices of meeting No. 2, and the composite transition matrix of the two meetings for committee A.

The second null hypothesis is identical to the first, with respect to committee B.

$$H_2: {}^{t+1}M_{B1} = {}^{t+2}M_{B1} = {}^{t+3}M_{B1} = {}^{t+4}M_{B1} = {}^{t+1}M_{B2} = {}^{t+2}M_{B2} = {}^{t+3}M_{B2} = {}^{t+4}M_{B2} = M_B$$

Inasmuch as committees A and B are very similar in terms of history, membership-role distribution, number of members, and source of power, we wanted to know if the two committees could be treated as the same process. To answer this question, we combined the two probability vectors, V_A and V_B, into a composite transition matrix, M_{AB}. The eight meetings of these two committees each were divided into four probability vectors, ${}^{t+n}V$, as we did in the first two null hypotheses. Each probability vector was transformed into a transition matrix, ${}^{t+n}M$. The resulting 16 transition matrices were then compared to the composite matrix, M_{AB}. The third null hypothesis, then, posits no statistically significant differences among the transition matrices, ${}^{t+n}M$, when compared to their composite, M, when the two university committees were treated as a single process.

$$H_3: {}^{t+1}M_{A1} = {}^{t+2}M_{A1} = {}^{t+3}M_{A1} = {}^{t+4}M_{A1} = {}^{t+1}M_{A2} = {}^{t+2}M_{A2} = {}^{t+3}M_{A2} = {}^{t+4}M_{A2} = {}^{t+1}M_{B1} = {}^{t+2}M_{B1} = {}^{t+3}M_{B1} = {}^{t+4}M_{B1} = {}^{t+1}M_{B2} = {}^{t+2}M_{B2} = {}^{t+3}M_{B2} = {}^{t+4}M_{B2} = M_{AB}$$

The fourth null hypothesis is identical to the first two, with respect to the three meetings of committee C.

$$H_4: {}^{t+1}M_{C1} = {}^{t+2}M_{C1} = {}^{t+3}M_{C1} = {}^{t+4}M_{C1} = {}^{t+1}M_{C2} = {}^{t+2}M_{C2} = {}^{t+3}M_{C3} = {}^{t+4}M_{C2} = {}^{t+1}M_{C3} = {}^{t+2}M_{C3} = {}^{t+3}M_{C3} = {}^{t+4}M_{C3} = M_C$$

Method

The four null hypotheses of source-mode stationarity, identified with the discrete Markov model, were tested by comparing the maximum likelihood estimates of the parameters of each matrix, ${}^{t+n}M$, with the maximum likelihood estimates of the parameters of the appropriate composite matrices, M. The maximum likelihood estimates are the relevant proportions for each case.

We used the test that Lewis (1970) employed in similar group research. Anderson and Goodman (1957) developed the likelihood ratio test, LR, specifically for Markov chain research, in which

$$LR = -2 \sum_{t,j} \left\{ n_{ij}^{(t)} \left[\log_e(\hat{P}_{ij}) - \log_e(\hat{P}_{ij}^{(t)}) \right] \right\} \quad [1]$$

where $\hat{P}_{ij}$ is the probability of the ij transition in the composite matrix; $\hat{P}_{ij}^{(t)}$ is the probability of the ij transition in the individual matrices, t; and $n_{ij}^{(t)}$ is the frequency of the ij transition in the individual matrix, t. This statistic has a chi-square distribution with degrees of freedom equal to m(m−1)(T−1), where m is the number of rows or columns of the matrices being compared, and T is the number of independent matrices being compared.

Because of the chi-square distribution of this statistic, an LR value significant at the specified alpha level (.05 in this study) means that the transition probabilities of the individual matrices, ${}^{t+n}M$, and the transition probabilities of the composite matrix, M, are statistically independent of one another. Stated another way, the individual matrices can be treated as if they were generated by a committee different from the one represented by the composite matrix; statistically significant LR values mean that the null hypotheses must be rejected. Conversely, LR values less than those stipulated at the .05 alpha level constitute support for the model-to-data goodness of fit.

Results

Table 1 presents the results of the tests of stationarity. As can be seen, the second null hypothesis was not accepted. The first, third, and fourth null hypotheses were accepted.

The four null hypotheses posited that the transition probabilities from *all* nine source-mode states in the individual transition matrices and the composite matrix were the same. When a statistically significant LR value was obtained, the

TABLE 1

LR VALUES FOR THE FOUR NULL HYPOTHESES TESTING THE ASSUMPTION OF STATIONARITY

Hypothesis Number	*Committee*	*Number of Meetings*	*LR*	*df*	*p*
1	A	2	434.5488	504	ns
2	B	2	600.5671	504	ns
3	A&B	4	1155.8872	1080	.05
4	C	3	392.6707	792	ns

null hypothesis involved could not be accepted. However, the source of the lack of stationarity could not be determined from the results; the source-mode state(s) responsible for the lack of stationarity was (were) not identified. Consequently, when statistically significant LR values were obtained, an additional maximum likelihood estimate procedure was followed. The procedure tested the null hypothesis that transition probabilities from *each* (instead of *all*) nine source-mode states in the individual transition matrices and the composite matrix were the same.

Table 2 presents the LR values for the tests of null hypotheses 2a through 2i. It is the *assert* mode for all three source-roles that accounts for the lack of stationarity in the two meetings of committee B.

When considered by itself, committee B cannot be treated as a decisioning process whose source-mode parameters remain stationary across two meetings when those meetings are subdivided into shorter probability vectors. Specifically, it is the transition probabilities from the states of *faculty assert, student assert,* and *chairperson assert* that lack stationarity.

The pattern of results is intriguing. That the meetings of committees A and C were stationary over time, in terms of transition probabilities from the nine source-mode states, is not difficult to explain. The most parsimonious explanation is that the order of talking and the function of the individual utterances never changed significantly during the times studied. *Who* talked when and *how* they talked remained stationary—for whatever reason(s).

Why, then, is H_3 accepted but H_2 is not? Recall that H_3 treated committees A and B as one process; the two meetings of committee A and the two meetings of committee B were treated as probability vectors generated by the same

TABLE 2

LR VALUES FOR THE NINE NULL HYPOTHESES TESTING THE ASSUMPTION OF STATIONARITY FOR EACH SPEAKER-MODE STATE FOR COMMITTEE B

Hypothesis Number	*Speaker-Mode**	*LR*	*df*	*p*
2a	FA	205.6467	56	.001
2b	SA	78.9615	56	.01
2c	CA	97.1401	56	.001
2d	FR	45.5272	56	ns
2e	SR	20.8475	56	ns
2f	CR	41.3355	56	ns
2g	FP	57.6448	56	ns
2h	SP	24.1942	56	ns
2i	CP	29.2705	56	ns

*The first letter represents speaker, the second letter represents mode.

F = Faculty A = Assert
S = Student R = Request
C = Chairperson P = Propose

process. Each of these four probability vectors was subdivided into four smaller probability vectors which, in turn, were transformed into transition matrices. Sixteen, rather than eight, matrices were compared to the composite transition matrix. In short, we were using a probability vector twice as long (i.e., twice as many coded utterances and corresponding transition probabilities) as the ones used to test the stationarity of committees A and B individually.

When committees A and B were treated as one process rather than two, the assumption of source-mode stationarity was supported; when treated as separate processes, the assumption was not supported for committee B. The most parsimonious explanation is that the variability of transition probabilities from the three source-mode states in question was small enough to lose its statistical significance when the vectors were combined (thereby increasing sample size), and the number of degrees of freedom for the resulting LR value was thereby increased.

TESTING ORDER

The order assumption of a discrete Markov chain model posits that the string of coded utterances are first order and not second or higher order in nature. For an indefinitely long string of discrete codes—say, . . . C, E, Q, A, O, L, . . . etc.—any code in that string can be maximally predicted from the single code preceding it. In our hypothetical string of codes, if we wanted to know with as much certainty as possible when an A will occur, all we have to do is know when a Q occurs because we know with as much certainty as possible that A's follow Q's. If the string were second order it would mean that A's could be predicted with more certainty by knowing the two preceding codes than by knowing only the single preceding code; i.e., knowing that both E and Q immediately precede A better enables us to predict A than if we just know Q to be the immediately preceding code.

The procedures for testing the first order assumption are as follows. First, the frequencies of the nine speaker-mode categories, taken individually, were listed then summed across the nine categories. The 81 possible paired combinations of the nine categories were then listed, and the frequencies were summed across the 81 pairs. The same was done for the 729 possible triplet combinations and the 6,561 possible quadruplet combinations of the original nine individual categories.

Second, these summed frequencies for singles, pairs, triplets, and quadruplets were converted into empirical proportions, p, to be used in the following formula (Attneave, 1959:20):

$$H_i = \sum \hat{p}_i \log \frac{1}{\hat{p}_i} \qquad [2]$$

where $\hat{H}_i$ is the information value of all individual categories, or all paired combinations, or all tripled combinations, etc., and $\hat{p}_i$ is the empirical proportion (as opposed to a priori probability) of the first, second, third, and fourth order combinations of the categories. Consequently, this procedure results in an H value for the string of coded utterances when treated as a first order, second order, third order, and fourth order chain.

Third, we determined the differences between the successive order values of H_i. In other words, we determined the amount by which H_2 (information value of pairs of categories) exceeded H_1 (information value of individual categories) in terms of the new information contributed by the second member of the pair. We were determining if knowledge of the two codes preceding a given code would increase its predictability (i.e., decrease the amount of new information it contains) more than if only one preceding code were taken into account.

Fourteen hypotheses were advanced, two for each of the seven meetings of the three committees. The first hypothesis for a meeting posited a statistically significant difference between H values for the first order and zero order analyses of the string of coded utterances. In other words, we hypothesized that the string was not random, but knowing the preceding code better enabled us to predict the next code than if we simply guessed. The second hypothesis for each meeting was a null and identified directly with the model. It posited no statistically significant differences between H values for the second and first order analyses. In other words, we posited that the string of coded utterances for the seven meetings were first order in nature. Specifically:

H_{5a}: $H_2 - H_1 \neq H_1 - H_0$ for committee A, meeting No. 1.

H_{5b}: $H_3 - H_2 = H_2 - H_1$ for committee A, meeting No. 1.

The remaining 12 hypotheses were identical in form to the above two with respect to the six other meetings of the three committees.

Method

The 14 order-related hypotheses were tested using procedures that Attneave (1959) proposed. He constructed a variant of the information statistic, H, to determine how much new information is contributed by adding more preceding units in terms of better predicting the immediately subsequent unit. He also provided an approximate chi-square test for determining statistically significant differences between successive orders of strings. The formula is based on the asymptotic relationship between the estimate of shared information, $\hat{T}$, and the measure of the significance of this estimate, X^2:

$$X^2 \cong 2(\log_e 2)n\hat{T} \quad [3]$$

where $2(\log_e 2)$ is equal to 1.3863, n is the number of coded utterances in the string, and T is the difference in H values of the successive orders being compared. The statistic has $(c-1)^2$ degrees of freedom for first order and $c^{i-1}(c-1)^2$ degrees of freedom for second or higher order analyses, where c is the number of discrete categories (see Chatfield, 1973).

Results

Table 3 presents test results of the order assumption. All 14 hypotheses were accepted. Recall that the a hypotheses were hypotheses of difference; they posited that first order analyses better predicted coded utterances than did zero order analyses. The b hypotheses were nulls positing no difference between first and second order analyses in terms of best predicting subsequent coded utterances.

We attempted to determine the power of these tests but were not completely satisfied. Cohen (1969) presents tables of power values for the chi-square statistic. He constructed his tables using four parameters of statistical inference: power, significance criterion, sample size, and effect size. Cohen (1969:14) contends that these four parameters "are so related that any one of them is a

TABLE 3
CHI SQUARE VALUES FOR THE 14 HYPOTHESES
TESTING THE ASSUMPTION OF ORDER

Hypothesis Number	*Committee*	*Number of Meetings*	*Chi Square*	*df*	*p*
5a	A	1	85.0075	64	.05
5b	A	1	257.3608	576	ns
6a	A	2	98.1974	64	.01
6b	A	2	67.3531	576	ns
7a	B	1	135.1764	64	.01
7b	B	1	262.2920	576	ns
8a	B	2	264.9815	64	.01
8b	B	2	453.8173	576	ns
9a	C	1	124.9261	64	.01
9b	C	1	127.6792	576	ns
10a	C	2	139.8565	64	.01
10b	C	2	126.2740	576	ns
11a	C	3	970.7924	64	.01
11b	C	3	138.7237	576	ns

function of the other three, which means that when any three of them are fixed, the fourth is completely determined."

Unfortunately for our purposes, he constructed the tables up to only 24 degrees of freedom; our chi-square values for the test of order began with 64 degrees of freedom. We interpolated a power value for our a hypotheses, whose respective chi-square values were based on a significance criterion of .05, sample sizes (in this study, sample size was the number of coded utterances in the zero-order string) ranging from 282 to 461, and a moderate effect size of .10. Using 350 as the average sample size, our best interpolated power value for 64 degrees of freedom was between .70 and .80. The power value for 24 degrees of freedom (the upper limit of the tables) with an alpha size of .05, an effect size of .10, and a sample size of 350 was .96.

Although we were reasonably confident of the interpolated power value for 64 degrees of freedom, we were not confident in interpolating power values for 576 degrees of freedom–the degrees of freedom value for our b hypotheses. Currently, we are searching for a procedure to more accurately determine the power of this approximate chi-square test. Our best guess is that the test is reasonably powerful at relatively low levels of degrees of freedom; it is difficult to determine the power of the statistic at much higher levels of degrees of freedom.

Given the above qualification of the power of our statistic, however, we concluded that our data could be treated as first order. Thus far, the decisioning committees appear to be stationary over time and exhibit first order properties.

TESTING HOMOGENEITY

The assumption of homogeneity posits that no subgroups in the population have substantially different transition probabilities. The procedures used to test the homogeneity assumption were very similar to those used to test the stationarity assumption. As with stationarity, each committee meeting was treated as a separate decisioning process. Committees A and B each generated two probability vectors, and committee C generated three. The homogeneity assumption posits that, given this interpretation, there are no significant differences in transition probabilities between meetings generated by the same committee.

The seven probability vectors, V, were transformed into seven transition matrices, M. The two transition matrices for committee A were combined to form a composite matrix, M, against which each of the two separate transition matrices could be compared. The same procedure was followed for the two meetings of committee B and the three meetings of committee C. Three null hypotheses were posited.

$$H_{12}: M_{A1} = M_{A2} = M_A$$

The null hypothesis reads as follows: there are no statistically significant differences in transition probabilities between meeting No. 1 of committee A, meeting No. 2 of committee A, and the composite of both meetings. Following are the other two null hypotheses identified with the homogeneity assumption of the discrete Markov chain model:

$$H_{13}: M_{B1} = M_{B2} = M_B$$

$$H_{14}: M_{C1} = M_{C2} = M_{C3} = M_C$$

Method

The three null hypotheses of source-mode homogeneity were tested, as were the stationarity null hypotheses, using Anderson and Goodman's (1957) maximum likelihood statistic. The statistic has a chi-square distribution; therefore, a statistically significant LR value means that the transition probabilities of the matrices representing the individual meetings and the composite matrix are statistically independent of one another. Statistically nonsignificant LR values constitute support for the model-to-data goodness of fit.

Results

Table 4 presents the results of the homogeneity tests. As can be seen, the first two null hypotheses were rejected; the third was accepted. As with the tests of stationarity, when a null hypothesis was rejected it meant that the transition probabilities from *all* nine source-mode states in the transition matrices being compared were independent of one another. When a null hypothesis was rejected, as was H_{12} and H_{13}, an additional maximum likelihood estimate procedure was followed to determine which states were responsible for the lack of homogeneity. The procedure tested the null hypothesis that the transition probabilities from *each* (instead of *all*) nine source-mode states in the individual and composite transition matrices are the same.

TABLE 4

LR VALUES FOR THE THREE NULL HYPOTHESES TESTING THE ASSUMPTION OF HOMOGENEITY

Hypothesis Number	*Committee*	*Number of Meetings*	*LR*	*df*	*p*
12	A	1&2	125.4188	72	.001
13	B	1&2	192.8154	72	.001
14	C	1,2&3	73.4588	144	ns

Eighteen additional null hypotheses were posited to determine the source of the lack of homogeneity made apparent by the rejection of H_{12} and H_{13}. The form of these 18 null hypotheses is as follows: the transition probabilities from *each* speaker-mode state in *each* of the matrices, for the meetings involved, are not significantly different from the transition probabilities from *each* speaker-mode state in the respective composite matrix. In other words, each of the nine speaker-mode states was tested individually for homogeneity with respect to committees A and B.

Table 5 presents the results of these tests. For committee A, the transition probabilities from *faculty assert, chairperson assert,* and *faculty propose* are not homogeneous. For committee B, the transition probabilities from *faculty assert, student assert, chairperson assert,* and *student propose* were not homogeneous. At this stage of our descriptive research, there are no a priori conceptual reasons for these particular speaker-mode states lacking homogeneity.

Considering the results of the stationarity tests together with the results of the tests of homogeneity, we may advisably conclude that committee meetings, similar to those studied here, are best analyzed separately. Although null

TABLE 5

LR VALUES FOR THE 18 NULL HYPOTHESES TESTING THE ASSUMPTION OF HOMOGENEITY FOR EACH SPEAKER-MODE STATE

Hypothesis Number	*Speaker-Mode**	*Committee*	*Number of Meetings*	*LR*	*df*	*p*
15	FA	A	1&2	36.1221	8	.001
16	SA	A	1&2	8.4418	8	ns
17	CA	A	1&2	26.7091	8	.001
18	FR	A	1&2	12.5785	8	ns
19	SR	A	1&2	0.0000	8	ns
20	CR	A	1&2	9.5347	8	ns
21	FP	A	1&2	23.4890	8	.005
22	SP	A	1&2	0.0000	8	ns
23	CP	A	1&2	8.5366	8	ns
24	FA	B	1&2	69.0274	8	.001
25	SA	B	1&2	22.2875	8	.005
26	CA	B	1&2	36.9923	8	.001
27	FR	B	1&2	12.8198	8	ns
28	SR	B	1&2	6.7561	8	ns
29	CR	B	1&2	14.7621	8	ns
30	FP	B	1&2	4.1807	8	ns
31	SP	B	1&2	20.8621	8	.01
32	CP	B	1&2	5.1237	8	ns

*The first letter represents speaker, the second letter represents mode.

F = Faculty A = Assert
S = Student R = Request
C = Chairperson P = Propose

hypothesis H_{14} was accepted–thus indicating that the three meetings of committee C and their composite transition matrix did not differ significantly from each other–it may be more prudent to treat each meeting as a separate decisioning process and to test each meeting for stationarity, order, and homogeneity.

That we did not satisfy the homogeneity assumption, as we operationally defined it, does not necessarily mean that our data cannot be mapped onto a discrete Markov chain model. It may mean that we need to consider a slightly different way of operationally defining homogeneity. It is also possible that not every meeting of every group will meet all three assumptions of the discrete Markov chain model. Had we investigated a greater number of committee meetings, we may have found that some committees generated homogeneous output whereas others did not. This, of course, remains an empirical question. There is evidence, however, that a discrete Markov chain can be used as an appropriate model even though not all groups meet all assumptions. For example, Lewis (1970) investigated the stationarity assumption of group discussions and concluded that the model was appropriate for certain descriptive purposes even though approximately one-third of the discussions did not satisfy the stationarity assumption.

Clearly, more work is needed to refine this particular modeling activity. Perhaps one way of proceeding is to go back to the coded transcripts and use discourse analysis techniques (Sacks, 1972; Schegloff, 1972) to develop more specific conceptual models of how people use utterances communicatively to build decisions. Another avenue is to continue using the discrete Markov chain as a model for decisioning activity, defining homogeneity as within-meeting rather than between-meeting homogeneity.

DISCUSSION

Assuming stationarity, order, and homogeneity, Kemeny and Snell (1960) identify various process characteristics that can be calculated from a transition matrix: (1) the mean and variance of the number of transitional steps necessary to move from any one coded utterance to any other, (2) the probability of moving from any one coded utterance to another in a specified number of transitional steps, (3) the mean and variance of the number of times that the process will move to any of the coded utterances in a specified number of steps starting with a specified utterance, and (4) the probability of "moving through" a specified utterance when moving from one utterance to another.

Such procedures are conceptually advantageous for several reasons. There is a sizable literature (e.g., Bales, 1950, 1972; Bales and Slater, 1955; Bennis and Shepard, 1956; Schutz, 1958; Tuckman, 1965; Fisher, 1970; Valentine and

Fisher, 1974; Ellis and Fisher, 1975) indicating that discussion groups move through different phases of activity in the course of discussing a problem. Fisher (1970) is the first to mention at what times groups change from one phase to another. He counted the number of utterances during a meeting and specified approximate points in the process when the group left one phase and entered the next.

For example, Fisher (1970) says that certain categories of utterances appear close together with relatively high frequencies during the orientation phase of a discussion. As the group enters the conflict phase, different categories frequently appear close together. Using a discrete Markov chain model would allow us to specify and predict such behavior with greater specificity. What is the mean and variance of the number of transitions needed to move from utterances characteristic of the orientation phase to utterances characteristic of the conflict phase, and so forth? The answer could tell us something about the *length* of respective phases. What is the probability of moving from one conflict utterance to another in a certain number of transitions during the conflict phase? The answer could tell us something about the *intensity* of the phase. What is the mean and variance of the number of times that the process will move to a specified utterance starting with another specified utterance? The answer could tell us something about the *rate* at which the process transforms itself into a new phase. What is the probability of the process moving through a certain utterance when moving from one utterance (or phase) to another? The answer could tell us something about the *constituency* of respective phases.

The more long-range theoretical implications of this research are for the eventual specification of "rules" of group decisioning. We are using the term "rule" in its constitutive and regulative, rather than prescriptive sense. In other words, what are the rules that, when adhered to, generate or constitute appropriate talk for making decisions?

But we are a long way from realizing these theoretical and methodological objectives. At present, all we have is evidence that a nine-state source-mode decisioning process is stationary, first order, and perhaps homogeneous if meetings are analyzed separately. The next set of studies in our research program analyzes more specific functions of assertions. That is the mode where homogeneity could not be assumed. We are now looking at the several functions of assertions, mapping these functions onto a similar model to determine if homogeneity can be assumed. If so, the model will continue to be used to answer the questions mentioned above. If not, the model will be modified.

REFERENCES

ANDERSON, T.W., and GOODMAN, L.A. (1957). "Statistical inference about Markov chains." Annals of Mathematical Statistics, 28:89-110.

ATTNEAVE, F. (1959). Applications of information theory to psychology: A summary of basic concepts, methods, and results. New York: Holt, Rinehart and Winston.

BALES, R.F. (1950). Interaction process analysis. Reading, Mass.: Addison-Wesley.

--- (1972). Personality and interpersonal behavior. New York: Holt, Rinehart and Winston.

BALES, R.F., and SLATER, P.E. (1955). "Role differentiation in small decision-making groups." In T. Parsons and R.F. Bales (eds.), Family socialization and interaction process. Glencoe, Ill.: Free Press.

BARTOS, O.J. (1967). Simple models of group behavior. New York: Columbia University Press.

BENNIS, W.G., and SHEPARD, H.A. (1956). "A theory of group development." Human Relations, 9:415-437.

CHATFIELD, C. (1973). "Statistical inference regarding Markov models." Applied Statistics, 22:16.

COHEN, J. (1969). Statistical power analysis for the behavioral sciences. New York: Academic Press.

ELLIS, D.G., and FISHER, B.A. (1975). "Phases of conflict in small group development: A Markov analysis." Human Communication Research, 1:195-212.

FISHER, B.A. (1970). "Decision emergence: Phases in group decision-making." Speech Monographs, 37:53-66.

GUETZKOW, H. (1950). "Unitizing and categorizing problems in coding qualitative data." Journal of Clinical Psychology, 39:47-50.

HERTEL, R.K. (1972). "Application of stochastic process analyses to the study of psychotherapeutic processes." Psychological Bulletin, 77:421-430.

HEWES, D.E. (1975). "Finite stochastic modeling of communication processes: An introduction and some basic readings." Human Communication Research, 1:270-283.

KEMENY, J.S., and SNELL, J.L. (1960). Finite Markov chains. New York: Van Nostrand.

LEWIS, G. (1970). "The assumption of stationary parameters in theories of group discussion." Behavioral Science, 15:269-273.

PARZEN, E. (1962). Stochastic processes. San Francisco: Holden-Day.

SACKS, H. (1972). "An initial investigation of the usability of conversational data for doing sociology." In D. Sudnow (ed.), Studies in social interaction. New York: Free Press.

SCHEGLOFF, E.A. (1972). "Notes on a conversational practice: Formulating place." In D. Sudnow (ed.), Studies in social interaction. New York: Free Press.

SCHUTZ, W.C. (1958). FIRO: A three dimensional theory of interpersonal behavior. New York: Rinehart.

TUCKMAN, B.W. (1965). "Developmental sequences in small groups." Psychological Bulletin, 6:384-399.

VALENTINE, K.B., and FISHER, B.A. (1974). "An interaction analysis of verbal innovative deviance in small groups." Speech Monographs, 41:413-420.

Chapter 12

INTERPERSONAL COMMUNICATION IN THE THERAPEUTIC SETTING: MARIAH OR MESSIAH?

Douglas R. Vaughn and Michael Burgoon

TO BE CONCERNED with communication in the therapeutic context is, as Rossiter (1975) maintains, to be concerned with communication that is "health-promoting." Lacking a generally agreed upon definition of those conditions that constitute health, however, practitioners in various health-related professions currently operate from independent, sometimes contradictory, frames of reference. The World Health Organization's commonly accepted definition of health as "a state of complete physical, mental and social well-being and not merely the absence of disease or infirmity" (WHO, 1958) is of little utility, for beyond suggesting a needed systemic approach it fails to specify any empirical indicators which might be used diagnostically as standards of health to identify problems or to evaluate treatment. We must accept at the outset that our approach to this problem is thus restricted to an ethnocentric point of view. Our standards of physical and psychological health are based upon numerous factors deeply rooted in the nature of this particular cultural tradition. These standards differ from society to society and, to a lesser extent, from group to group across socioeconomic classes within the same society (Walker, 1973). In Barclay's (1971:48) analysis of the philosophical underpinnings of modern approaches to counseling and therapy, the central role of sociocultural determinants is emphasized:

AUTHORS' NOTE: We would like to thank James G. Hiett, Jr., and Edward C. Hutchinson for sustaining, maintaining, and reinforcing our interest in the content area represented by this chapter.

> The purposes of culture appear to be related to the establishment of stable patterns of human behavior. One of the first necessary requisites for existence in a social community is some general prescriptions about behavior. Relationships must be established on a firm and predictable basis. Individuals in a group cannot feel secure unless they know that certain types of stimuli will elicit certain types of responses. Assessment, the prediction of dependable behavior, and the determination of effective behavior are functions of culture that exist in some form or other in every social group.

The implications of this position have been delineated by Fabrega (1975) in his call for an "ethnomedical" science which would start from the recognition that those syndromes recognized as pathologies in any given culture are closely tied to the social functions which are altered or disrupted. Though Fabrega operates from a medical viewpoint and Barclay from a psychotherapeutic and counseling perspective, both locate the critical reference point for standards of "health" as being the social functioning of individuals as judged by the norms and standards of their particular cultural and social milieu. This is similar to Parsons' (1951) conception that illness is, in one of its major aspects, to be defined as a form of deviant behavior.

Such an approach should appeal to communication scholars because the emphasis on disrupted social functioning highlights the role of communication in the origin, expression, recognition, diagnosis, prognosis, and treatment of a wide range of organic and behavioral "pathologies." Because of the centrality of communication to social functioning it is possible to view disrupted social functioning as "disturbed communication" (Ruesch, 1957). Communication may be disturbed in many ways, but in order to be so judged, it must deviate perceptibly from some expected norm, as perceived by the individual and/or others, thus making predictable interaction difficult and obviating some or all of the normal modes of social influence. Parsons (1951) maintains that therapy becomes necessary when the control mechanisms inherent in the reciprocities of ordinary human relationships break down. These control mechanisms are intimately bound up with human communication, for it is primarily through communication that individuals influence and are influenced by one another (King, 1975). Only by observing the constraints of a particular set of socially agreed upon behaviors can the individual hope to communicate (Harré and Secord, 1973). Thus, communication as a mode of social influence is central to the well-being of both the individual and the larger social unit; both depend upon it for their existence.

The relative stability and security provided by norms or tacit rules of interaction allow individuals in a given community to make more or less accurate predictions concerning the way others will behave in normal human intercourse, and, in turn, this accuracy allows them a certain amount of control and influence over others. It also, of course, allows influence to be exerted in return. It is this question of bidirectional influence in human interaction which we believe to be central to a clear understanding of interpersonal communication in the therapeutic process.

As we conceptualize them, the therapeutic and helping professionals are primarily concerned not with individuals *per se* but with *individuals as they interact with others in their particular sociocultural milieu.* What this implies is that the traditional "medical model" of disturbed social functioning, with its suggestion of some dysfunction *in* the individual (perhaps caused by some agent *in* the environment) is both misleading and inadequate: inadequate because it fails to appreciate fully the dynamic ongoing process of organism-environment interaction through which disturbed communication is generated, maintained, recognized, and responded to, and misleading because it has encouraged an approach to therapy that frequently stigmatizes the individual as being mentally ill or deviant, while at the same time legitimizing his or her behavior as representing some recognizable, classified syndrome. This latter consideration is important because the fallacy of reification, when applied to questions of human behavior, can have unforeseen reflexive consequences (Fabrega, 1975:974):

> Definitions and understanding of disease partially shape the behavioral forms of disease and they quite naturally also dictate medical practices. These practices logically entail, order, program and regulate certain forms of social relations. And what gets exchanged in them eventually has a feedback on disease that affects how it is viewed, treated, and evaluated, and how the behavioral form of disease itself comes to be structured. The social relations implicated in diagnosis and treatment, when viewed in their totality, underlie and partially shape or pattern the pathways of disease occurrences in the group at large. Furthermore, these relations and pathways themselves energize and challenge and are constrained by macrosocial arrangements and structures which have a historical and ecological basis and which directly affect and have a feedback on disease and medical care.

What is true of medical practice generally is even more true of the helping professions which deal with the so-called "psycho" and "socio" pathologies. In overly simplistic terms, the "myth of mental illness" contributes to the "manufacture of madness" (Szasz, 1961). Many have considered the serious consequences of our initial conceptualizations upon the subsequent behavior of clients, clinicians, and society at large (Laing, 1962; Guerney et al., 1971). Among the many unfortunate consequences of the medical or "personal defect" model is the legitimation of such roles as "mental patient," "delinquent," "alcoholic," or "stutterer." These roles have particular expectancies associated with them so that those who assume or who are assigned such labels are treated according to the constraints imposed by that particular definition of social reality. We have in many cases a self-fulfilling prophecy. More important is the fact that in our society, these roles are themselves associated with other institutionalized roles (psychotherapist, counselor, speech therapist, etc.) whose professional responsibility it is to care for, correct, rehabilitate, or facilitate the adjustment of those in the deviant roles. The various helping relationships thus become an institutionalized activity, carried out at specified times in official surroundings by a trained and licensed professional *outside the normal social milieu of the client.* We strongly believe that this is often an inappropriate and ineffective response to the actual behavioral problem because it misrepresents the nature and locus of the problem. It is also potentially, and in some cases actually, detrimental to the well-being of the client and to society at large (see, e.g., Goffman, 1961; Leifer, 1969).

In the subsequent analysis we will present a reconceptualization of therapeutic and helping relationships and of the place of interpersonal communication in those relationships. While the discussion will primarily center on psychotherapy, speech therapy, and counseling, it is also applicable to medical doctors, social workers, teachers, and others concerned with the question of "deviant" behavior and disrupted social functioning.

INTERPERSONAL COMMUNICATION

Since the subject of this chapter is interpersonal communication in the therapeutic and helping relationship, it is important that we distinguish interpersonal from noninterpersonal communication at the outset. To view interpersonal communication as all face-to-face, spoken, symbolic interaction is, we believe, both misleading and analytically useless. For our purposes, the conceptualization offered by Miller and Steinberg (1975) seems more appropriate. Their approach is based on the assumption that all communicative situations require the communicator to make predictions about the effects of his communicative behaviors on those with whom he wishes to communicate. Specifically, one chooses from one's available communicative repertoire those specific behaviors, verbal and nonverbal, which seem to have the best chance of being understood and responded to in the way intended. There are at least three distinct levels of information available to the communicator that may provide the basis for such predictions: cultural, sociological, and psychological (personal or idiosyncratic). Communication based on the first two levels of information is dependent upon cultural norms and social stereotypes as a basis for prediction and is defined as noninterpersonal. Only those communicative behaviors based upon idiosyncratic infromation concerning the receiver of the message are considered interpersonal.

Furthermore, one must distinguish between interpersonal *communication* and interpersonal *relationships* (Miller and Steinberg, 1975:55). In any communicative transaction the interactants may be operating at any or all of these levels of predictive information. Thus, one individual may be communicating interpersonally whereas the recipient of his communication may be basing communicative predictions upon cultural or sociological information (resulting in what Miller and Steinberg call a mixed-level relationship). There is reason to believe that this is commonly the case in the therapeutic and helping relationship. In contrast, an interpersonal relationship is one in which both parties predominantly base predictions upon "personal" information. Thus, while interpersonal communication plays a part in the therapeutic relationship, that relationship is not an *interpersonal* one in the present sense.

Although this conceptualization of interpersonal communication may not please some, we feel it has certain advantages in the present context. The emphasis on prediction allows us to focus on problems concerning behavioral control and social influence as these relate to the etiology, diagnosis, and treatment of a wide range of problems for which people seek professional help. Also the distinction drawn concerning levels of information available for making predictions provides a potential framework for distinguishing between appropriate and inappropriate forms of communication in the various helping relationships; not all need to utilize interpersonal communication to the same degree or in the same manner. Finally, the distinction between interpersonal communication and interpersonal relationships allows us to consider some of the confusions and contradictions that have evolved from a failure to distinguish interpersonal communication in professional and helping relationships from "therapeutic" communication in nonprofessional interpersonal relationships. This last consideration is especially important since one of the dominant influences in modern therapy and counseling is the assumption that the therapist provides a concentrated dose of what should naturally occur under optimal conditions (Carson, 1969:267). Maslow (1965), for example, has maintained that all human interactions may have either a "psychotherapeutic" or a "psychopathogenic" influence on the participants, and other theorists of diverse persuasion have echoed that point (Ruesch and Bateson, 1951; Jourard, 1971). What seems to be at issue is the extent to which "therapeutic communication" as a naturally health-promoting aspect of effective human interaction is isomorphic with interpersonal communication in the professional therapeutic relationship. We do not believe that the two are necessarily equivalent, and failure to distinguish one from the other has contributed substantially to the problems faced by the helping professions. Specifically, the reluctance to deal comprehensively with questions of social influence, regulation, and control as these relate to normal and disturbed communication *in the natural social environment of particular clients* is a distinct handicap to both accurate assessment of the problem and to successful corrective action.

COMMUNICATION, SOCIAL INFLUENCE, AND DEVIANCE

What makes an individual subject to social influence of a particular sort and what factors account for differential reaction to the same basic mechanisms of social control and regulation are complex questions. Students of human behavior influenced by the medical model have waged a long and not terribly productive search for the chimerical "pathogenic factor" that is presumed to cause some individuals to react unpredictably or unacceptably to environmental forces in ways that are labeled deviant (Carson, 1969:221). A more fruitful approach to the question of deviance is to face it squarely as a "problem" only as it is so defined by the priorities of a given human community and, within that context, to recognize that any "solution" must be judged in terms that are acceptable and meaningful to that community. Because most scientific-clinical approaches to the issue of deviant behavior or social dysfunctionality are couched in terms that are not meaningful to the community at large, the "problem" becomes, in all its aspects, one that it is assumed can only be handled by professionals possessing the specialized skills and knowledge with which to treat the problem person. The value of this approach can be seen in the progress that medical science has made in the treatment of a wide range of physical disorders. Yet even here there is growing doubt that the medical model is sufficiently comprehensive to deal with the full range of human physical complaints, especially as these are related to psychological and social factors outside the scope of a physician's immediate control (see, e.g., Leifer, 1969). In terms of dealing with communicative and behavioral problems, we believe that the medical model, especially as manifested by the failure of traditional psychiatric and psychoanalytic methods (Eysenck and Rachman, 1965), is neither practical, nor expedient, nor very realistic.

In contrast, a systemic approach emphasizing the transactional nature of organism-environment interaction appears to offer a broader base for understanding "health" problems generally. Such an approach has the advantage, as previously indicated, of focusing attention upon the central role of all forms of human communication, especially interpersonal, in explaining the origin (Bateson et al., 1956; Laing, 1962), recognition (Zola, 1966), diagnosis (Ruesch, 1957), epidemiology (Fabrega, 1975), and treatment (Carkhuff and Berenson, 1967) of many of the problems dealt with by the therapeutic and helping professions. This is, of course, neither a new nor an original idea. In the absence of a comprehensive systemic framework, however, interested researchers and theorists have drawn from a number of different fields in an effort to overcome the myopic tendencies inherent in the traditional medical model.

One promising approach with application to psychotherapy, suggested by Carson (1969), combines the interaction theories of personality and personality disorders (Sullivan, 1953) with basic concepts drawn from social exchange theory (Thibaut and Kelley, 1959) and various learning theories (e.g., Krasner,

1962; Goldiamond and Dyrund, 1968). This "system" provides a basic conceptualization of human communicative interaction amenable to practical application in therapeutic and helping relationships and having the advantage of focusing on questions concerning the control and regulation of interaction outcomes by the individual and those with whom he or she normally interacts in natural social environments. Human interaction may be controlled (influenced, regulated) by the participants because it is a socially determined activity which is, in large part, constrained by the "rules" that interactants recognize as being operative at any one moment in time (Harré and Secord, 1973). These rules include both linguistic and other relevant sociocultural norms and constitute the "definition of the situation" as understood by each participant (Goffman, 1959).

While a complete treatment of the numerous factors presumed to contribute to mutually agreed upon definitions of a situation transcends the scope of the present discussion, research indicates that two primary dimensions of judgment are involved in defining the nature of the *relationship* between interactants within a given situation (Carson, 1969). These are (1) judgments concerning the affective nature of the interaction (friendly-hostile) and (2) an evaluation of the relative status of the interactants (dominant-submissive). To the extent that individuals have developed preferred stances with respect to these dimensions or that relevant role expectancies are involved, part of the information exchanged (especially on the covert or nonverbal level) will usually consist of cues designed to affirm one's own definition and/or prompt complementary responses from the other. According to social exchange theory, the predictability offered by a mutually accepted definition of the situation serves the interests of the interactants by allowing them to engage in personal communicative transactions that are jointly rewarding and to avoid those that are costly. Transactions are rewarding to the extent that positively valued consequences accrue to the persons involved; these may be such consequences as the ability to engage in preferred behavior, need-satisfaction, consensual validation of attitudes, or feelings of personal acceptance by another. A "cost," on the other hand, is any negatively valued consequence such as the amount of effort required to make a particular response, anxiety, embarrassment or other unpleasant emotions, or conflicting or noncomplementary responses. Exchange theory makes the reasonable assumption that "every individual voluntarily enters and stays in any relationship only as long as it is satisfactory in terms of rewards and costs" (Thibaut and Kelley, 1959:37).

In light of the foregoing considerations, a "healthy" individual may be conceptualized as one who is able to function within the constraints of his particular community and engage in transactions with others that are jointly rewarding and mutually satisfying. In other words, such a person is able to exercise a certain amount of control over the rewards that he receives from interacting with others because he provides them with rewards in return. This reciprocity is often obviously affected in those cases that society defines as disturbed or deviant. Certain individuals may, for example, fail to obtain sufficient rewards from others either because they cannot or will not "abide by the rules" of conventional interaction (Argyle, 1967:173-179). Thus, their communicative behaviors may be judged as deviant by others because they respond inappropriately, either unpredictably or in rigid patterns, regardless of the demands of changing circumstances. On the other hand, they may judge their own situations as being disturbed if they recognize that they are receiving insufficient rewards and are frustrated in their efforts to satisfy their needs. *The concern of those in the therapeutic and helping professions is thus to aid such individuals in satisfying their own needs by helping them to accommodate the needs of others with whom they must deal.*

THERAPEUTIC AND HELPING RELATIONSHIPS

As stated previously, we view the therapeutic and helping professions as being concerned with the social functioning of individuals in their particular sociocultural milieu. As should be clear by this point, the professional helper is concerned with basic questions of social influence as these relate to the functioning of individuals in normal interaction. We agree with Costello (1972:423) that a therapist should be primarily interested in "the relationship between an individual and his social environment and how this relationship is formed, maintained, and changed in and through communication." In actual practice, however, there is reason to believe that this transactional perspective is seldom pursued realistically.

> Therapeutic failure in the face of counteracting natural influences, though common, is largely undocumented. Only recently have the professions faced it as a phenomenon. Most surprising, however, has been the failure of the professions to develop ways of directing the forces of the natural environment toward therapeutically congruent ends. Rather than involve the environment in therapeutic reorganization, and, hence, harness the enormous influence on behavior available there, the professions have established the natural environment as the enemy of therapeutic intervention. [Tharp and Wetzel, 1969:7]

One major reason for this bias lies in the influence of the medical model, with its emphasis on a professional relationship between client and clinician in an institutional setting. Goffman's (1961) enlightened exposition of the "moral career of the mental patient" highlights the essentially counterproductive nature of "total institutions" as vehicles for therapeutic change. Rather than help the individual develop sufficient control over his or her own social environment, the institutional rule structure substitutes a new "social milieu foreign to the individual, bizarre by outside standards, or inadequate as a relearning device," and the result "often is increased disorganization of social behavior rather than its acquisition or reorganization" (Tharp and Wetzel, 1969:8). While it is true that the vast majority of professional and helping relationships are not confined to "total institutions" (mental hospitals, correctional facilities, etc.), they are nevertheless typically divorced from the natural social environment of the client. Furthermore, they are institutionalized in the sense that the role expectancies involved are legitimized by legal and professional priorities and further constrained by sociocultural stereotypes associated with the (doctor-patient) medical model.

Thus, the role of the professional helper is one vested with considerable status, authority, and power. The role of the client, in contrast, is one of subservience, weakness, and impotence. There is no doubt that in the hands of a competent therapist these expectancies can be used strategically to help the client change, as Ruesch (1961:140) suggests, but there is also the very real danger that they will, even when beneficial within the context of the therapeutic setting, not translate to the patient's natural social environment. One basic reason for this lack of transfer is that the therapist becomes a substitute for what the client cannot find in his actual life experience (Carkhuff and Berenson, 1967:3). The client depends upon the therapist for the rewards and reinforcement that are not forthcoming from his interactions with others. Despite what may appear to be real progress within the therapeutic context, often little change (thus little benefit) is observed outside that context.

This problem is not confined to psychotherapy. Speech therapists have been concerned with it in relation to treating stuttering and other basic communicative disorders, and the dependency of the client on the therapist is often given as one reason for the failure of those who show progress in the clinical environment to demonstrate those same successful behaviors in their normal interactions with others (Emerick and Hood, 1974:50). In the classical psychotherapeutic approach, exemplified by psychoanalysis, such dependency is actually encouraged as a way of heightening the process of "transference" in which the analyst becomes a substitute figure for some significant person (usually a parent) in the patient's real world. It is presumed that by "working through" their feelings with this substitute, clients will be able to resolve their "inner" conflicts and thus function more realistically in the real world (Patterson, 1966:317). Unfortunately, the approach does not seem to work. Despite the profound influence which psychoanalytic theories have had on the helping professions generally, especially in terms of the therapeutic techniques involved (dyadic interaction, verbalizing, free association to reveal repressed feelings, emphasis on inner conflict and past traumatic experiences), neither the techniques nor the theoretical foundations have ever been systematically evaluated, and their influence is based solely on "a certain compelling face validity" (Williams, 1972:8).

To rely on a method of treatment for so long and on such a large scale merely on the basis of face validity and in the absence of clear empirical support seems an unconscionable breach of professional responsibility. After reviewing the available evidence, Eysenck (1952) concluded that not only psychoanalysis but also most other forms of psychotherapy were ineffective in helping either the disturbed child or the neurotic or disabled adult. Frank (1961) further observed that statistical studies of the supposed benefits of traditional forms of psychotherapy consistently demonstrate that while approximately two-thirds of all neurotic patients seem to improve regardless of the type of therapy they receive, a comparable percentage of those with the same complaints improve over the same period of time *with no therapy at all.* Truax and Carkhuff (1967:5) conclude that "*average* counseling and psychotherapy as it is currently practiced does not result in average client improvement greater than that observed in clients who receive no special counseling or psychotherapeutic treatment." Furthermore, when the differing effectiveness of individual therapists was analyzed, the conclusion was reached that certain individuals seemed consistently to have a beneficial effect on their own clients, thus leading to the inescapable conclusion (given the overall finding of no *average* difference) that some therapists are actually harmful to their clients. Lister (1970:37) goes even further and claims that "it is fair to conclude that at least half of the counseling relationships in which the typical school counselor participates are apt to have harmful consequences to the student who comes for help." (For a comprehensive review of the literature on the effects of psychotherapy, see Meltzoff and Kornreich, 1970.)

We consider all this to be a serious indictment of the therapeutic and helping professions, in that neither the utility of the theoretical basis nor the particular method of any one traditional approach has been clearly demonstrated. Rather, the evidence indicates that some specific therapists, *irrespective of theoretical or methodological persuasion,* are truly helpful to the client, while some are actually harmful. Since it is virtually axiomatic to members of the helping professions that the unique relationship between a particular client and therapist is the most important factor in treatment (Combs et al., 1971:5), one might reasonably ask why more has not been done, and sooner, to determine exactly what is at work in successful therapeutic relationships. What kinds of communication transactions benefit clients and what kinds further impair their functioning?

Common sense might dictate that what is therapeutic in the client-clinician relationship is the same as what is basically health-promoting in normal, rewarding human relationships. Many therapists have taken exactly this position (Rogers, 1951; Ruesch, 1961; Jourard, 1968). One widely accepted notion that follows from this stance is that the client has the capacity to deal with his own problems if he can be provided with a friendly, nonthreatening atmosphere. Thus, the counselor need not explain, direct, evaluate, or prescribe behaviors for the client and, indeed, is presumed less effective to the extent that he does so (Rogers, 1951). To the extent that they actually practice what they preach, such "client-centered" or "nondirective" therapists are operating on the assumption that rewarding human interaction is, itself, health-promoting.

Although this position appears to have considerable appeal, we feel that it is unacceptable as a rationale for a professional and helping relationship. Professionals are commonly expected to possess specialized skills and knowledge, yet in the case of nondirective therapy, the basic posture of the therapist is exactly the opposite of what one expects of a professional. The direct application of special knowledge is specifically eschewed by refusing to evaluate, analyze, inform, persuade, motivate, or direct the client, irrespective of the client's wishes in this regard. Any improvement of the client is assumed to result from his or her own ability to change in a positive way when provided with a supportive relationship with another human being, even though "the counselor is not supportive in the usual sense of the word" (Patterson, 1966:416).

The inescapable conclusion seems to be that if warm, nondirective human relationships per se constitute the sole therapeutic ingredient, then the guise of professionalism is inappropriate. Untrained, unskilled persons who are naturally warm, empathic, and nonjudgmental could become more economical and practical substitutes. That those in the helping professions do not seriously consider such an approach is testimony to the fact that more is involved in the counseling process than is being acknowledged. However, empirical evidence strongly suggests that the use of paraprofessional workers in what have traditionally been considered professional roles (requiring advanced degrees and laborious preparation) is not only feasible but, in many cases, actually preferable to the use of professionals (see, e.g., Grosser, 1969; Williams, 1972). We feel that this idea has merit. Furthermore, since existing evidence does not support the value of current practices involved in training and certification of professional therapists and counselors (Bergin and Solomon, 1963; Lister, 1970), a reevaluation of contemporary approaches is imperative. Standards of either public or professional accountability are woefully lacking (Truax and Carkhuff, 1967:14):

> Inasmuch as the available evidence indicates that the average ineffectiveness of psychotherapy and counseling, as currently practiced, is due to the presence of large numbers of practitioners who have negative effects offsetting the equally large number of those who have positive effects, it would seem sensible for professional organizations, clinics, schools, hospitals and other interested agencies to attempt to identify the effectiveness of individual practitioners. In that way, and only in that way,

can the patient's welfare and the public good be best served. Unfortunately, this has almost never been done. Almost never do individuals or agencies keep even crude outcome measures of a given therapist's effectiveness! In the licensing or certification or the employment of an individual practitioner, he is almost never asked to give evidence of his average effect on patients. Whether he has a long history of helping or harming clients seems to have no bearing—in most cases, no one even asks or bothers to keep records. As things stand today, a counselor or therapist receives his doctorate from a university, becomes licensed by his state, employed or enters private practice, and even passes specialty board examinations in his profession without anyone making a systematic evaluation of his actual effects (for better *or* for worse) on his all-too-human clients!

From their own investigations as well as a comprehensive review and analysis of both relevant theory and research, Truax and Carkhuff (1967) have isolated what they feel are the three essential ingredients of the therapist's personality which facilitate positive change by the client: (1) accurate empathy or understanding, (2) nonpossessive warmth or respect for the client, and (3) genuineness or authenticity. These qualities are obviously important in human relationships generally, and Carkhuff and Berenson (1967) are probably correct in identifying them as the aspects of normal human interaction that are facilitative of personal growth and satisfaction.

But we doubt that this is all there is to successful counseling and psychotherapy. While therapeutic communication in both normal and professional contexts must manifest these qualities to be truly helpful, it would be a mistake to confuse therapy as the purchase of friendship. *The role of the professional must be justified by the possession and effective use of specialized skills and knowledge which the client needs in order to change his current mode of behavior.* The client seeks the professional because of a problem that impairs effective social functioning. If the client is lucky enough to encounter a therapist who possesses the desirable qualities mentioned earlier, he or she may begin to feel better. But if there is no change of behavior in dealing with others outside the therapeutic setting, the client has not been helped.

The problem of dependency in therapeutic relationships illustrates this point well. Dependency reflects the client's failure to find the satisfactions needed in everyday life. Consequently, for a substitute, the client turns to the therapist and the security provided by the institutionalized role expectancies. After all, the therapist *has* to listen to the client's problems and try to understand them—that is the therapist's role—while the patient's role is to be helpless and cared for. If the therapist cannot help the client to learn new behaviors and new ways of relating to the social world in order to function independently and to accept responsibility for actions, then the therapist has not done the job.

The therapist's job, as we see it, is to assist individuals to change in whatever ways are necessary and by whatever means are available so that their communicative behaviors allow them to function within the constraints of their particular communities and engage in transactions with others that are jointly rewarding and mutually satisfying. This means that therapists must become absolute pragmatists in relation to the problem. They cannot presume that what is needed by one client will suffice for another, though this is what the medical model of treatment often suggests. Nor can they presume that a warm human relationship is all the client needs: the client may, indeed, need such, but the therapist's concern is to teach the client how to build relationships in real life situations, not to provide ready-made relationships for the client. The therapeutic milieu is, after all, artificial (not "real") in terms of what clients must normally deal with in their natural environment. As Berne (1966:63) has said, "If the patient is to be cured by love, that should be left to a lover." The therapist is not a lover.

Nor is the therapist, as Carson (1969:267) correctly observed, a "horticulturalist" who merely provides the appropriate "atmospheric conditions essential to the unfolding of the client's heretofore blocked but wholly self-determined personhood." The *growth* of the person, the central theme of the human potential movement in therapy, is surely a rightful concern of therapists, but to encourage "growth" in some unspecified, highly abstract way with no thought to the actual environment wherein such changes must be sustained and supported is not only doomed to failure but also likely to impair the individual's ability to interact with those who do not provide the "good vibes" that he is erroneously led to expect. Encounter group casualties who find that their normal environment is intolerable and disconfirming after the uplift of the liberating group experience are a case in point.

Finally, we most emphatically disagree that the task of therapy should be to seek "subjective improvement" in contradistinction to "objective improvement" (Ruesch, 1961:6). The two are inseparably linked, as are individuals and their social environments. Subjective complaints are recognized as problems only when they deviate from what the individual has previously experienced as normal in ongoing, real life experiences. Even the "perception of losing one's mind is based on culturally derived stereotypes as to the significance of symptoms" (Goffman, 1959:132). Thus, many of those individuals who, in increasing numbers, are seeking professional help for what appear to be low levels of anxiety and depression are probably responding to erroneous social stereotypes which lead them to believe that no one should ever be unhappy, anxious, or depressed unless he or she is "sick." As a number of recent trends in therapy suggest (Ellis, 1962; Glasser, 1965), often all that is needed is a more realistic orientation; but to provide it, therapists must utilize all the techniques of social influence and information control at their disposal. Even if the client's "problem" is a mistake (i.e., false, inadequate, or distorted information), it does represent the present state of reality as he or she understands it. As Ruesch (1961:457) has observed, any "information," true or false, guides the conduct of the person because it is thought to be true. Wiener (1961:17-18) further emphasizes the role of information in controlling the mutually accommodating and constantly changing organism-environment interaction:

> Information is a name for the content of what is exchanged with the outer world as we adjust to it, and make our adjustment felt upon it. The process of receiving and using information is the process of our adjusting to the contingencies of the outer environment, and of our living effectively within that environment. . . . To live effectively is to live with adequate information. Thus, communication and control belong to the essence of man's inner life, even as they belong to his life in society.

THE ROLE OF INTERPERSONAL COMMUNICATION IN THE THERAPEUTIC RELATIONSHIP

It should surprise no one that we view the therapeutic and helping relationship as a directed, deliberate application of the psychology of behavior change in which communication as a form of social influence is both the primary object of attention and also the principal vehicle for inducing the desired change (Goldstein et al., 1966). The nature of the changes sought will depend upon the particular problem conditions that bring client and therapist together, for these will indicate those elements of information exchange between individual and environment in need of corrective attention. The focus on behavior is important because the overt, everyday communicative behavior of the client is the best index of the adequacy of his or her "information" and also the most direct route for changing that information-behavior link. The therapist must accept responsibility for making certain basic decisions that will change the client's life. This burden is unavoidable, for if the client does not change, nothing has been accomplished. The therapist cannot pretend to be a mere "facilitator," leaving the responsibility for changes to the client. Regardless of the particular stance adopted, the therapist is going to influence the client, for better or worse, and must realize the extent to which his or her own values, beliefs, and personal characteristics are implicated in the influence process. No good can come from the affectation of a passive role by the therapist (Tharp and Wetzel, 1969:12).

To apply this concept to the traditional dyadic model of therapy is to recognize the tremendous advantage that the therapist has over the client in terms of the control of essential information. If interpersonal communication is distinguished from noninterpersonal to the extent that predictions of communicative outcomes are based on "personal" information about the other, then the therapist is in a much better position to make such predictions than the client.

In other words, clients normally are encouraged to self-disclose at great length and in much detail so that the discerning therapist has access to a great deal of extremely potent information. Conversely, clients seldom have access to such information about the therapist and are thus not in a position to predict the likely responses to their communicative efforts. Therefore, the therapist is in a position to *move* the client, to touch sensitive spots and to manipulate thoughts, feelings, and actions. Directly and indirectly the therapist encourages the client to adopt particular ways of relating to the world, thereby imposing a definition of what it is to be "healthy." The therapist is, in a very real sense, a teacher who "guides the client toward implicitly or explicitly determined goals" (Carson, 1969:267). If the client refuses to accept the therapist's world view, the therapist is without influence. One suspects that this is often what happens in the "total institution," where the client as unwilling inmate of an alien environment finds it impossible to see the therapist as anything but the enemy—one of *them,* one of the *others* who contribute to the problem (Laing, 1962). It is at this point that the "facilitative conditions" of respect, empathy, and genuineness are obviously important (Truax and Carkhuff, 1967). These conditions contribute to the client's basic trust in the therapist, a necessary but not sufficient element for the exercise of influence. Furthermore, to the extent that he or she believes that these conditions are indicative of healthy social functioning, it ill behooves the therapist not to manifest them behaviorally. As indicated previously, such failure can only lead to further deterioration of the client's communicative behavior.

Since the ultimate aim of therapy is to improve the social functioning of the client *outside the therapeutic context,* the nature of the information conveyed during therapy sessions is crucial. Such information "can best be compared to a small-scale model of the self and of the world which enables a person to predict events, to correct his own behavior, and to partially alter the shape of the environment" (Ruesch, 1961:457). Since the usual candidate for therapy is someone whose communicative behaviors are disturbed as a function of a distorted self-environment model, successful therapeutic intervention depends upon changing that model through *new learning* that provides the client with "a different and more adequate set of *beliefs* about himself and his life" (Carson, 1969:273). Frank (1961) has called attention to the potential of the therapist's official role expectancies as a source of influence, and Truax and Carkhuff (1967) have emphasized the potent positive reinforcing aspects of the core facilitative conditions manifested by the therapist. The former provide the therapist with a certain amount of expert and legitimate power and the latter with reward and referent power. The therapist must use such power within the therapeutic context to frustrate the client's erroneous expectations and the resultant inappropriate behaviors. According to Carson (1969:280), this is a "cardinal therapeutic tactic":

> The therapist must avoid the adoption of an interpersonal position complementary to and confirmatory of the critical self-protective position to which the client will almost invariably attempt to move in the course of the therapeutic interaction.

In other words, for the client to learn and to change, the therapist must avoid reinforcing those behaviors which caused the client to seek therapy in the first place (Wolpe and Lazarus, 1968; Levis, 1970). This is a problem recognized by speech pathologists as well; disrupting the homeostatic balance of maladaptive behaviors is a necessary first step to replacing them with newly learned, more acceptable behaviors (Emerick and Hood, 1974). Thus, the therapist does not *respond* to the client's promptings, but rather *uses* these as a means of calling the client's attention to inappropriate behaviors. Because many clients are quite skillful manipulators of others, it is often difficult for the therapist to avoid responding in ways that reinforce undesired behaviors. Carson (1969:282) maintains that learning to manage this problem is the "greatest stumbling block in the education of new therapists." Furthermore, evidence suggests that clients can manipulate the response patterns of counselors who manifest low levels of the facilitative conditions (respect, empathy, and genuineness), but cannot manipulate counselors operating at high levels (Truax and Carkhuff, 1967). Truax and Carkhuff also note that successful counselors actually improved their functioning (in terms of the facilitative conditions) when confronted with a manipulative strategy on the part of the client.

These considerations imply that if the therapist is to *use* interpersonal communication as an instrument of therapeutic change, *he must often prevent the client from being able to communicate on an interpersonal basis in return.* If he does not, the focus of the relationship shifts from the problem as manifest in the client's real environment to the "problem" as a pretext for maintaining a surrogate relationship with the therapist. In this latter case, the therapist becomes a part of the problem—something which the evidence on therapist effectiveness suggests happens rather frequently.

BEYOND THE THERAPEUTIC RELATIONSHIP

Although the foregoing discussion has emphasized the importance of the dyadic model of therapeutic and helping relationships, this focus should be construed more as a result of traditional theory and practice (based on the medical model) than as a justification for its necessary importance as a process of change. Since we have emphasized the social functioning of the individual in his natural sociocultural milieu, we must consider the question of the transfer of learning from the traditional therapeutic setting to the everyday experiences of the client and also consider the related question of whether there is a more effective method for inducing beneficial change than the currently dominant one-to-one relationship. We are thus concerned with both the context and the techniques of therapy, and we feel that current theory and research suggest a convergence of these concerns in taking experimentally developed techniques derived from learning theory and applying them to actual situations in the client's own social community.

The movement away from the clinical setting has been facilitated by the increasing popularity of group treatment methods, especially as these focus on actual social units such as families (see, e.g., Mishler and Waxler, 1968). This approach deemphasizes the client-clinician relationship while focusing attention on communicative transactions between those who, in real life situations, constitute the "problem." Even in group treatment which does not focus on real life social units, clients obtain multiple feedback and opportunities to practice and evaluate their communicative behaviors with a variety of individuals rather than with a single therapist. Yet even here there is a danger of formalizing the experience into a traditional "institutional" approach with all the limitations already referred to (Berne, 1966:76). Recently the helping professions have focused on larger aspects of the actual community situation which may be contributing to the problems of individuals (Costello, 1972). This approach forces the "community therapist" to deal directly with many of the ethical, legal, and social concerns that traditional therapists have been able to ignore. However, since the therapeutic and helping professions typically seek to correct problems of "deviance," these issues can be ignored only at the risk of further exacerbating the problem, for the question of whose criteria are to constitute the standards for determining deviant behavior is often more crucial than any other aspect of the problem (see, e.g., Scheff, 1967).

To the extent that a clear behavioral problem does exist and is recognized as such by the client and by significant others in his or her social environment, the application of behavior modification techniques based on various learning theories offers numerous advantages over traditional approaches to therapy. From our present perspective, the main advantages seem to be: (1) these approaches are based on empirical evidence; (2) they focus on changing specific behaviors; (3) they emphasize the client's real-life problem; and, most importantly, (4) they work (Ullmann and Krasner, 1966). While the evaluation of traditional forms of therapy is often problematic, the criterion for success in behavior therapy is clear, i.e., the criterion is the extent of change in specified overt behaviors. Currently, such approaches to therapy are reporting a success rate far in advance of that claimed by traditional forms of therapy. Furthermore, the most often cited objection to dealing with the behavior directly rather than with the supposed underlying problem–i.e., the fear of "symptom substitution"–seems to be unfounded (Ullmann and Krasner, 1966:15).

One especially interesting and innovative form of behavior therapy is applied behavior analysis, an application of behavior modification techniques in the natural environment of the client (Tharp and Wetzel, 1969). The problems associated with transfer of learning and client dependence upon the therapist are eliminated by doing away with the traditional relationship entirely. In this approach the "therapist" is really a professional "consultant" who aids in modifying the behavior of an individual through scheduled reinforcement provided by some "mediator" who is a significant figure in the client's natural environment. Similar techniques have been employed to teach speech to autistic children by training parents to provide the appropriate conditions and to reinforce the appropriate behaviors (Risley and Wolf, 1967). Applied behavior analysis can also be used to train clients to be the "mediators" in changing the behaviors of others with whom they have a problem; thus, problem students have been trained in behavioral techniques designed to elicit more satisfactory responses from teachers and other authority figures with whom they must deal (Phillips et al., 1973). Such an approach is consonant with the National Institute of Mental Health's avowed aim to "regard as constructive anything which makes it possible to communicate and relate, and destructive anything which interferes with or distorts these capacities" (Williams, 1972:4). To the extent that techniques derived from learning theories can be so employed, we feel that they will have the salutory effect of forcing all concerned parties (client, clinician, and community) to accept their own fair share of responsibility for the problem and for its solution.

Clearly, many assumptions about the therapeutic communication situation lead to faulty clinical practices and unfortunate outcomes. Obviously, not everyone will be happy with our conceptualization of therapeutic and helping relationships as rhetorical and suasive in nature. However, it is our claim that such an approach might have real value when the concern is for the improved interpersonal communication behavior of the client in normal situations rather than the happiness of the therapist in a uniquely nonnormal context.

REFERENCES

ARGYLE, M. (1967). The psychology of interpersonal behavior. Baltimore: Penguin.

BARCLAY, J. (1971). Foundations of counseling strategies. New York: Wiley.

BATESON, G., JACKSON, D., and HALEY, J. (1956). "Toward a theory of schizophrenia." Behavioral Science, 1(October):251-264.

BERGIN, A.E., and SOLOMON, S. (1963). "Personality and performance correlates of empathic understanding in psychotherapy." Paper presented at the convention of the American Psychological Association, Philadelphia.

BERNE, E. (1966). Principles of group treatment. New York: Oxford University Press.

CARKHUFF, R., and BERENSON, B. (1967). Beyond counseling and therapy. New York: Holt, Rinehart and Winston.

CARSON, R. (1969). Interaction concepts of personality. Chicago: Aldine.

COMBS, A.W., AVILA, D., and PURKEY, W.W. (1971). Helping relationships: Basic concepts for the helping professions. Boston: Allyn and Bacon.

COSTELLO, D. (1972). "Therapeutic transactions: An approach to human communication." Pp. 420-435 in R. Budd and B. Ruben (eds.), Approaches to human communication. New York: Spartan.

ELLIS, A. (1962). Reason and emotion in psychotherapy. New York: Lyle Stuart.

EMERICK, L., and HOOD, S.B. (1974). The client-clinician relationship. Springfield, Ill.: Charles C Thomas.

EYSENCK, H.J. (1952). "The effects of psychotherapy: An evaluation." Journal of Consulting Psychology, 16(July):319-324.

EYSENCK, H.J., and RACHMAN, S. (1965). Causes and cures of neurosis. San Diego: Robert Knapp.

FABREGA, H. (1975). "The need for an ethnomedical science." Science, 19(September): 969-975.

FRANK, J.D. (1961). Persuasion and healing. Baltimore: Johns Hopkins University Press.

GLASSER, W. (1965). Reality therapy: A new approach to psychiatry. New York: Harper and Row.

GOFFMAN, E. (1959). The presentation of self in everyday life. New York: Doubleday.

--- (1961). Asylums: Essays on the social situation of mental patients and other inmates. Chicago: Aldine.

GOLDIAMOND, I., and DYRUND, J. (1968). "Some applications and implications of behavioral analysis for psychotherapy." Pp. 54-89 in J.M. Shlien (ed.), Research in psychotherapy (vol. 3). Washington, D.C.: American Psychological Association.

GOLDSTEIN, A.P., HELLER, K., and SECHREST, L. (1966). Psychotherapy and the psychology of behavior change. New York: Wiley.

GROSSER, C. (1969). Nonprofessionals in the human services. San Francisco: Jossey-Bass.

GUERNEY, G., GUERNEY, L., and STOLLACK, G. (1971). "The potential advantages of changing from a medical to an educational model in practicing psychology." Interpersonal Development, 2(October):238-245.

HARRE, R., and SECORD, P.F. (1973). The explanation of social behavior. Totowa, N.J.: Littlefield, Adams.

JOURARD, S. (1968). Disclosing man to himself. Princeton, N.J.: Van Nostrand.

--- (1971). The transparent self. New York: Van Nostrand.

KING, S. (1975). Communication and social influence. Reading, Mass.: Addison-Wesley.

KRASNER, L. (1962). "Behavior control and social responsibility." American Psychologist, 17(April):199-204.

LAING, R.D. (1962). The self and others. Chicago: Quadrangle.

LAZARUS, A.A. (1972). Clinical behavior therapy. New York: Brunner/Mazel.

LEIFER, R. (1969). In the name of mental health: The social functions of psychiatry. New York: Science House.

LEVIS, D. (ed., 1970). Learning approaches to therapeutic behavior change. Chicago: Aldine.

LISTER, J. (1970). "School counseling: For better or for worse?" Counseiller Canadien, 4(January):33-39.

MASLOW, A. (1965). Eupsychian management. Homewood, Ill.: Dorsey.

MELTZOFF, J., and KORNREICH, M. (1970). Research in psychotherapy. New York: Atherton.

MILLER, G.R., and STEINBERG, M. (1975). Between people: A new analysis of interpersonal communication. Palo Alto, Calif.: Science Research Associates.

MISHLER, E., and WAXLER, N. (1968). Interaction in families. New York: Wiley.

PARSONS, T. (1951). The social system. New York: Free Press.

PATTERSON, C. (1966). Theories of counseling and psychotherapy. New York: Harper and Row.

PHILLIPS, E.L., PHILLIPS, E.A., FIXIEN, D., and WOLF, M. (1973). "Behavior shaping for delinquents." Psychology Today, 7(June):74-79.

RISLEY, T., and WOLF, M. (1967). "Establishing functional speech in echolalic children." Behavior Research and Therapy, 5:73-88.

ROGERS, C. (1951). Client-centered therapy. Boston: Houghton-Mifflin.

ROSSITER, C. (1975). "Defining therapeutic communication." Journal of Communication, 25(summer):126-130.

RUESCH, J. (1957). Disturbed communication. New York: Norton.

--- (1961). Therapeutic communication. New York: Norton.

RUESCH, J., and BATESON, G. (1951). Communication: The social matrix of psychiatry. New York: Norton.

SCHEFF, T. (1967). Mental illness and social process. New York: Harper and Row.

SULLIVAN, H.S. (1953). The interpersonal theory of psychiatry. New York: Norton.

SZASZ, T. (1961). The myth of mental illness. London: Secker and Warburg.

THARP, R., and WETZEL, R. (1969). Behavior modification in the natural environment. New York: Academic Press.

THIBAUT, J., and KELLEY, H. (1959). The social psychology of groups. New York: Wiley.

TRUAX, C., and CARKHUFF, R. (1967). Toward effective counseling in psychotherapy: Training and practice. Chicago: Aldine.

ULLMANN, L., and KRASNER, L. (1966). Case studies in behavior modification. New York: Holt, Rinehart and Winston.

WALKER, H. (1973). "Communication and the American health care problem." Journal of Communication, 23(summer):349-360.

WIENER, N. (1961). The human use of human beings. New York: Doubleday.

WILLIAMS, R. (1972). Perspectives in the field of mental health. Rockville, Md.: National Institute of Mental Health.

WOLPE, J., and LAZARUS, A. (1968). Behavior therapy techniques. New York: Pergamon.

World Health Organization (1958). The first ten years of World Health Organization. Geneva: Author.

ZOLA, I. (1966). "Culture and symptoms: An analysis of patients presenting complaints." American Sociological Review, 31(October):615-630.

ABOUT THE CONTRIBUTORS

JAMES F. ALEXANDER received his Ph.D. in clinical psychology from Michigan State University in 1967. He is currently an Associate Professor and Director of Clinical Training in the Department of Psychology, University of Utah. A member of the 1974 National Institute of Mental Health Task Force on Research Training and currently a consultant to the National Institute of Drug Abuse Task Force on the Family and Substance Abuse, Dr. Alexander has done research and practice in family interaction and therapy, interpersonal communication, and program evaluation.

IRWIN ALTMAN is a social psychologist with a Ph.D. from the University of Maryland, 1957. He has been Professor and Chairman of the Psychology Department at the University of Utah since 1969. He has held teaching positions at the University of Maryland and the American University and held a research position with the Naval Medical Research Institute, Bethesda, Maryland. His research interests encompass the development and management of interpersonal relationships and environmental psychology. He is the author of many journal articles and has authored the following books: *Small Group Research* (with J.E. McGrath, 1966); *Social Penetration: The Development of Interpersonal Relationships* (with D.A. Taylor, 1973); *The Environment and Social Behavior: Privacy, Personal Space, Territory and Crowding* (1975).

CHARLES R. BERGER is Associate Professor of Communication Studies and Director of the Communication Research Center at Northwestern University. He received his Ph.D. in communication from Michigan State University. His areas of research interest are the development and disintegration of interpersonal relationships, attribution processes in interpersonal relationships, and interpersonal knowledge processes.

MICHAEL BURGOON is Associate Professor of Speech at the University of Florida. He received his Ph.D. in communication from Michigan State University. His research interests are in language and social change.

JOSEPH N. CAPPELLA, who received his Ph.D. from Michigan State University, is an Assistant Professor and the Director of the Center for Communication Research at the University of Wisconsin-Madison, Department of Communication Arts. His research interests include interpersonal processes, attitude change, human information processing, and mathematical modeling.

ROBERT T. CRAIG, who received his Ph.D. from Michigan State University, is Assistant Professor of Speech Communication at Pennsylvania State University. His research interests include communication theory, interpersonal communication, cognitive structure and communication, and the analysis of verbal behavior.

DONALD P. CUSHMAN, who received his Ph.D. from the University of Wisconsin-Madison, is Associate Professor of Communication at Michigan State University. His research interests include principles of causal systems, rules theory construction, interpersonal communication, and the analysis of verbal behavior.

STEVE DUCK is Lecturer in Psychology at Lancaster University, where he teaches social psychology. His main research interests are friendship formation and acquaintance and interpersonal attraction, and he has recently also become interested in the effects of production techniques used on television. He has published several articles and books in these areas, including *Personal Relationships and Personal Constructs: A Study of Friendship Formation* (1973), *Theory and Practice in Interpersonal Attraction* (in press), and *Dynamics of Television* (in press). He takes his surname seriously and is a keen ornithologist.

JOSEPH M. FOLEY, who received his Ph.D. from the University of Iowa, is Associate Professor of Communication at the Ohio State University. His major areas of research include public policy regarding the regulation of telecommunication and the use of computers to study communication processes.

ROYCE R. GARDNER is a Ph.D. candidate in the Department of Communication Studies at Northwestern University. She received her M.A. degree from the Department of Speech and Theatre at the University of Illinois at Chicago Circle. Her primary research interests are in the area of interpersonal communication theory, primarily relationship development and attribution processes.

SHIRLEY J. GILBERT, who received her Ph.D. from the University of Kansas, is Assistant Professor of Speech Communication at the University of Denver. In addition to a love for teaching and students, she enjoys doing research in interpersonal communication, family communication, and communication in the therapeutic setting.

RANDALL P. HARRISON, who received his Ph.D. from Michigan State University, is Professor of Communication at Michigan State University and Research Psychologist at the University of California Medical Center, San Francisco. His research interests include facial, pictorial, and nonverbal communication.

LEONARD C. HAWES, who received his Ph.D. from the University of Minnesota, is Associate Professor of Communication at the Ohio State University. His research interests include mathematical modeling of human communication, logical analysis of ordinary conversation, and certain aspects of logic and argument in everyday settings.

FRANK E. MILLAR, who received his Ph.D. from Michigan State University, has taught at Indiana State University and Montana State University. He is now with the Department of Communication of Cleveland State University. His major research interests include interpersonal and organizational communication, and he has recently coauthored an interpersonal book titled *Messages and Myths.*

GERALD R. MILLER, who received his Ph.D. from the University of Iowa, is Professor of Communication at Michigan State University. His major research interests are in the areas of interpersonal communication and persuasion, and he recently received a Joint Resolution of Tribute from the Michigan legislature for his research dealing with the use of videotape in courtroom trials. The author of seven books and many articles in journals of communication, psychology, and law, he is presently editor of the journal *Human Communication Research.*

TERU L. MORTON received a Ph.D. in clinical psychology from the University of Utah and is now at the University of Hawaii. Her major research and training emphases include intimate communication, marital and family therapy, and program evaluation. She pursued a long-standing interest in cultural variables in these areas during her internship at Hawaii State Hospital.

MALCOLM R. PARKS received his B.A. in speech communication from the University of Montana and his M.A. in communication from Michigan State University and is completing his Ph.D. from Michigan State. In the fall of 1976 he joined the faculty of the Department of Communication Studies at Northwestern University. His major areas of interest are family communication and interpersonal communication as it relates to relational development and termination processes.

W. BARNETT PEARCE graduated from Carson-Newman College (B.A.) in 1965, attended Southwestern Baptist Theological Seminary, and received the M.A. and Ph.D. degrees from Ohio University in 1968 and 1969. He taught at the University of North Dakota and the University of Kentucky and presently is Associate Professor of Communication Studies at the University of Massachusetts. He describes his present work as attempting to construct a general theory of interpersonal communication. He wrote *Communicating Personally: A Theory of Interpersonal Communication in Human Relationships* (with Charles Rossiter, 1975), *An Overview of Interpersonal Communication and Relationships* (1976), and articles in the *Journal of Communication, Communication Research, Human Communication Research, Intellect, The French Review,* and other journals. In real life, he reads and writes science fiction, enjoys observing and reflecting about the human condition generally, and plays several sports.

L. EDNA ROGERS, who received her Ph.D. from Michigan State University, has taught various social science disciplines at the Ohio State University, Universidad de Los Andes in Columbia, and Michigan State University. Dr. Rogers' major research interest lies in family communication, and she is presently the codirector of a research project dealing with this area and sponsored by the National Institute of Mental Health.

MICHAEL E. ROLOFF, who received his Ph.D. from Michigan State University, is Assistant Professor of Human Communication at the University of Kentucky. He coauthored the study-activity guide which accompanies the Miller and Steinberg interpersonal text, *Between People.* His major research interests include the areas of conflict resolution and persuasive message strategies.

LINDA SCHULMAN is a Ph.D. candidate in the Department of Communication Studies at Northwestern University. She received her M.A. degree in the Department of Speech at the University of Florida. Her primary research interests are ingratiation, relationship development, and attribution processes as they relate to interpersonal communication theory.

DOUGLAS R. VAUGHN recently completed his Ph.D. in Speech at the University of Florida. His research interests include therapeutic communication and accuracy in assessing interpersonal communication.